Arc Left From Istanbul
A Photographic Exploration

Scott Shaw

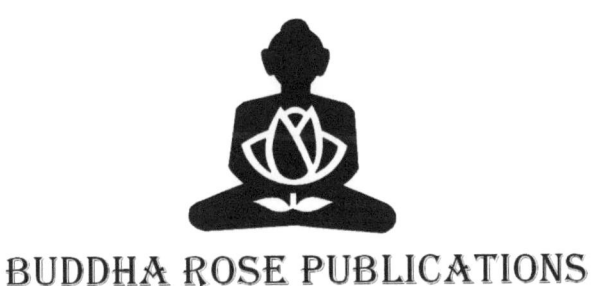

BUDDHA ROSE PUBLICATIONS

Arc Left from Istanbul: A Photographic Exploration
Copyright © 1984 and 2012 by Scott Shaw
www.scottshaw.com
All Rights Reserved

No part of this book may be reproduced in any matter without the expressed written consent of the author or the publishing company.

Photographed with a vintage Leica camera.

First Edition 2012

ISBN: 1-877792-57-8
ISBN 13: 978-1-877792-57-1

Printed in the United States of America

10 9 8 7 6 5 4 3 2 1

ARC LEFT FROM ISTANBUL

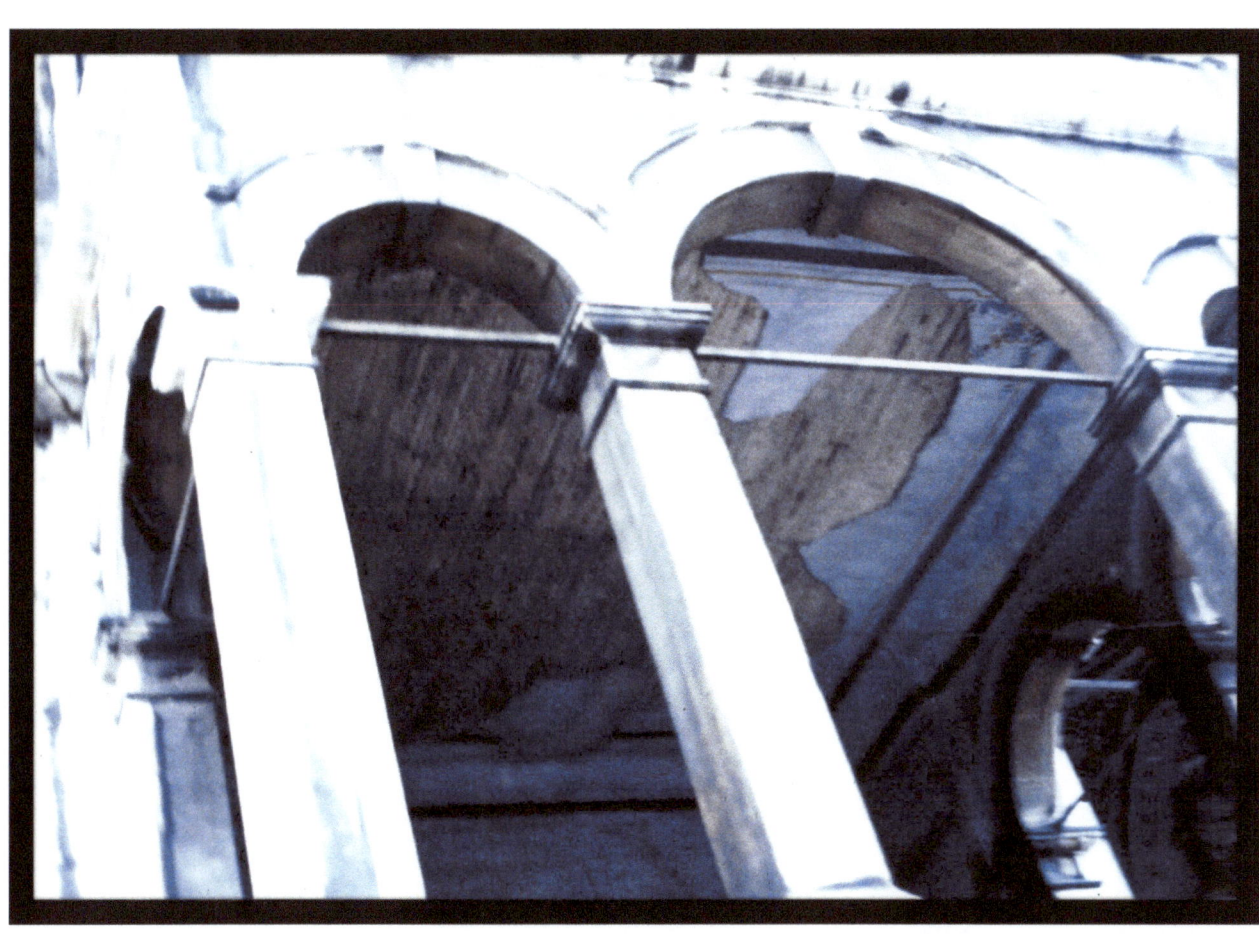

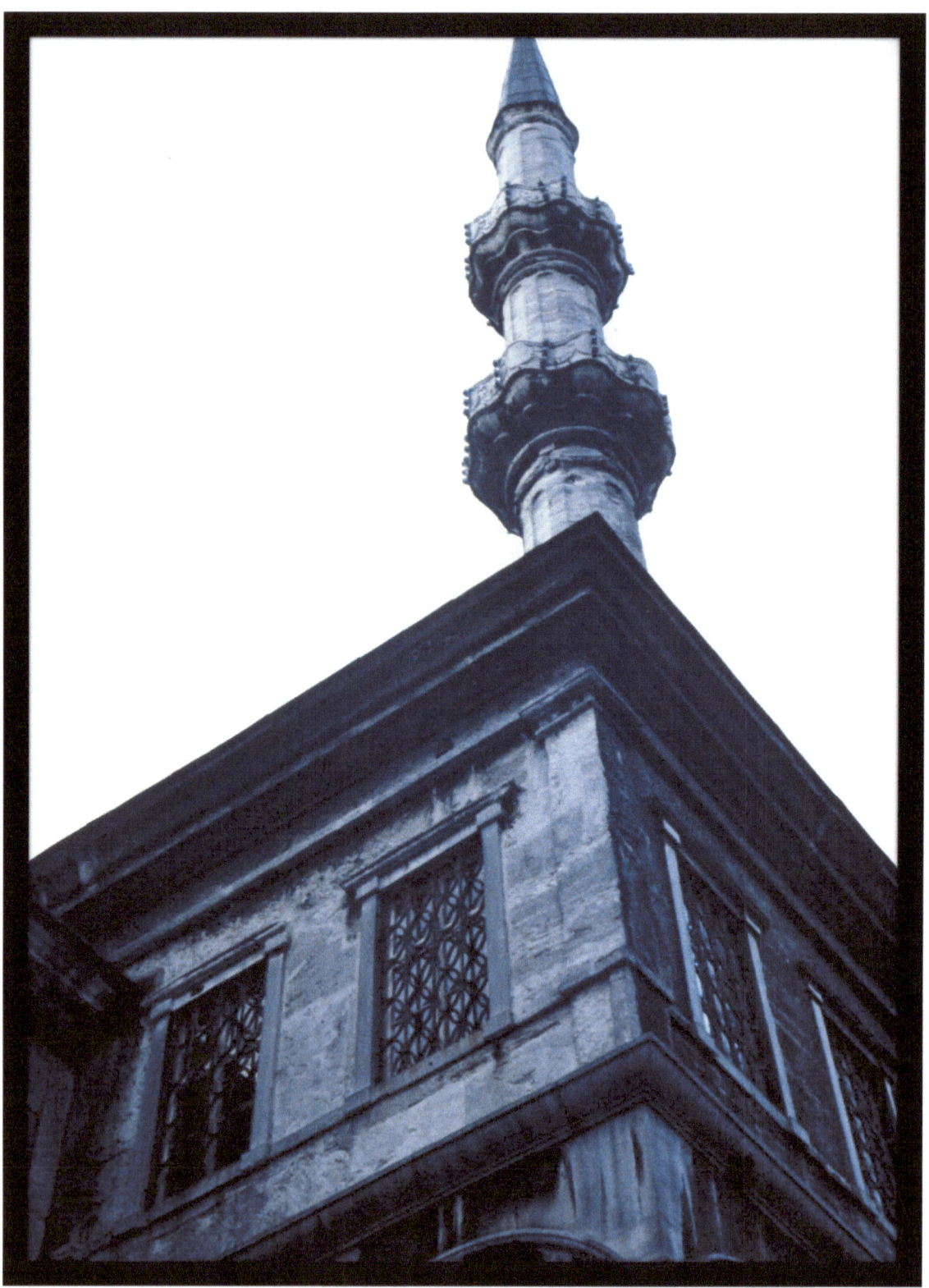

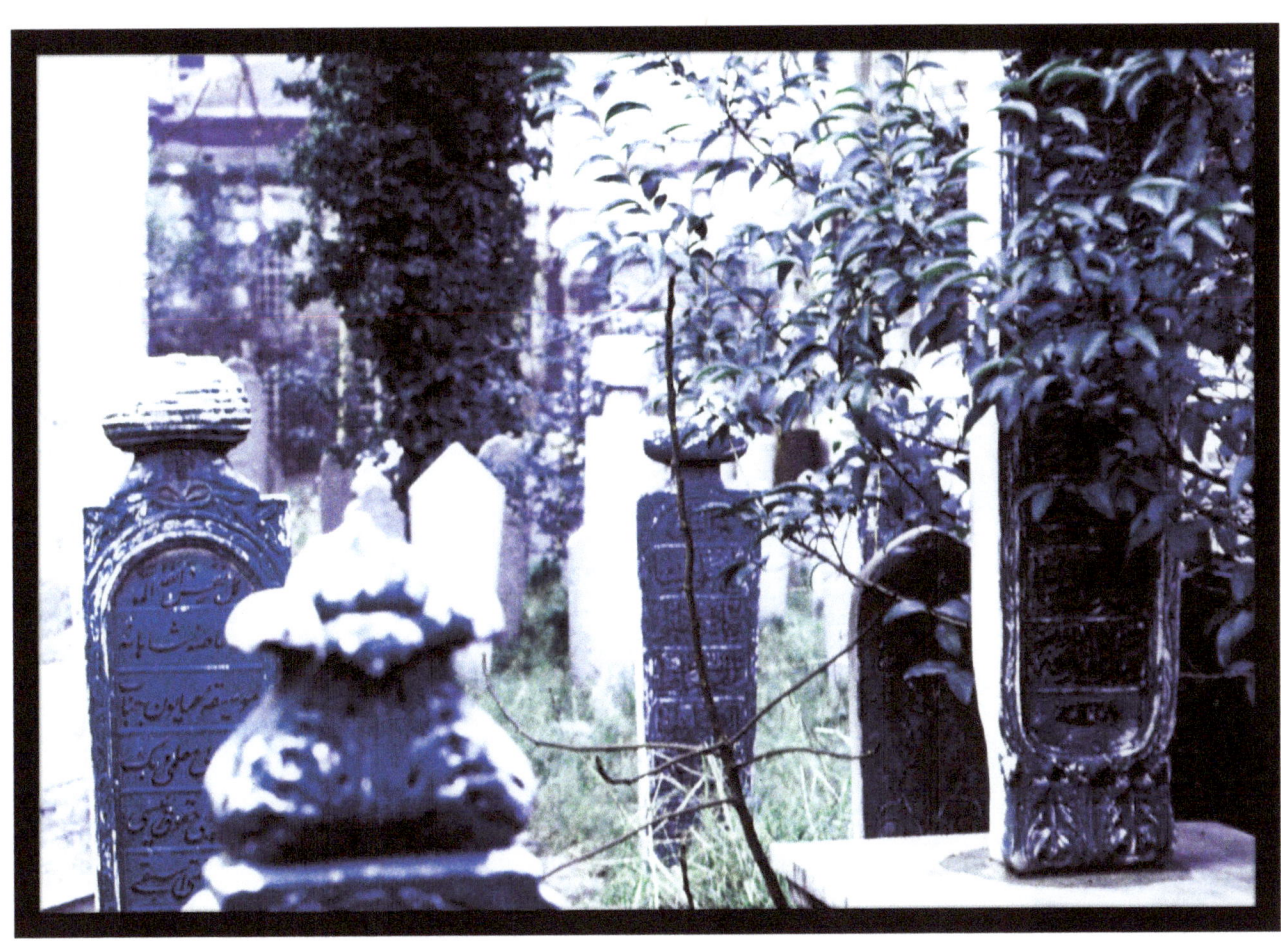

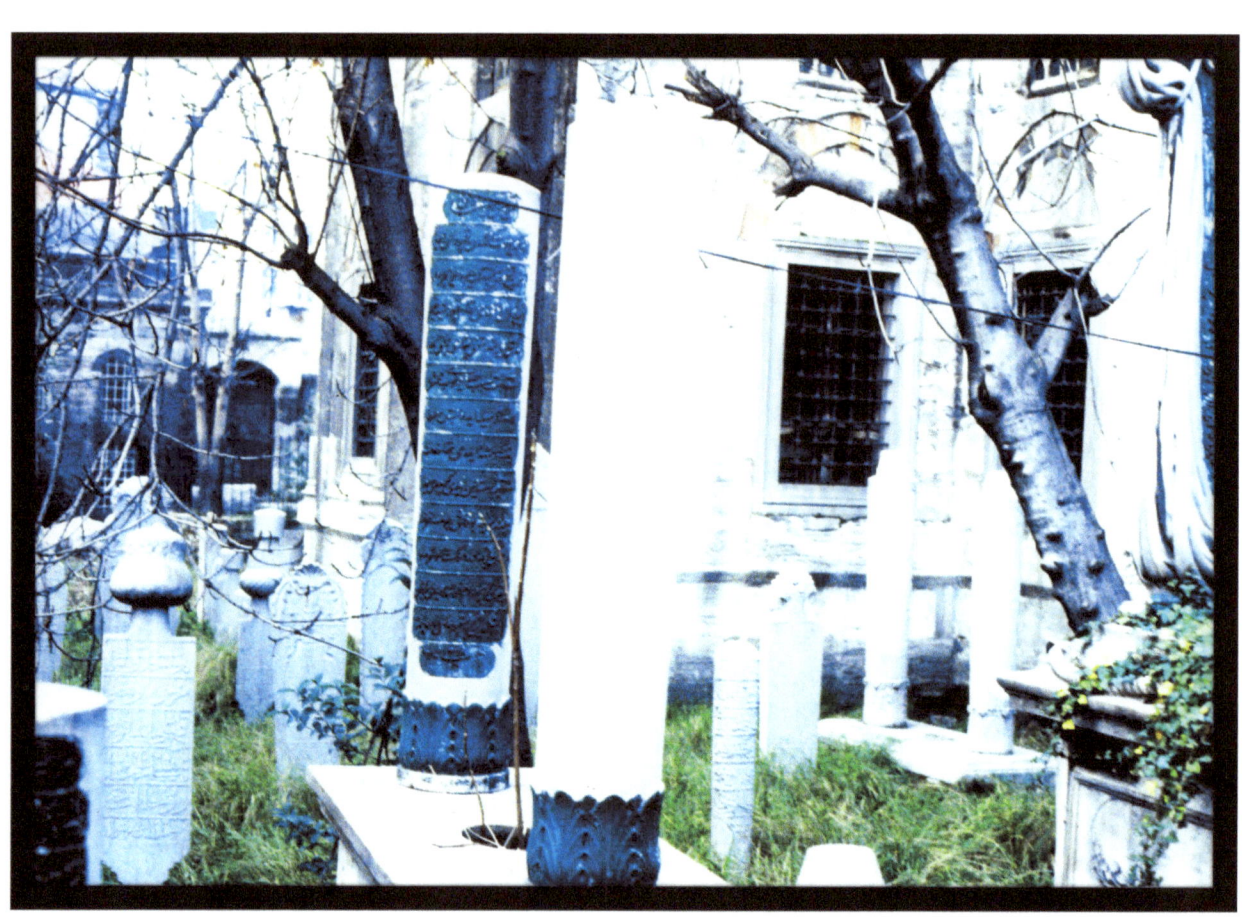

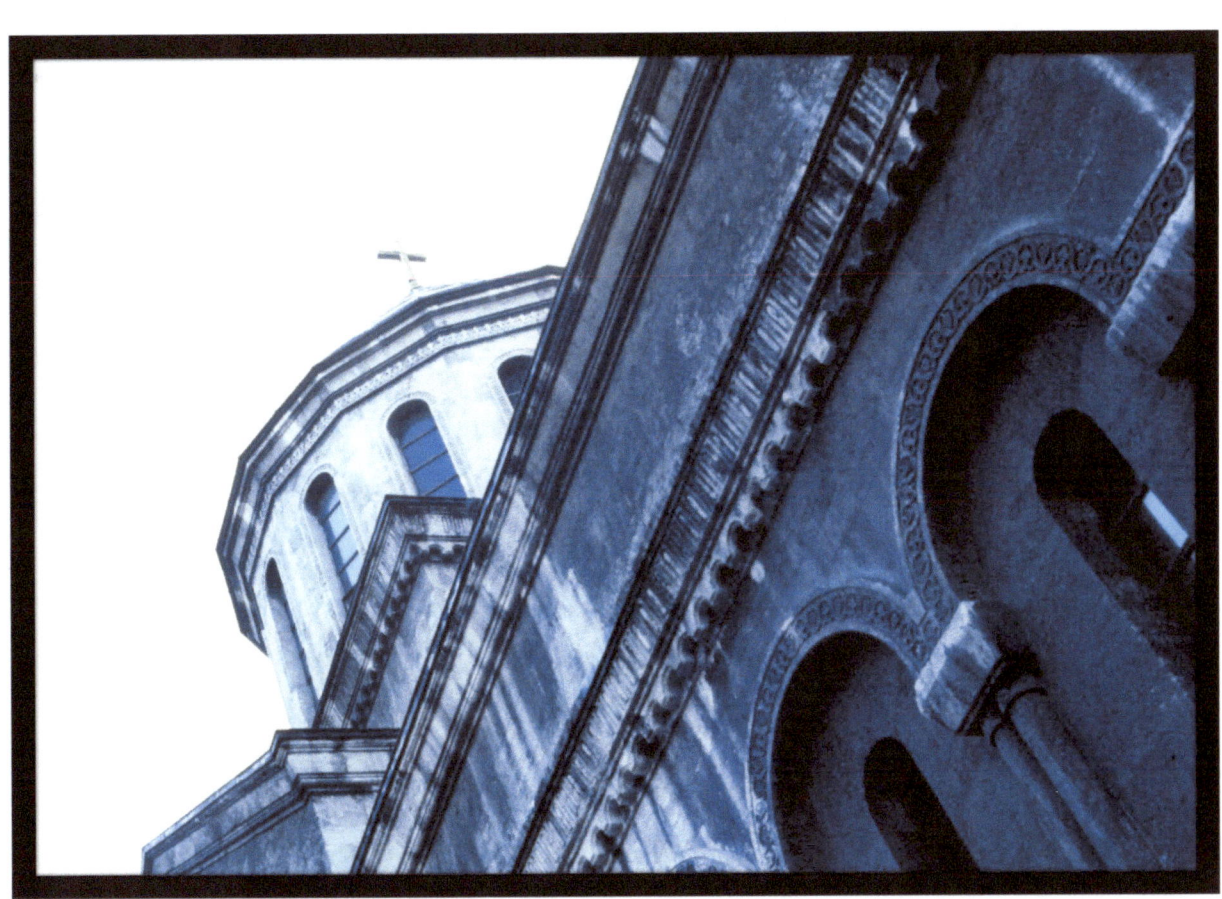

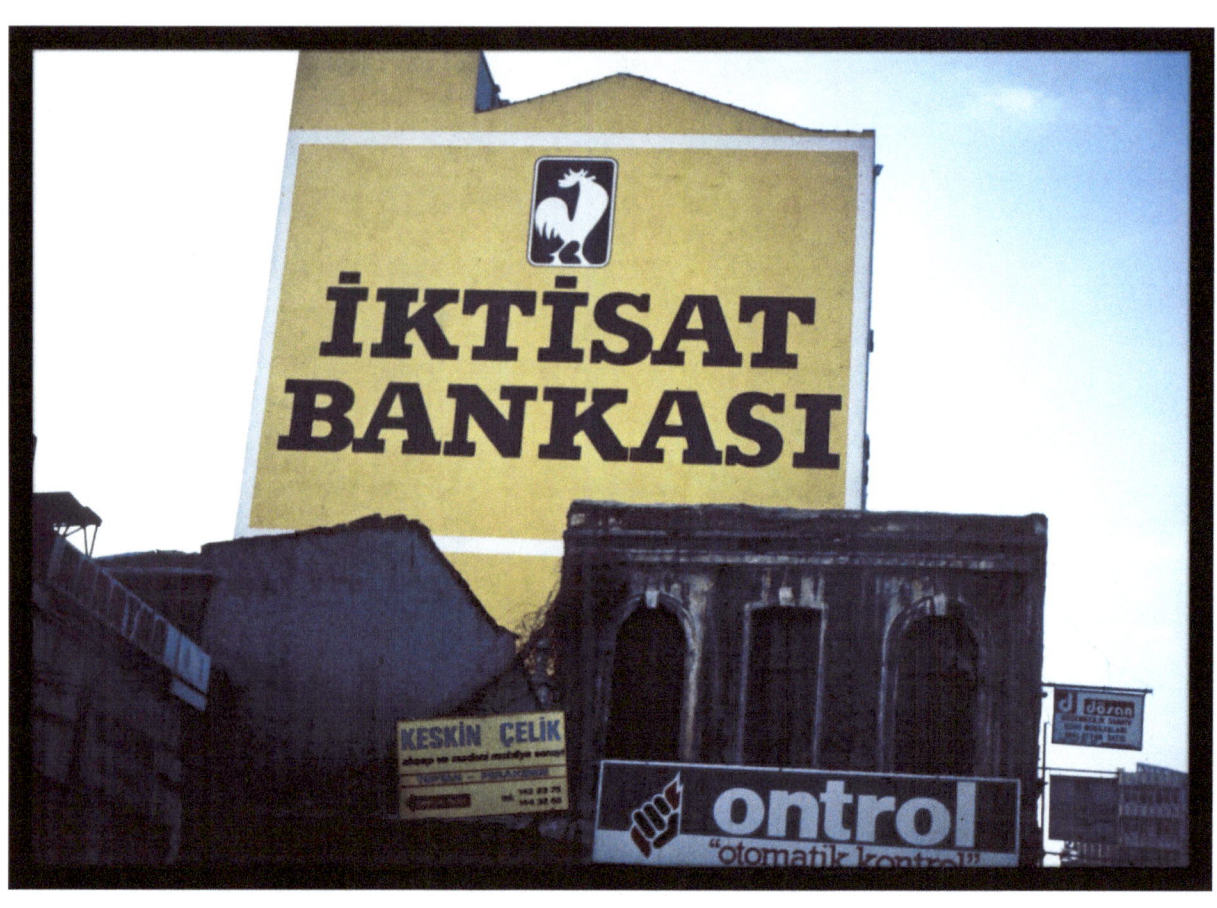

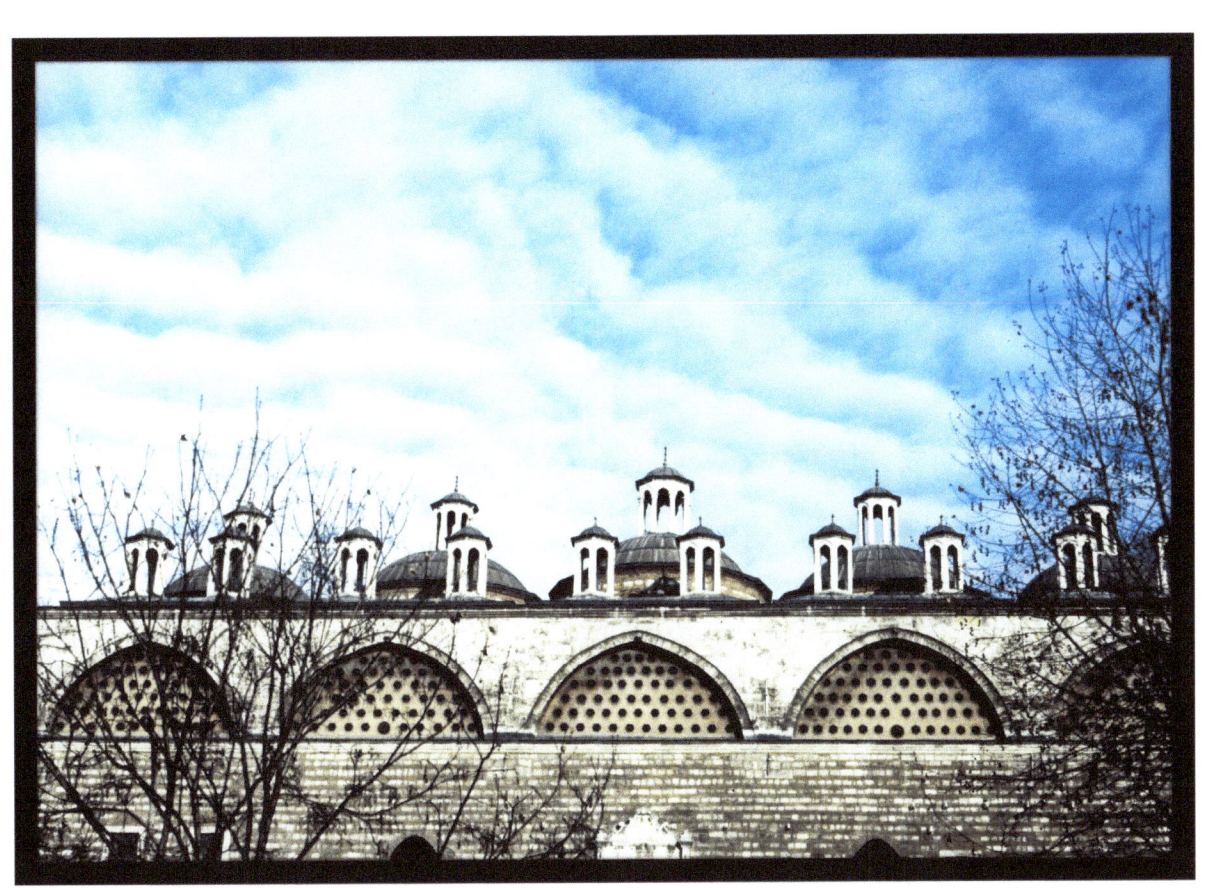

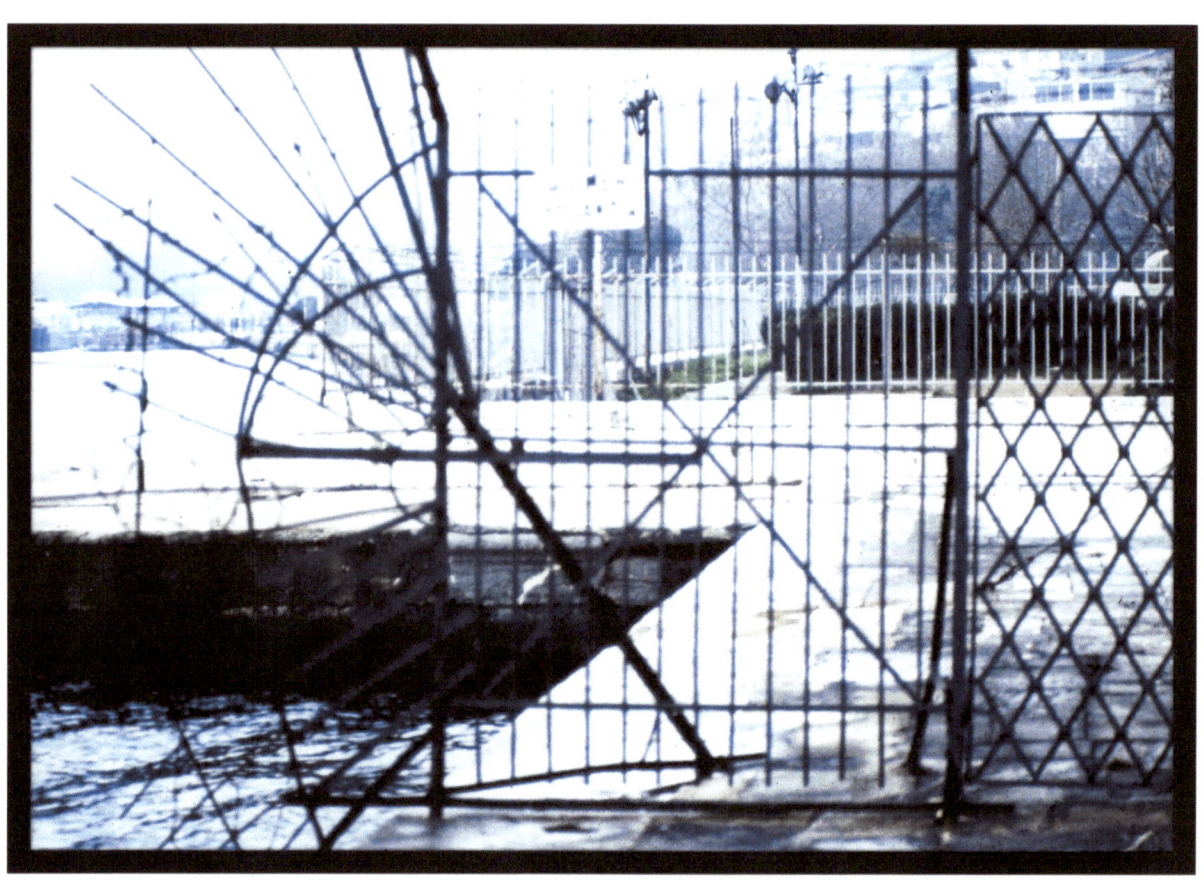

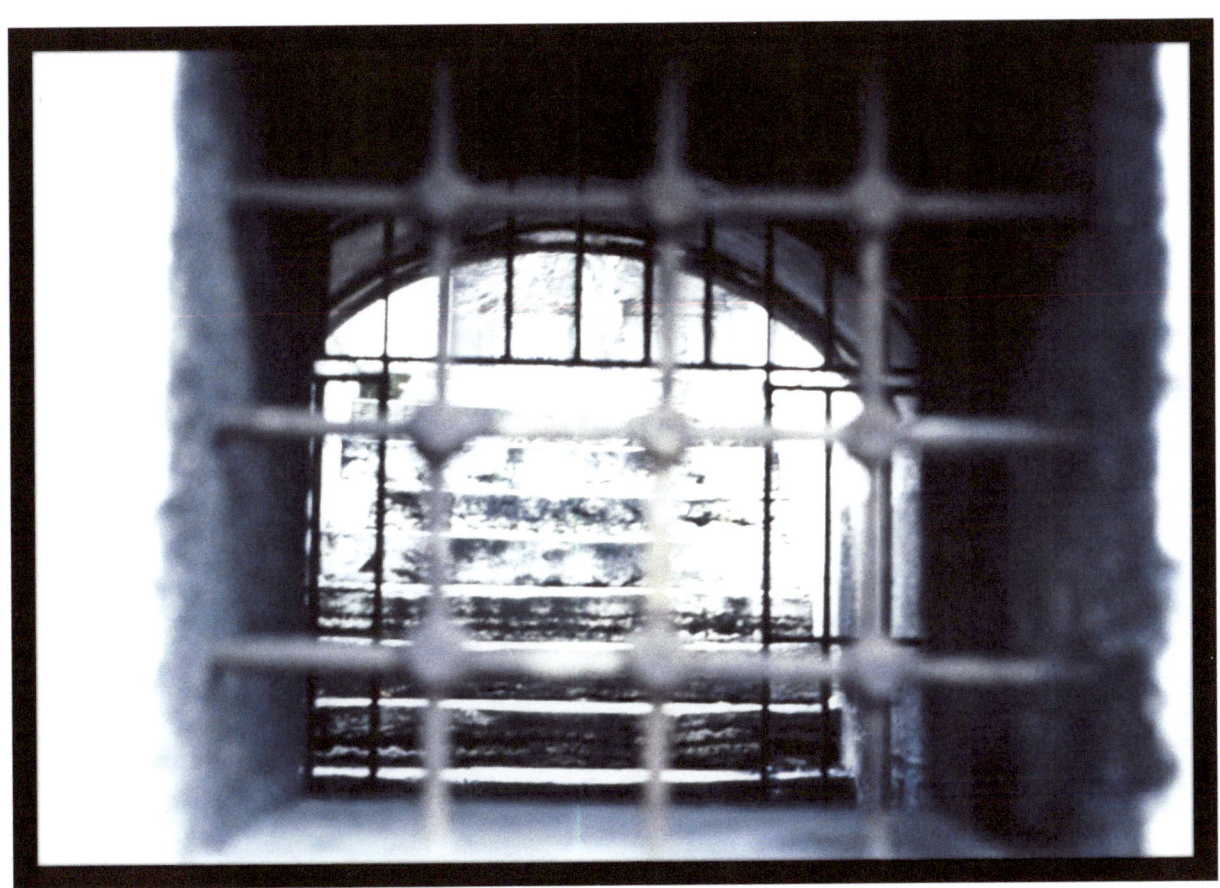

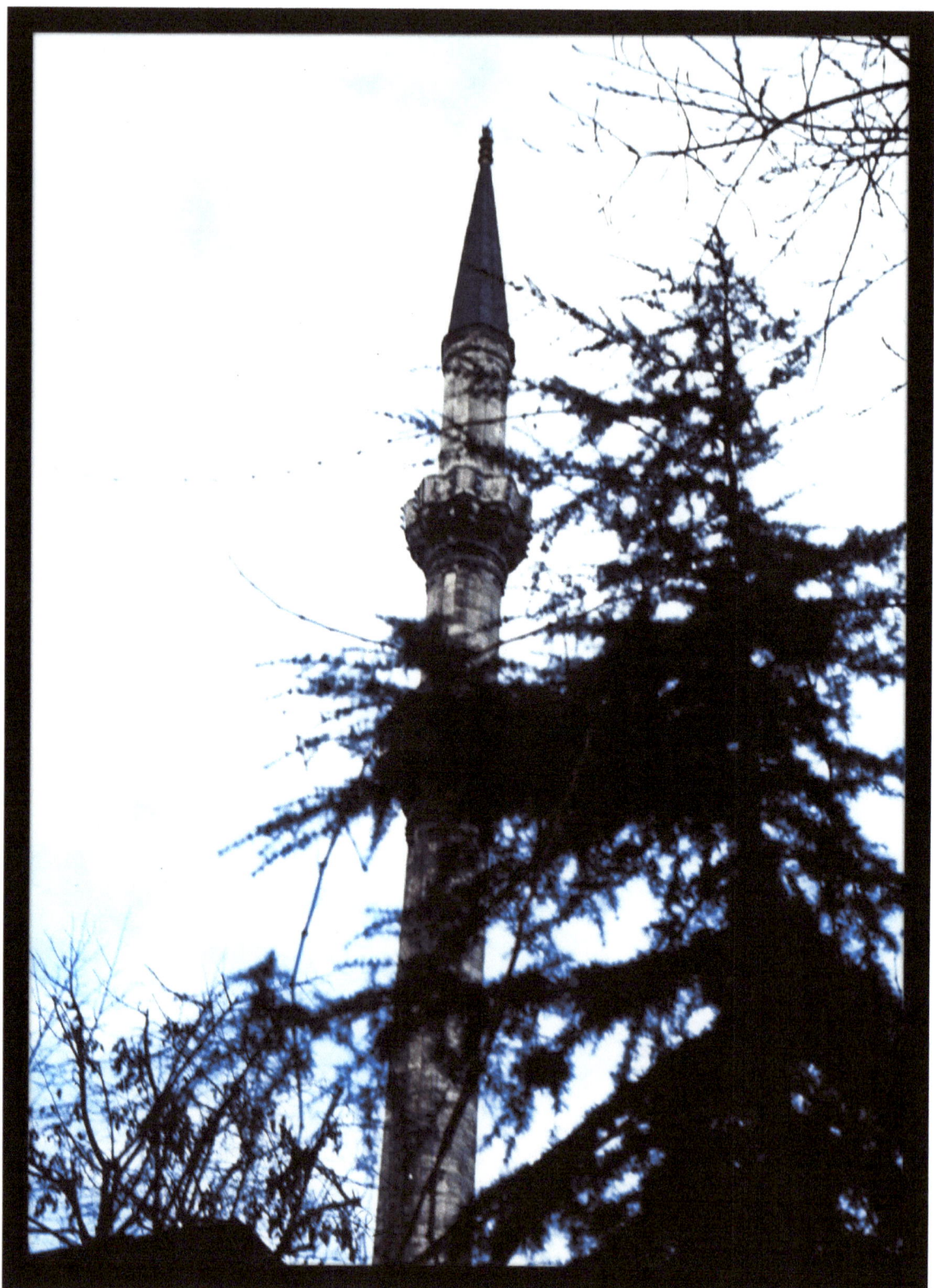

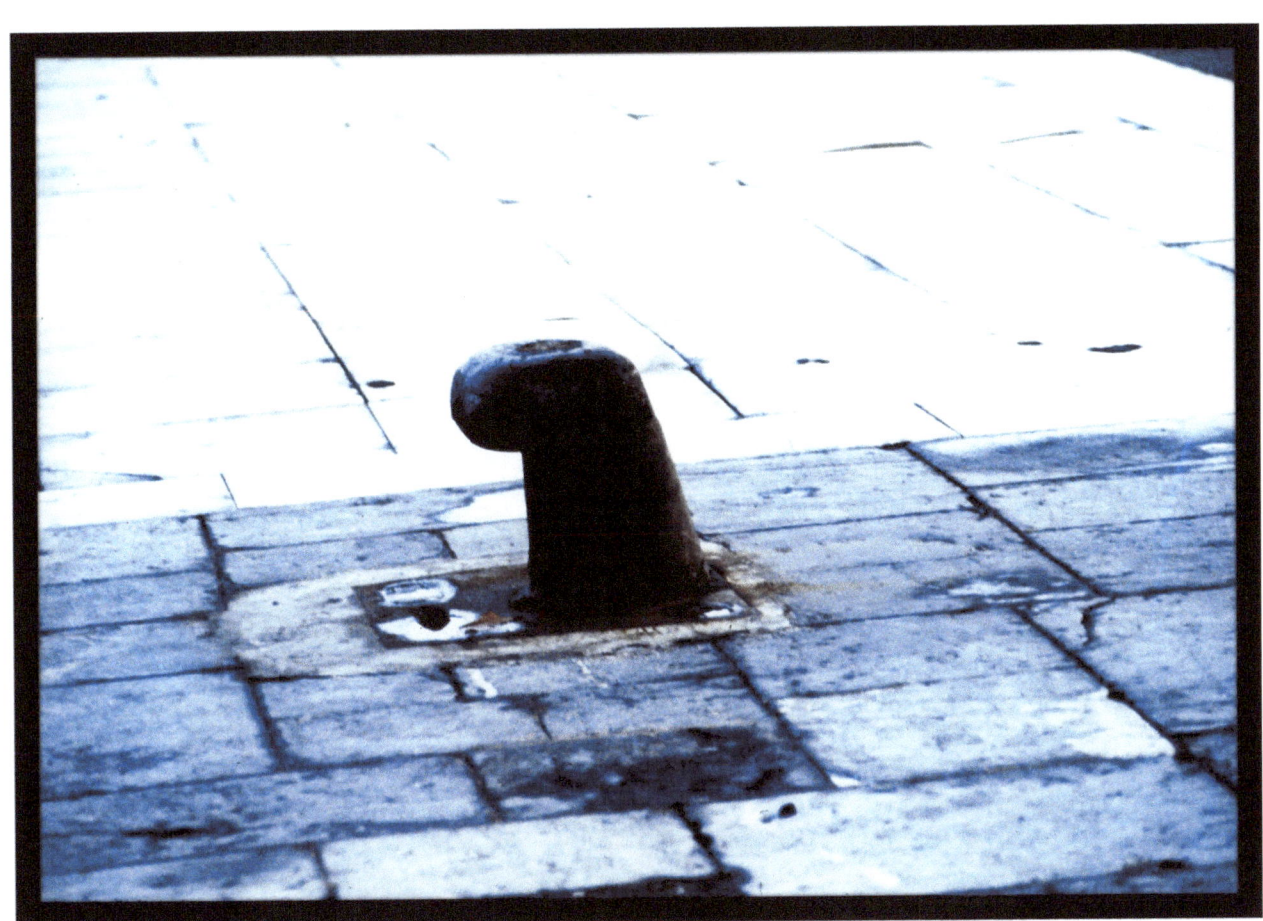

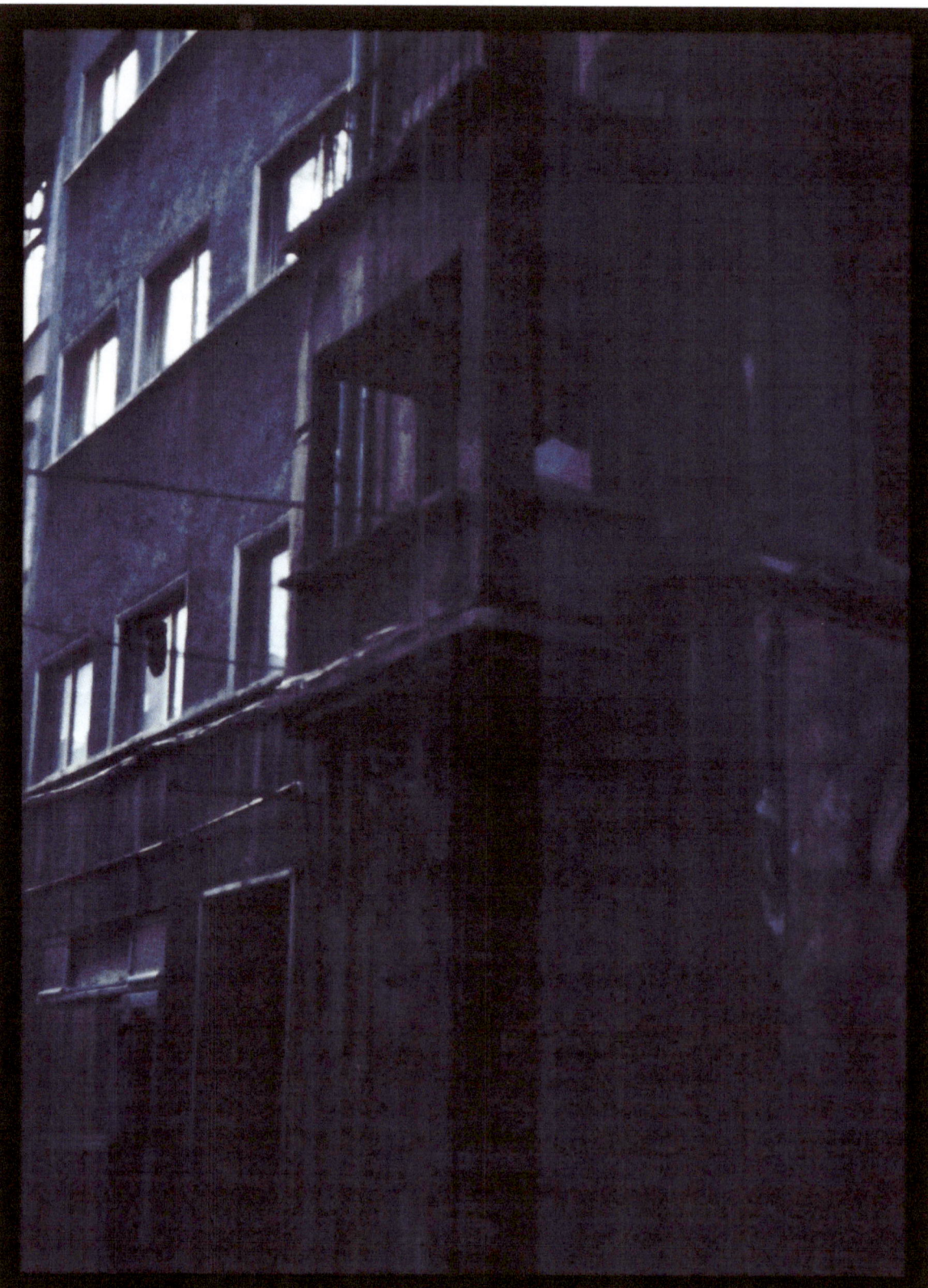

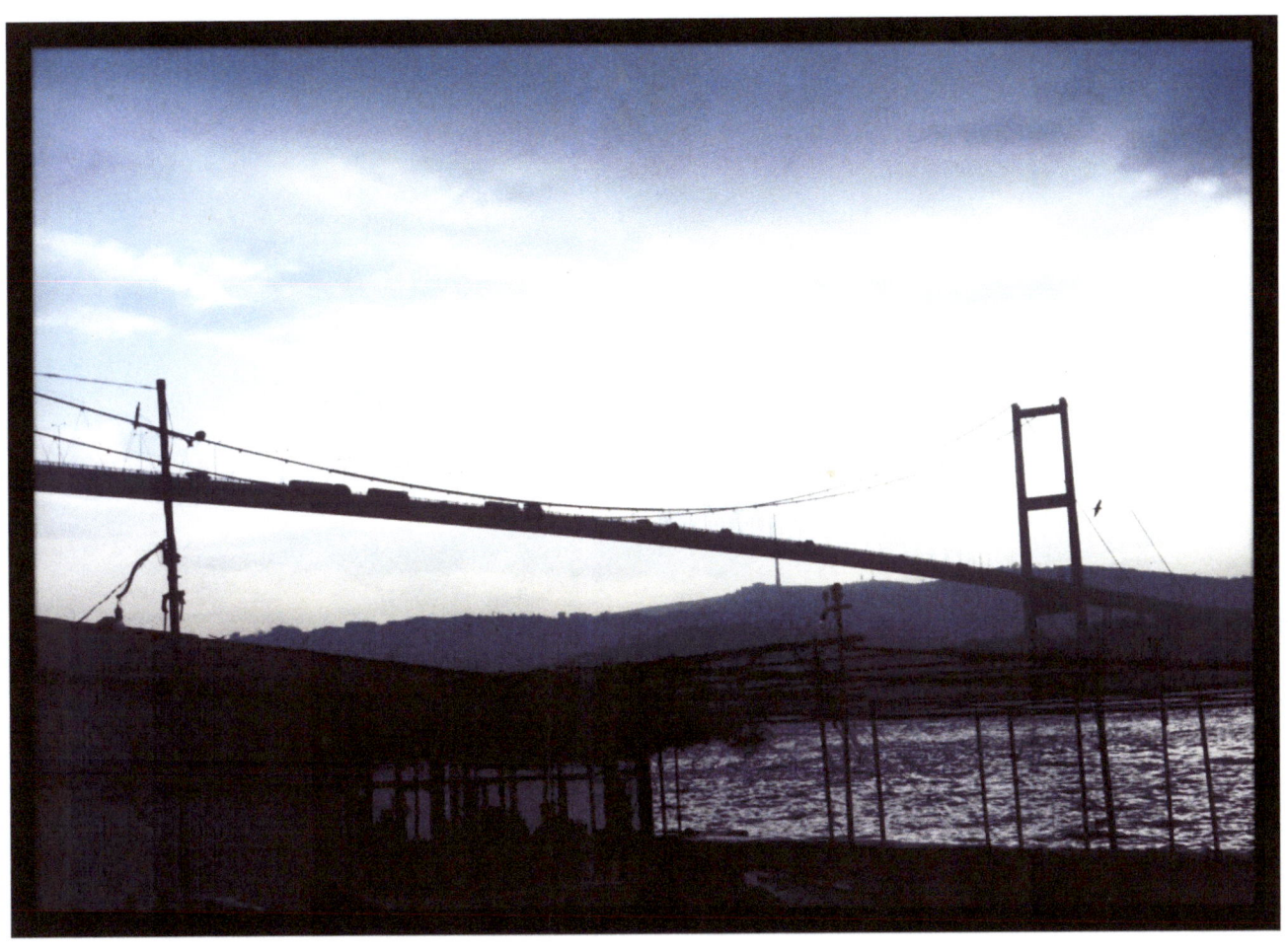

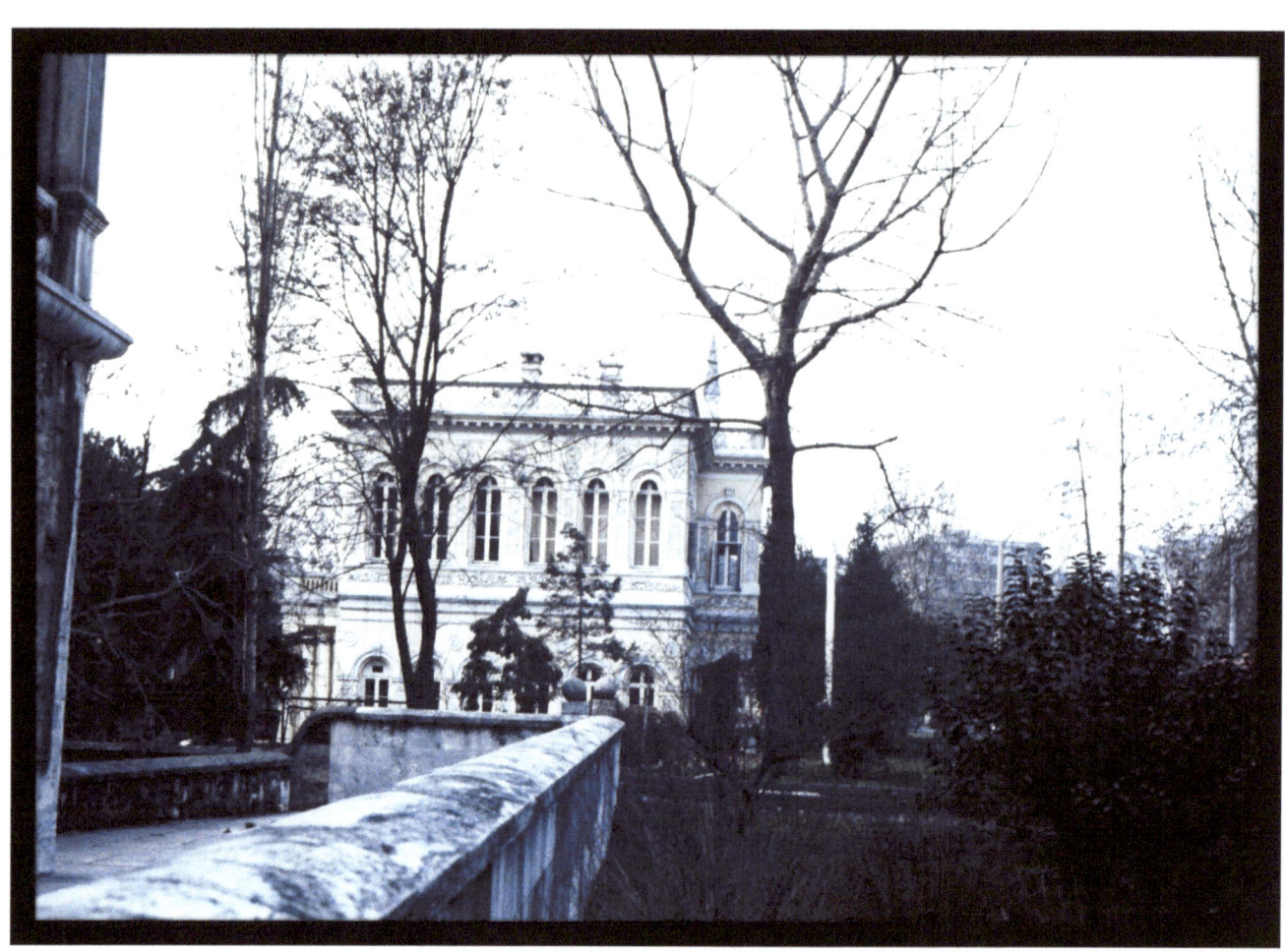

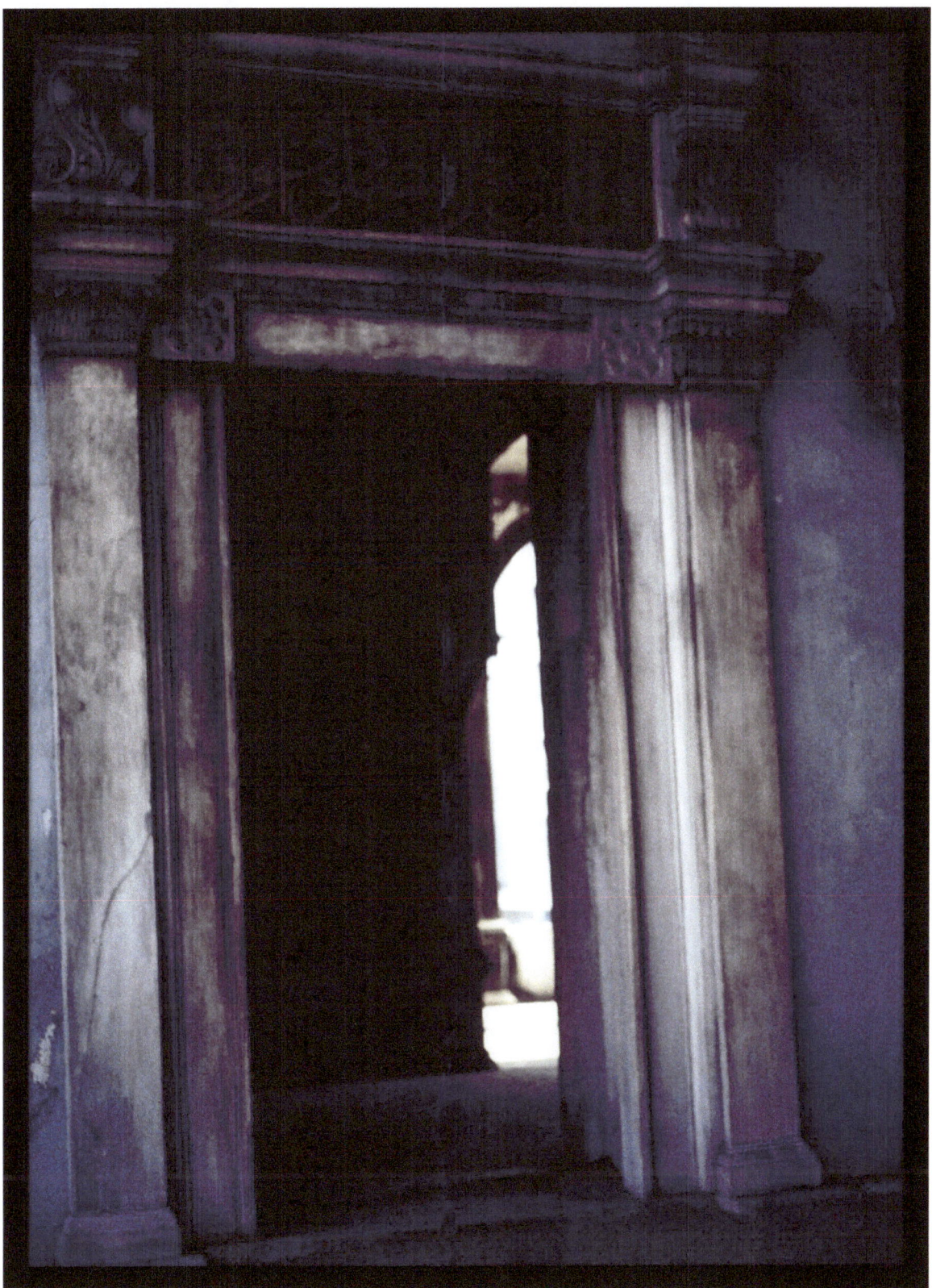

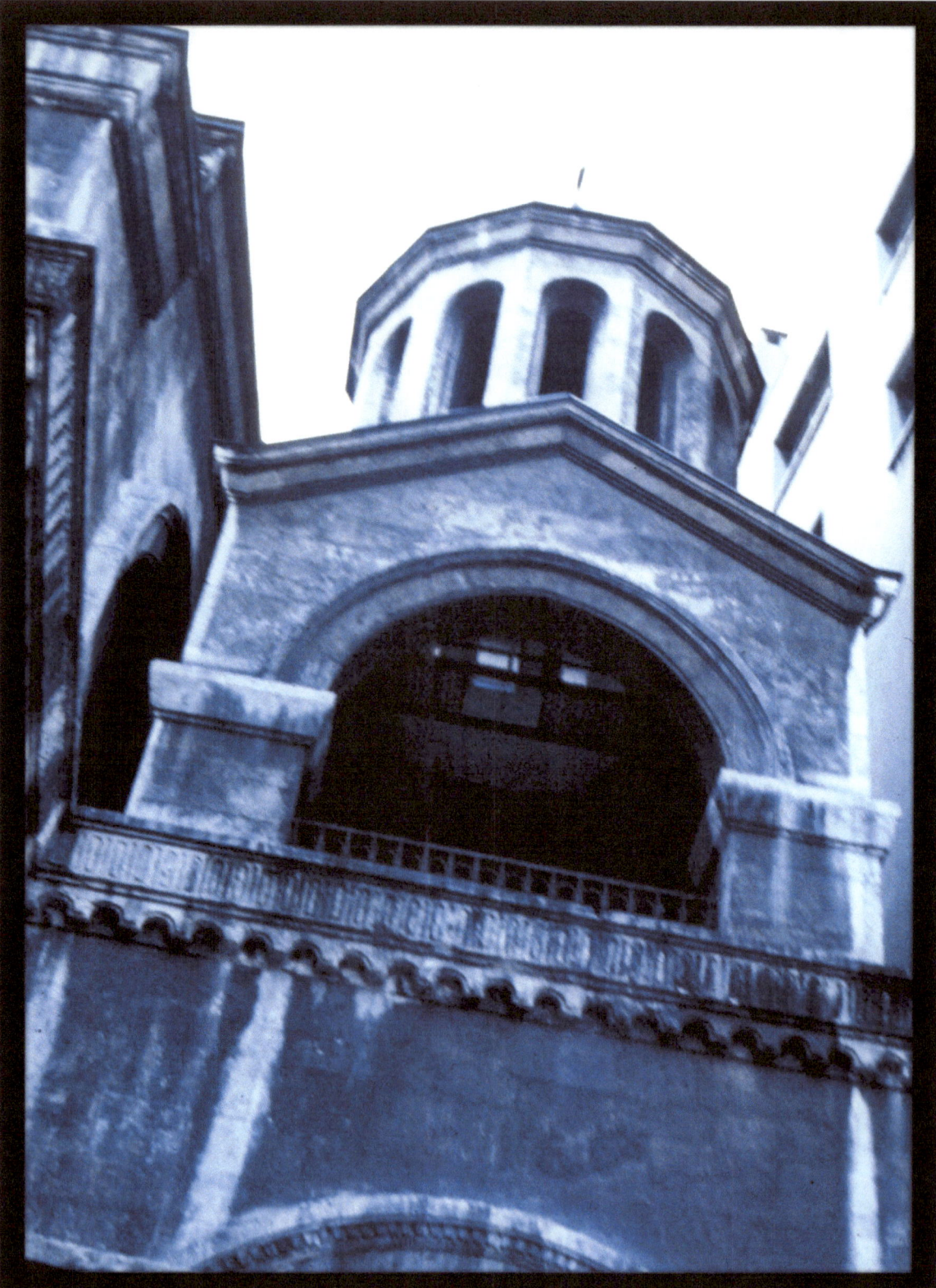

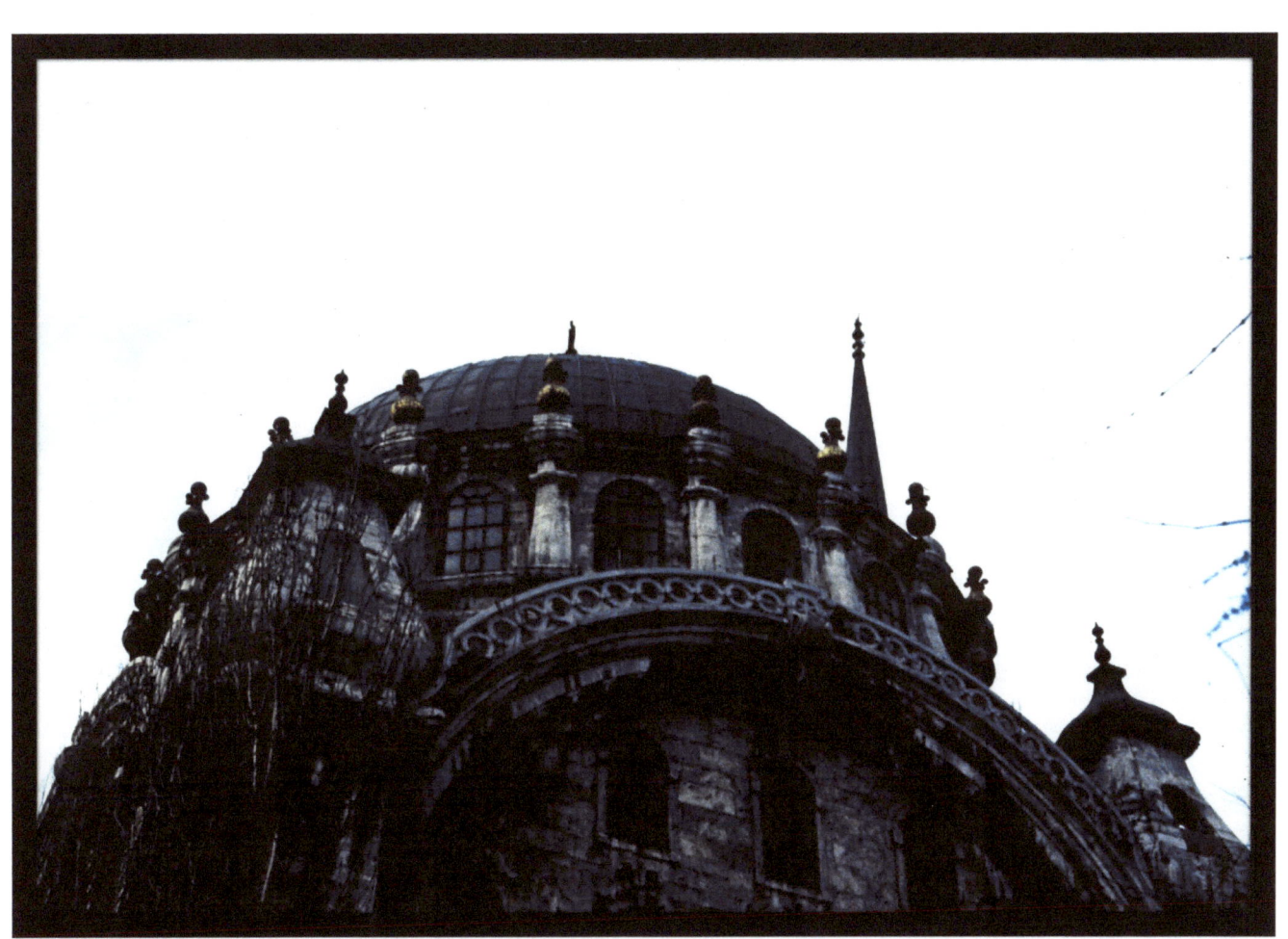

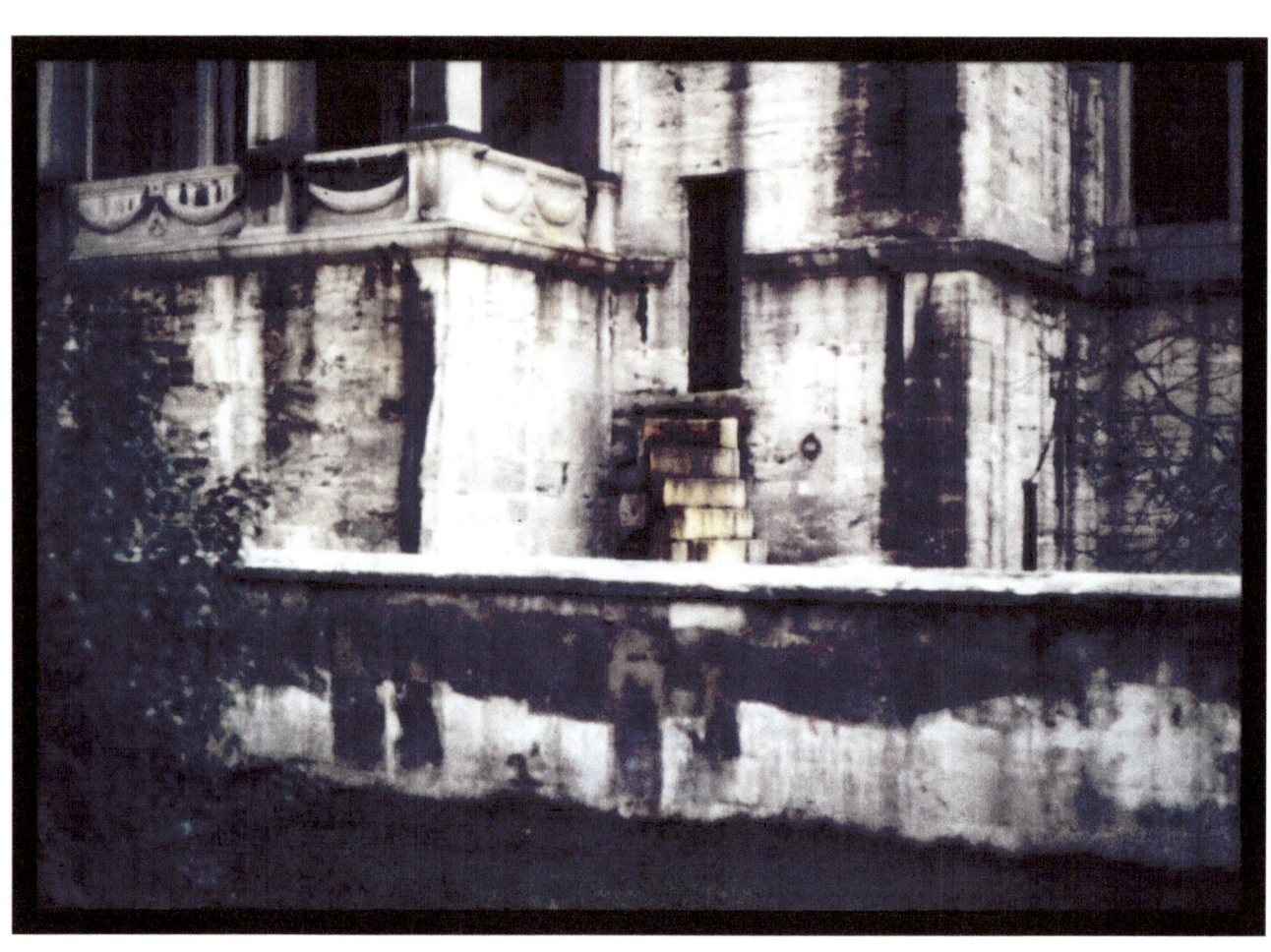

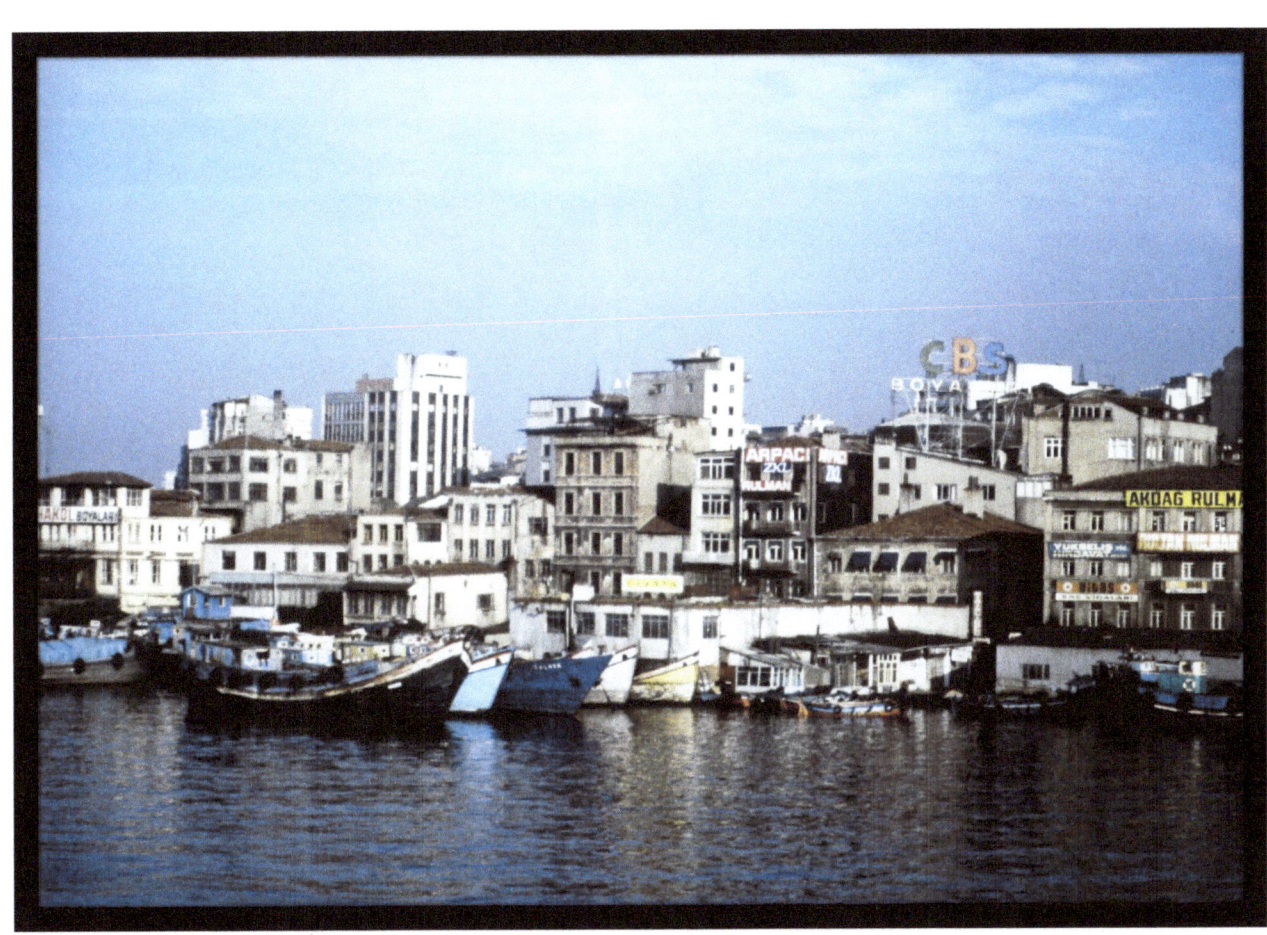

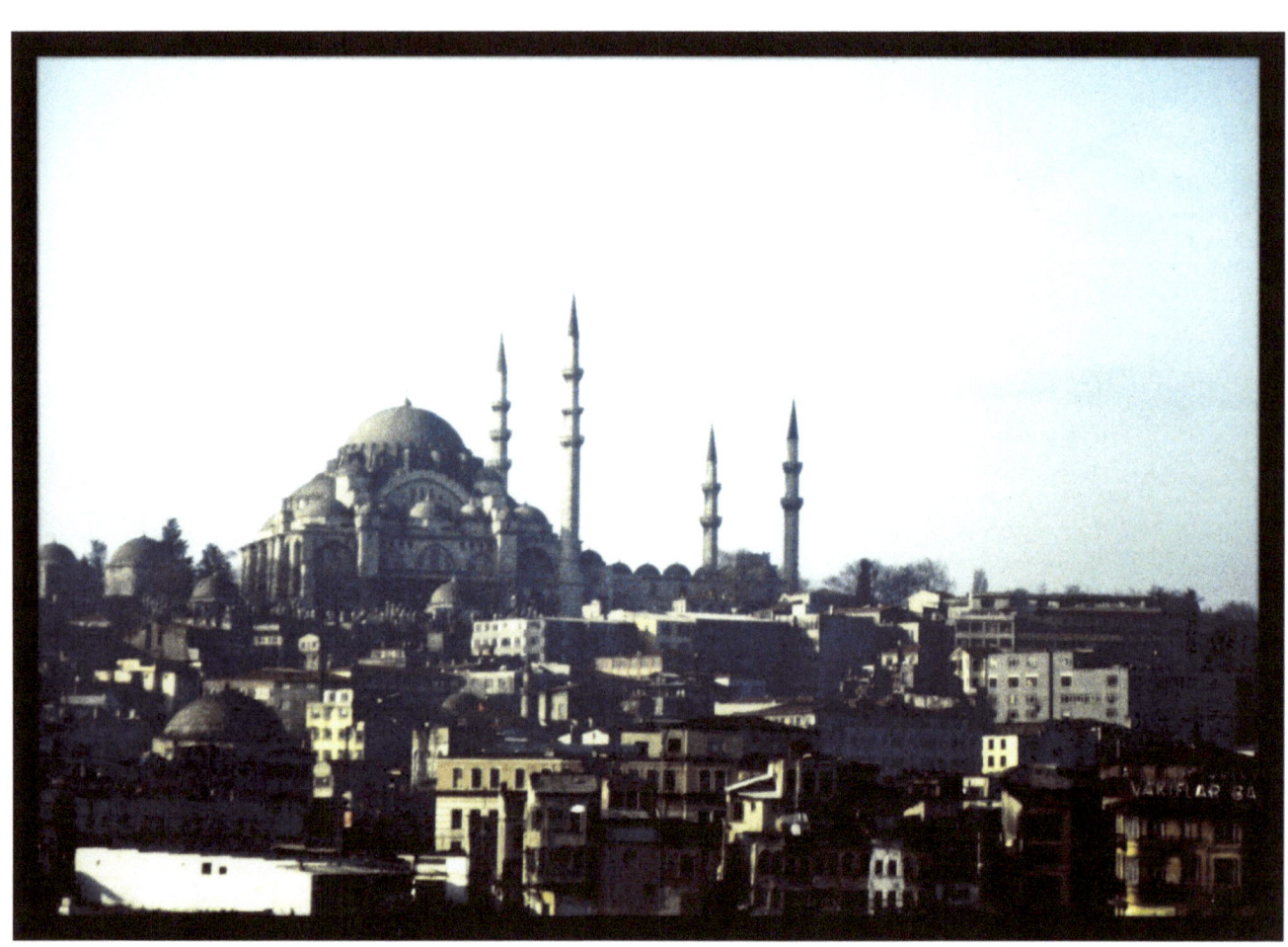

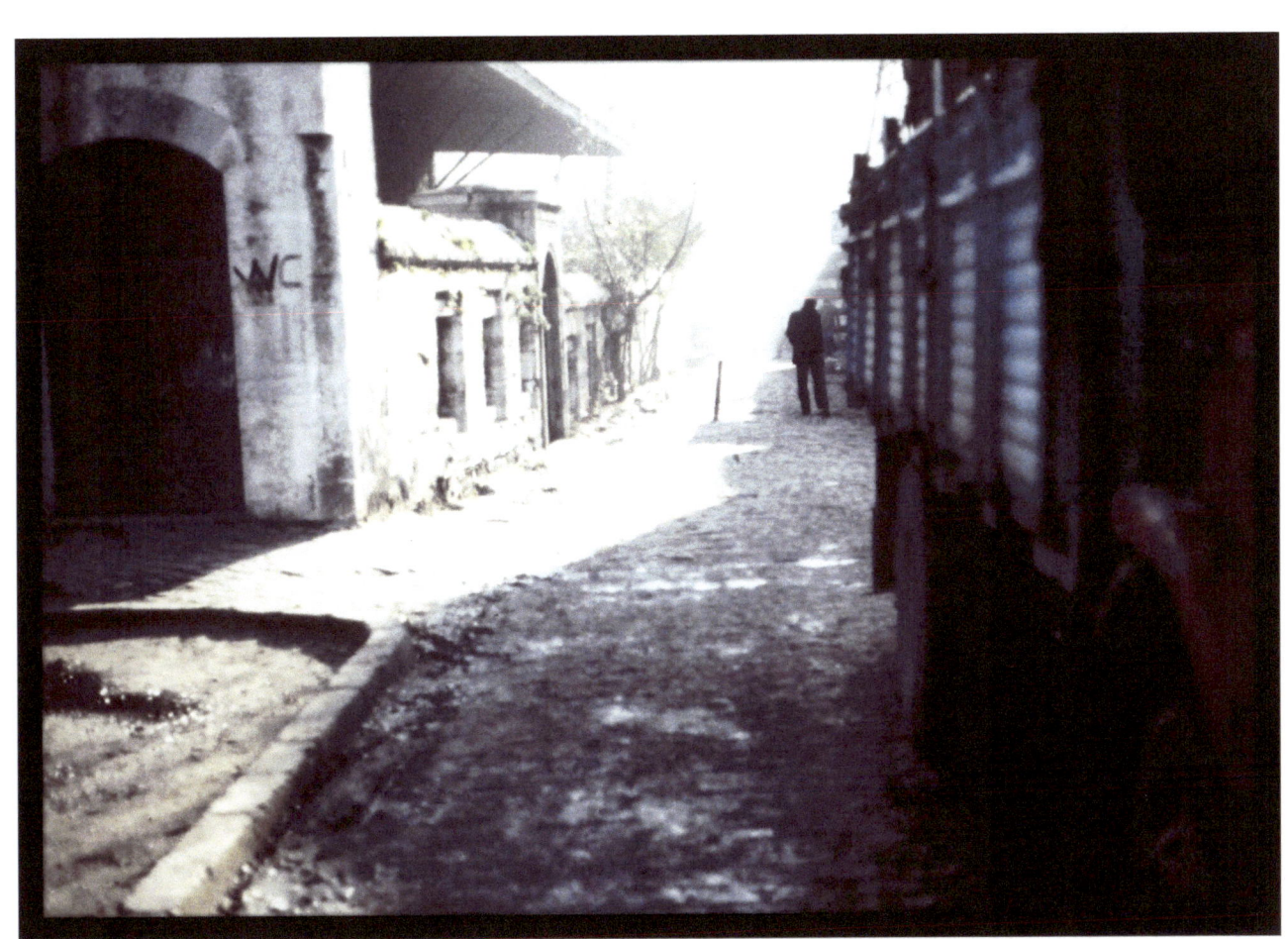

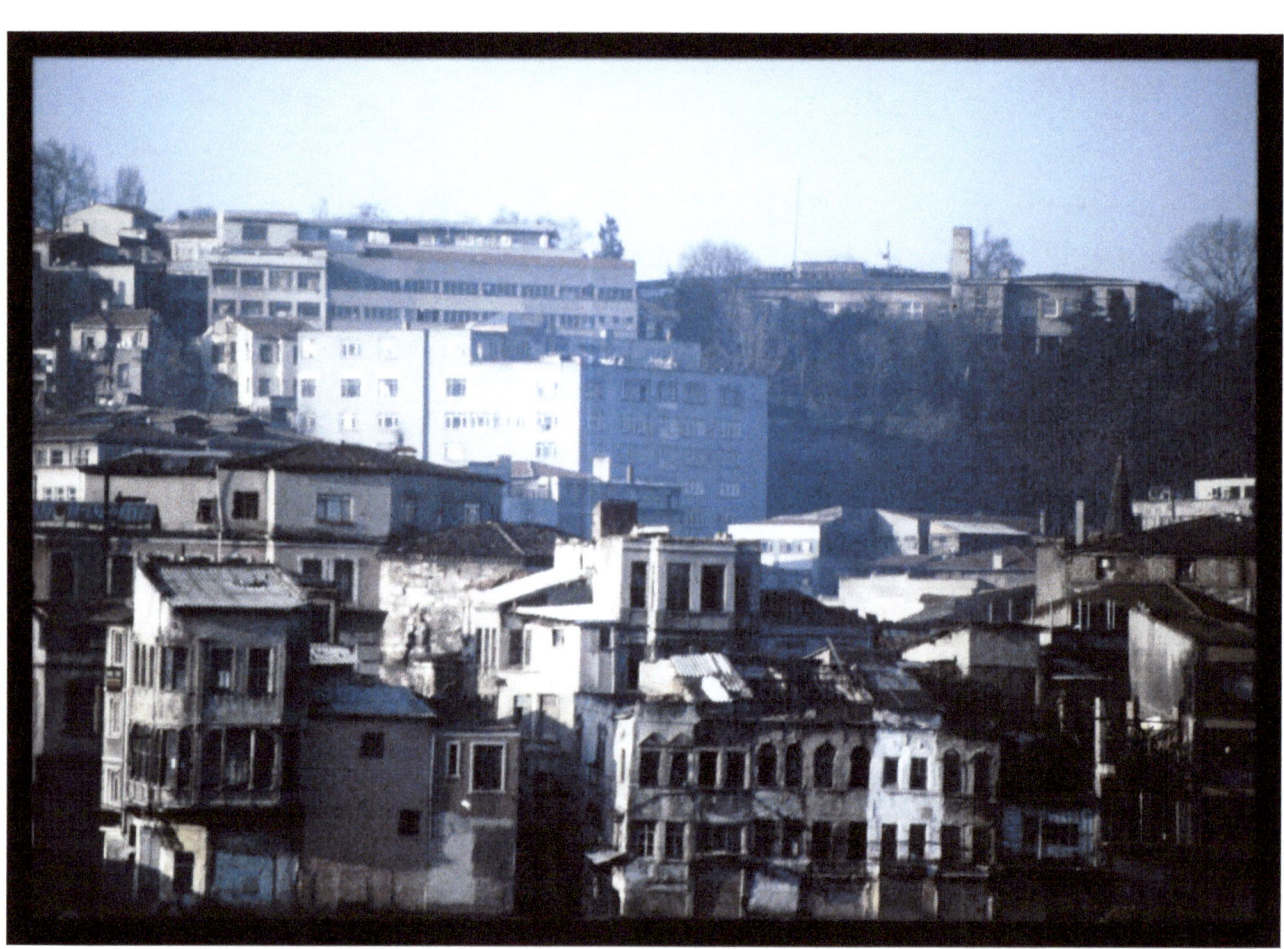

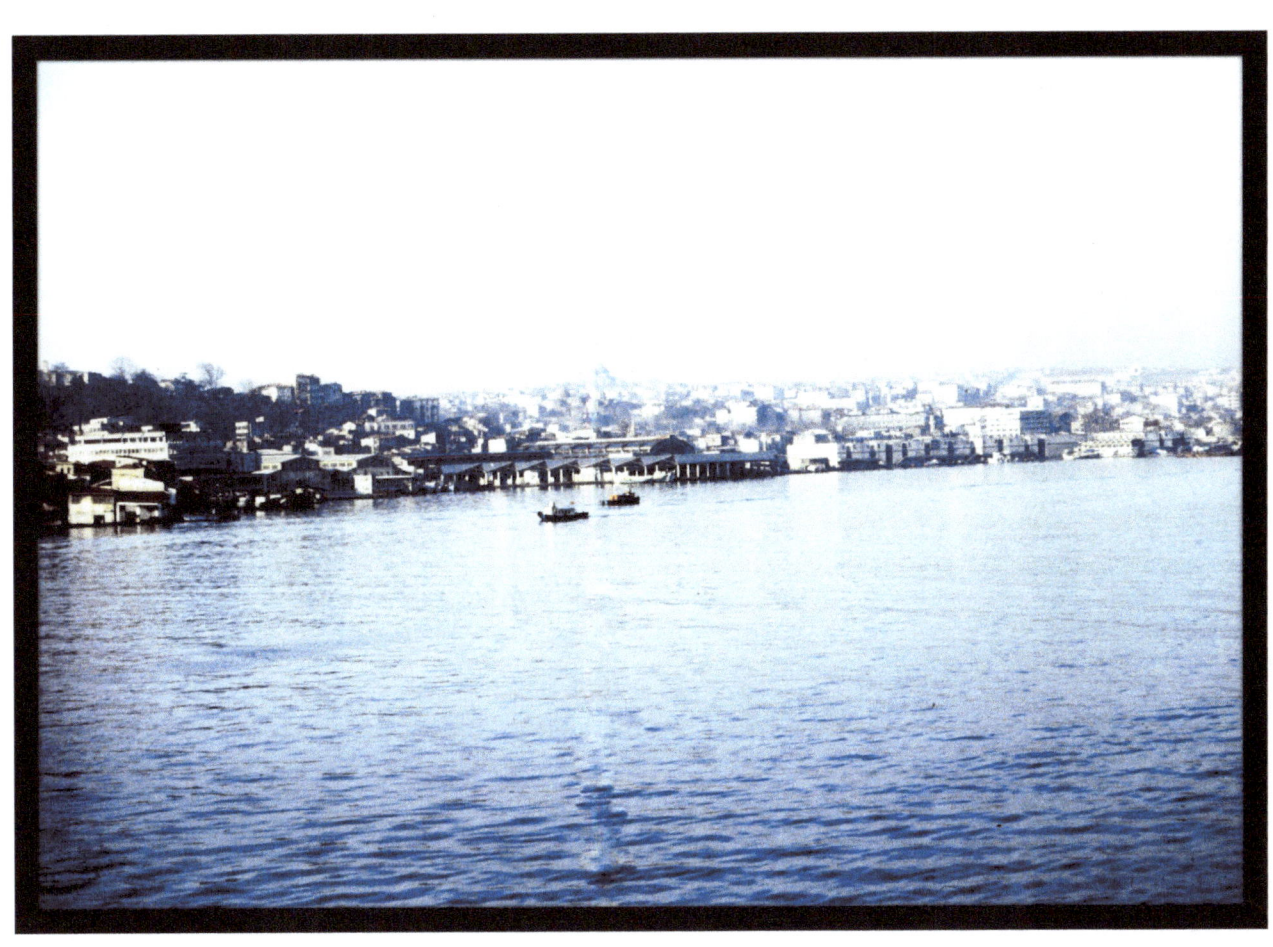

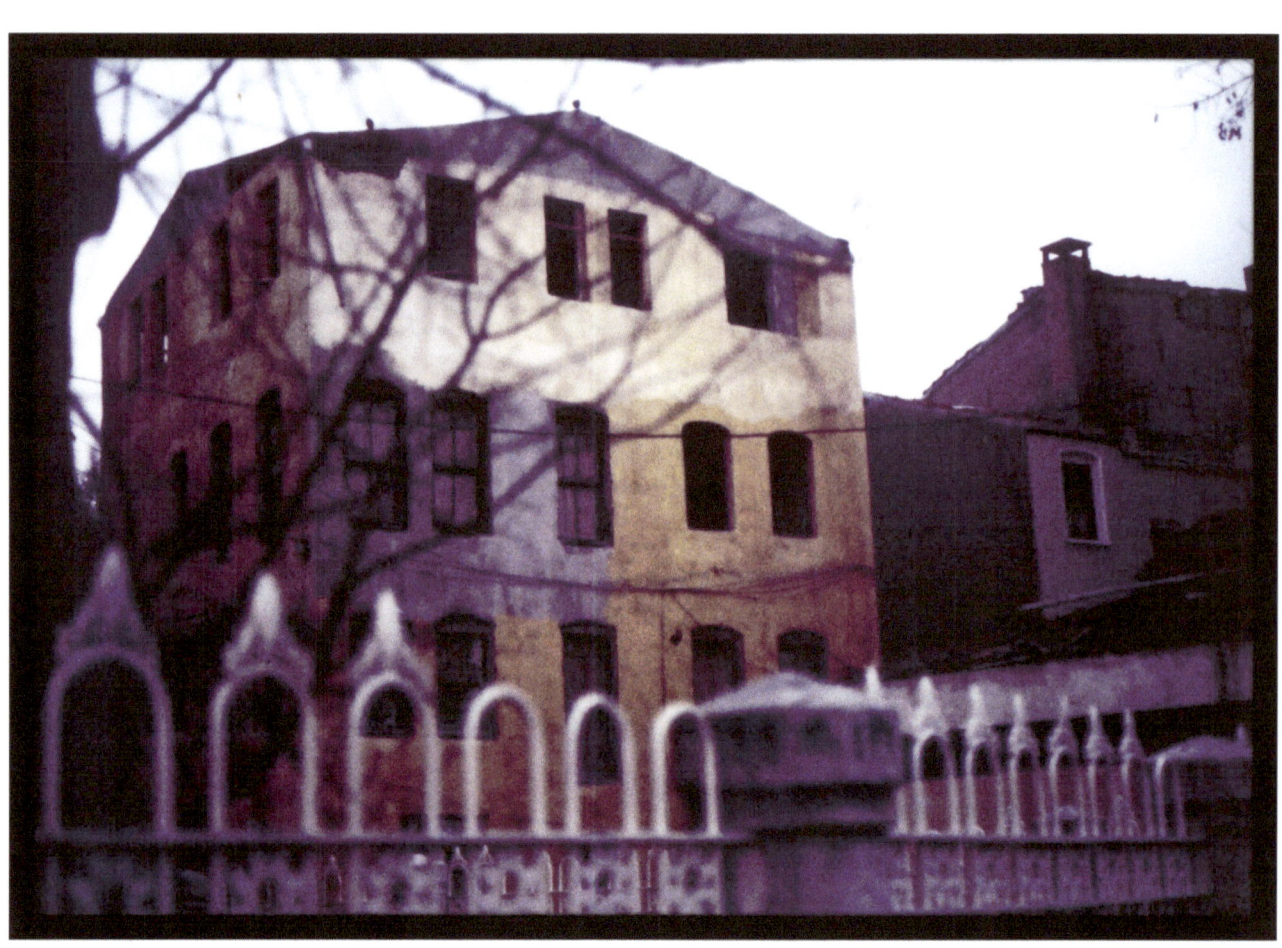

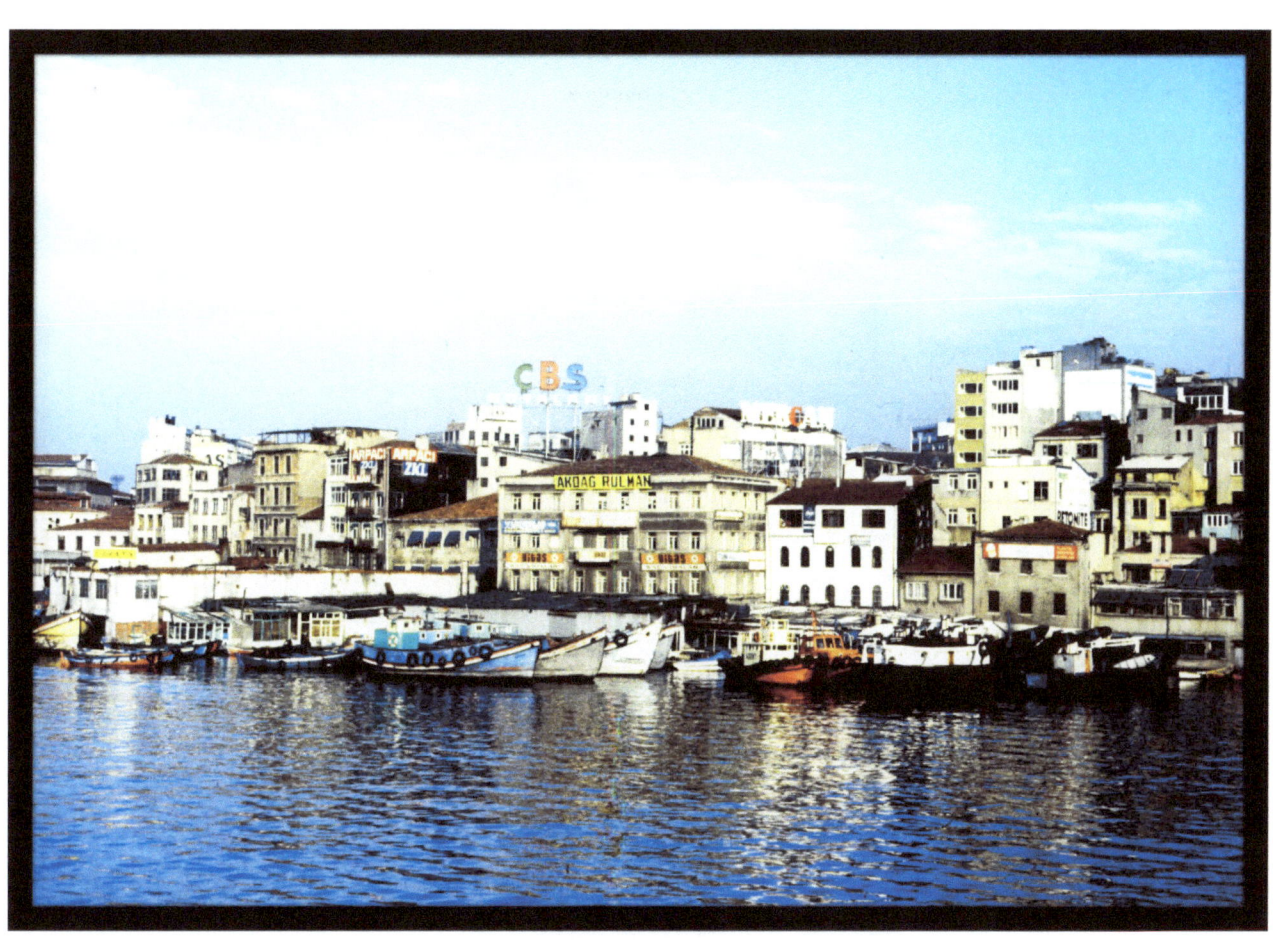

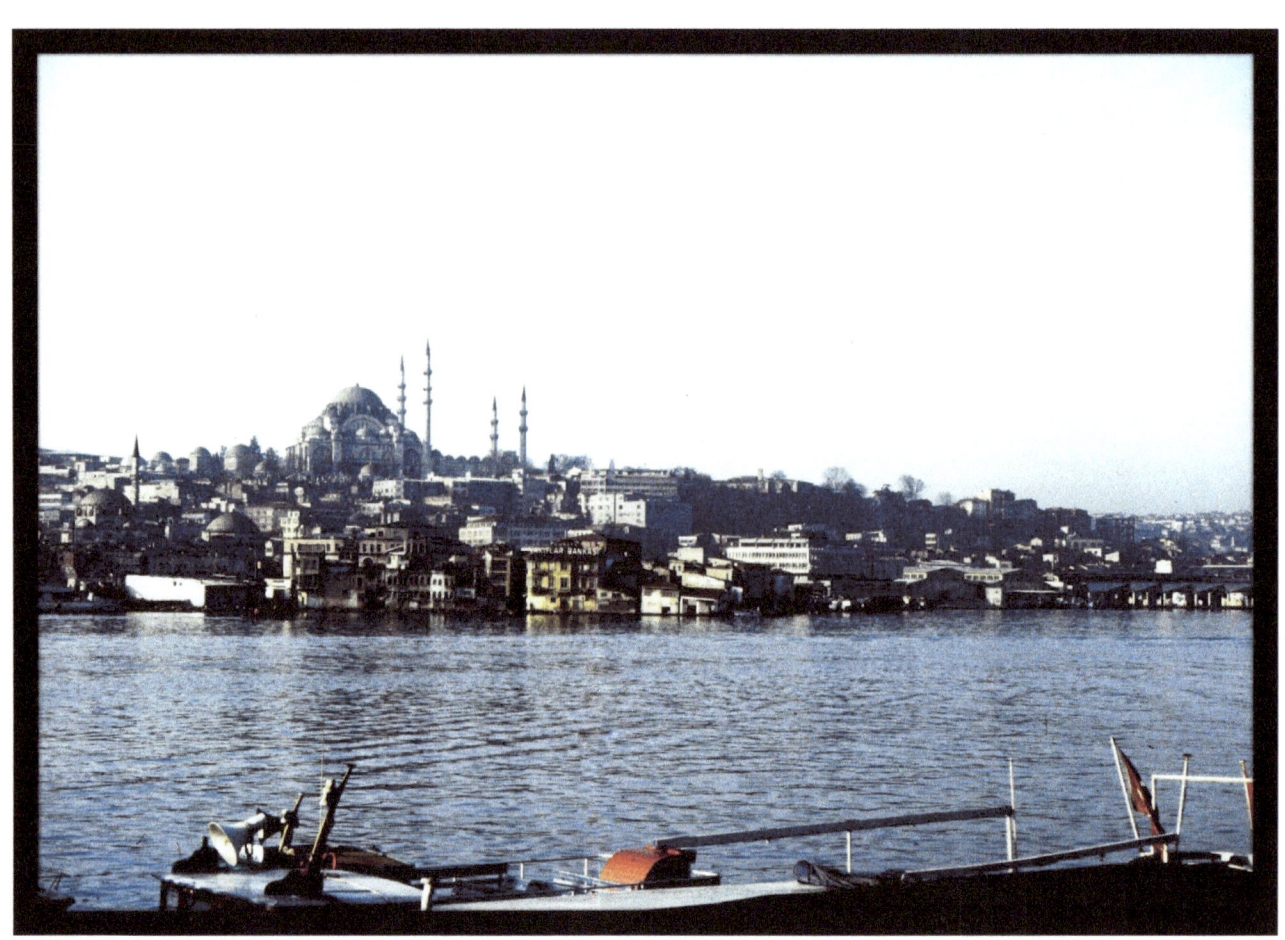

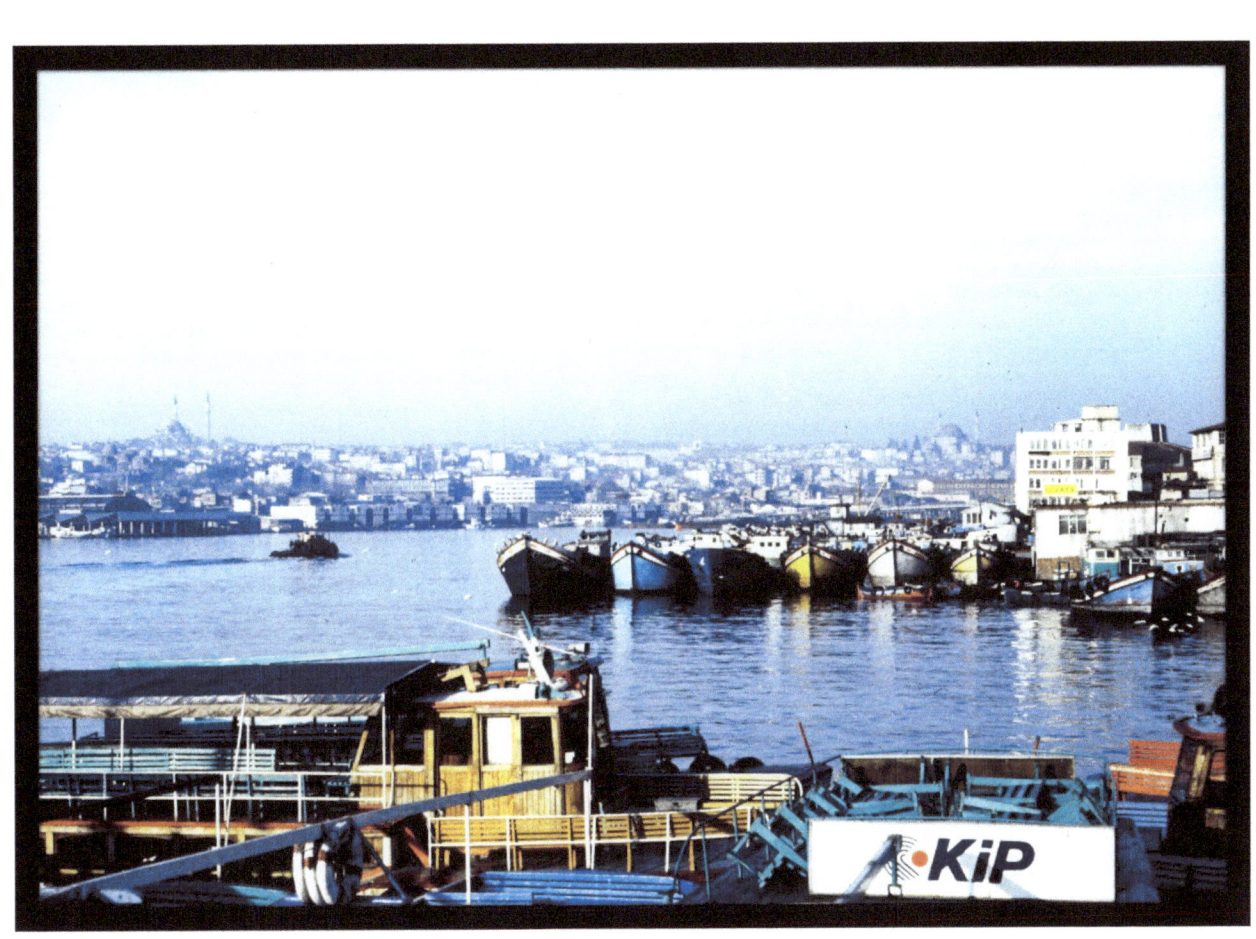

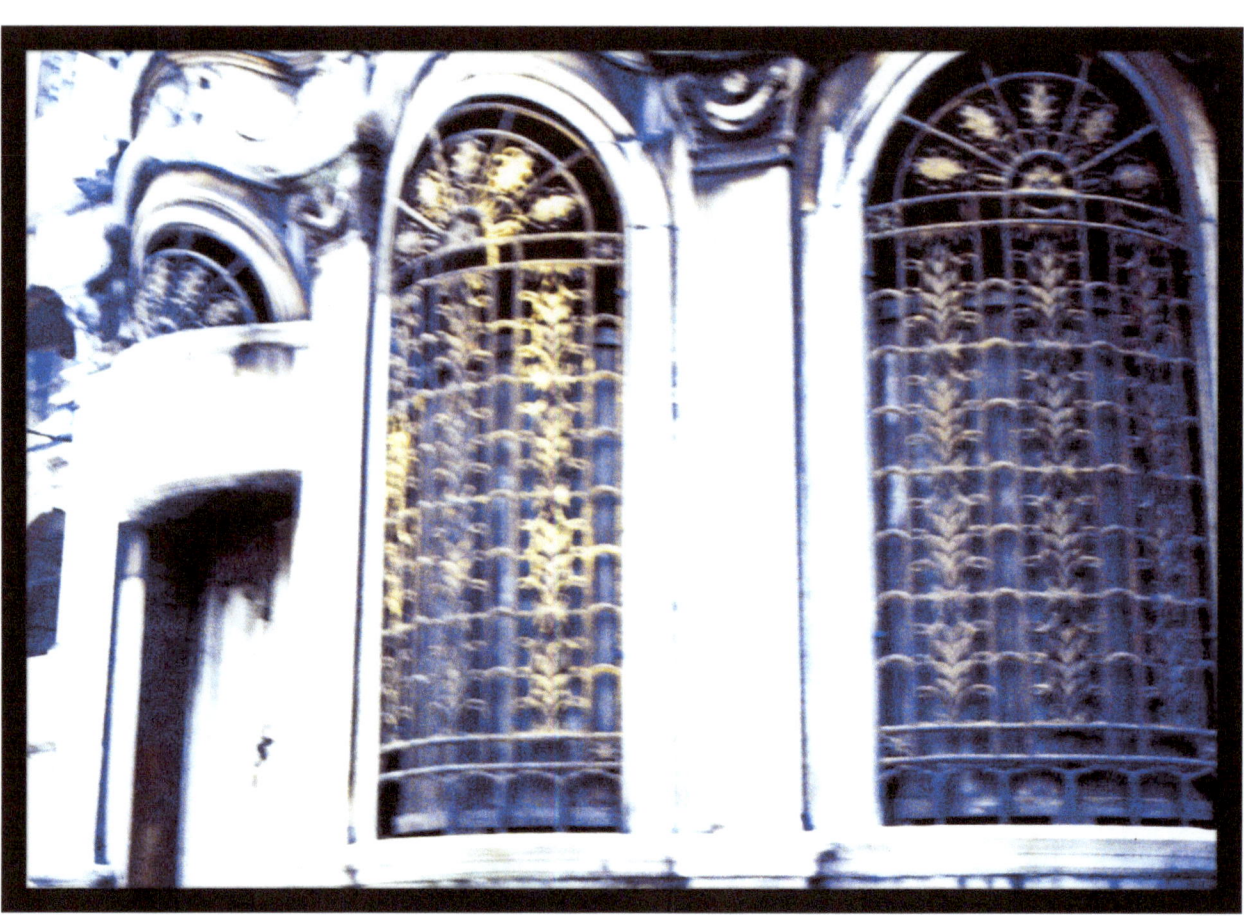

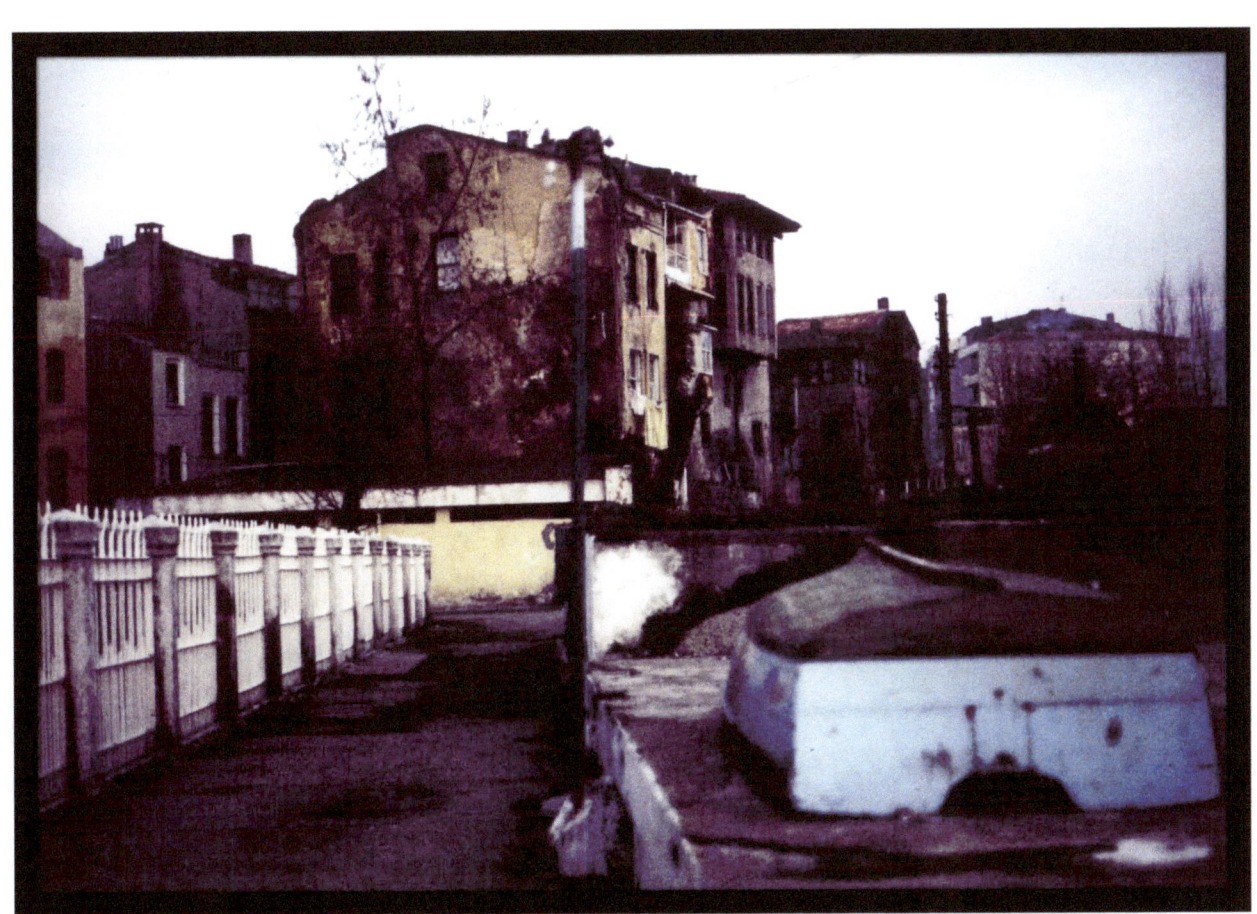

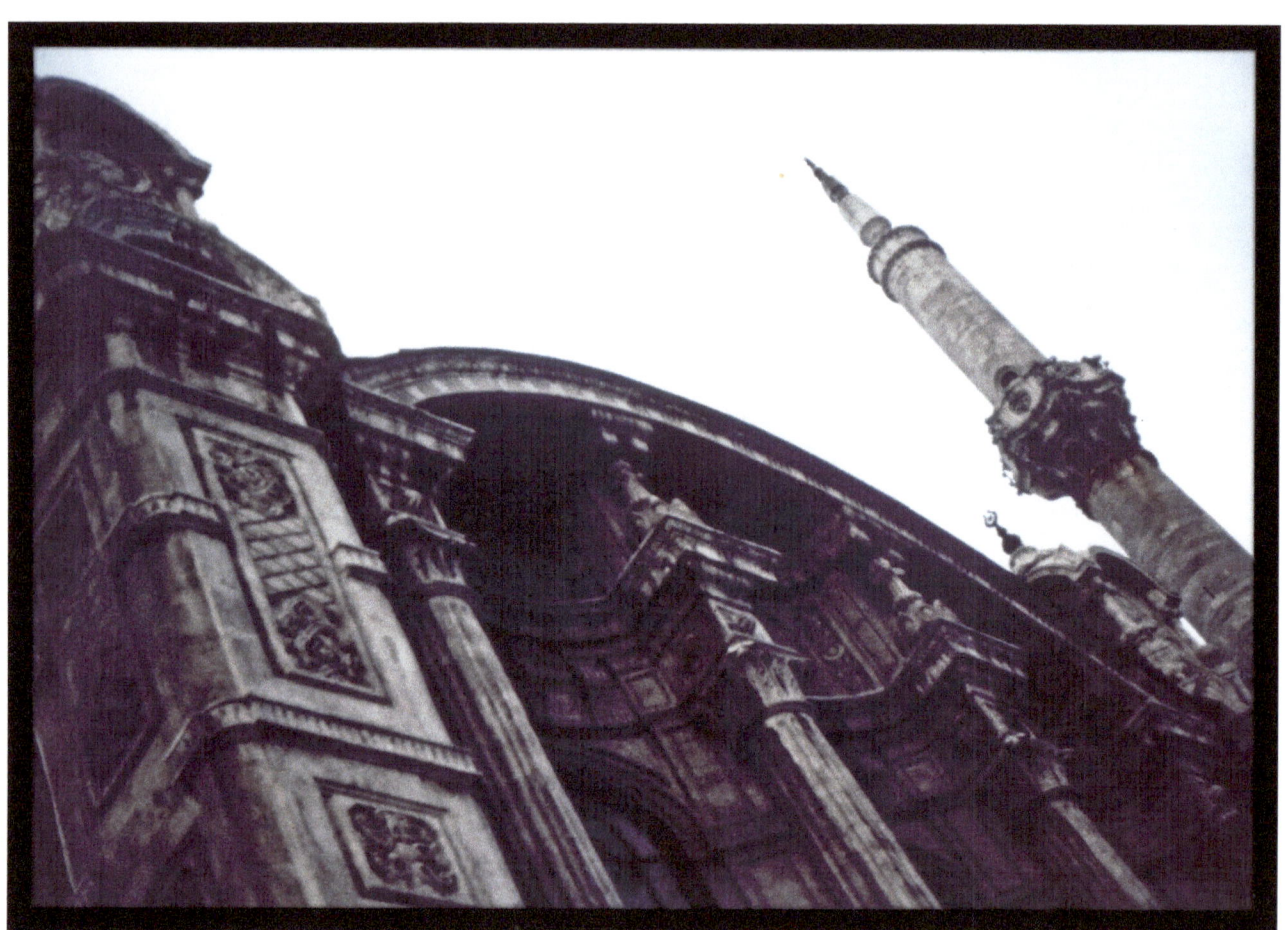

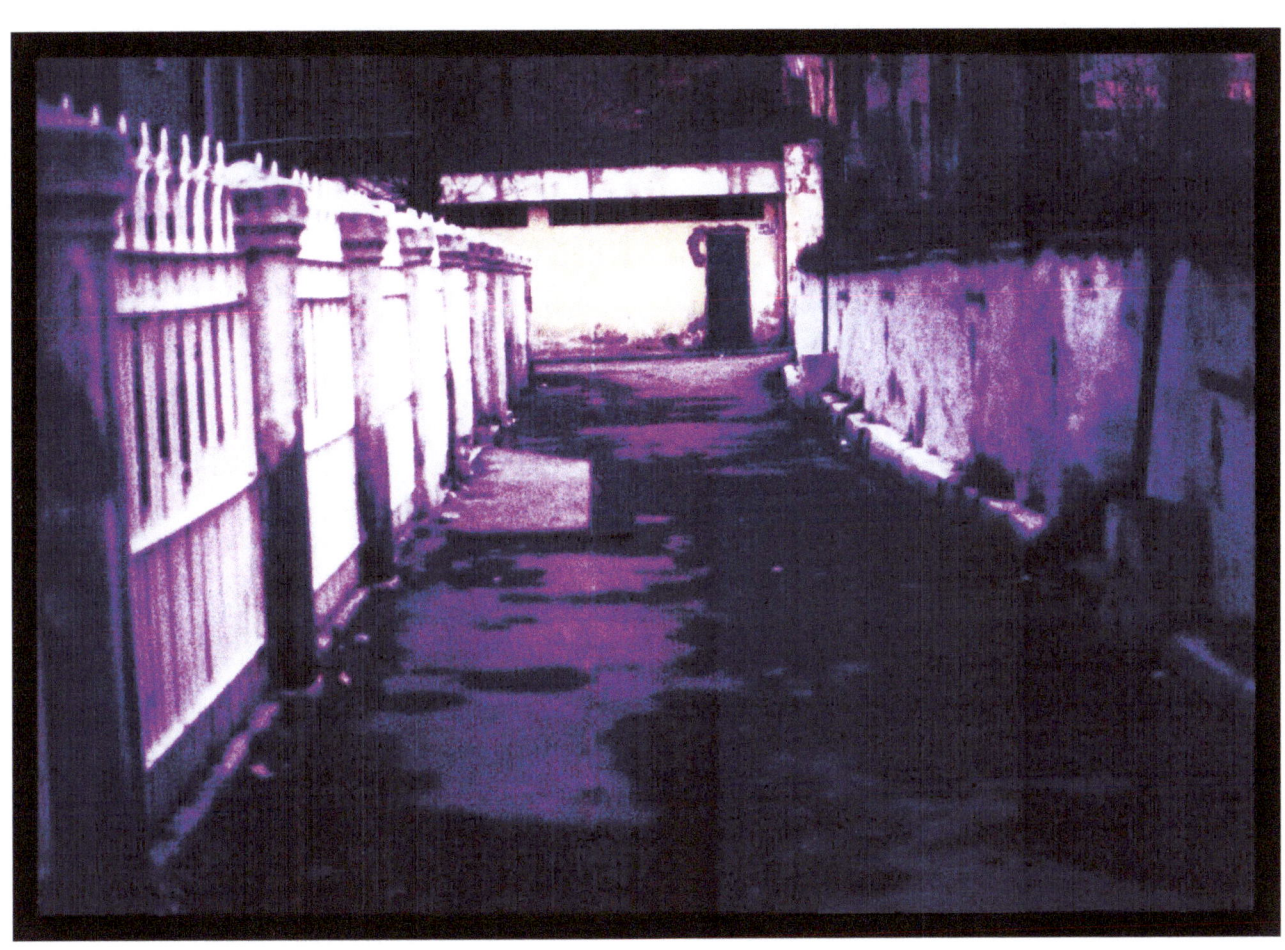

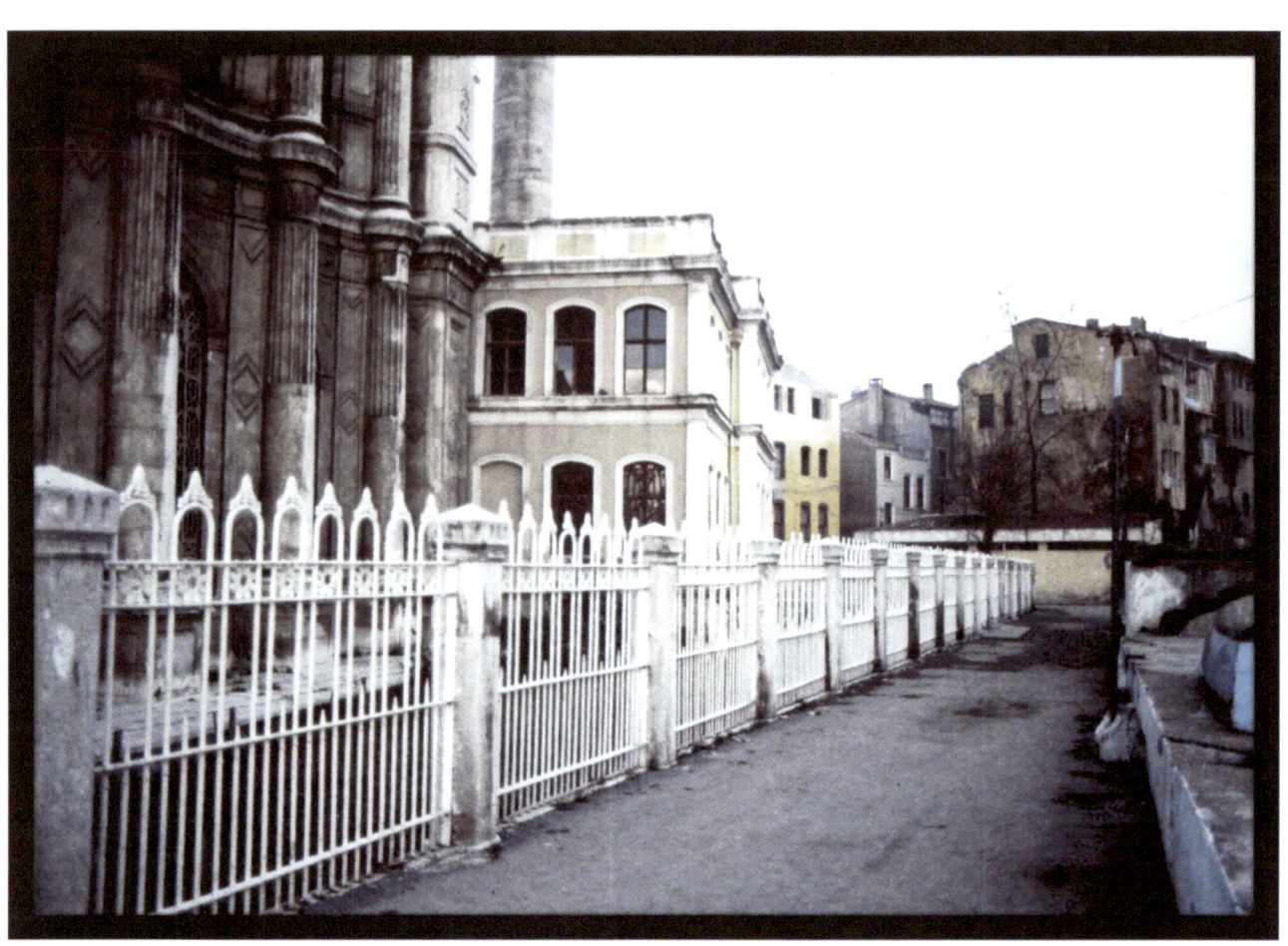

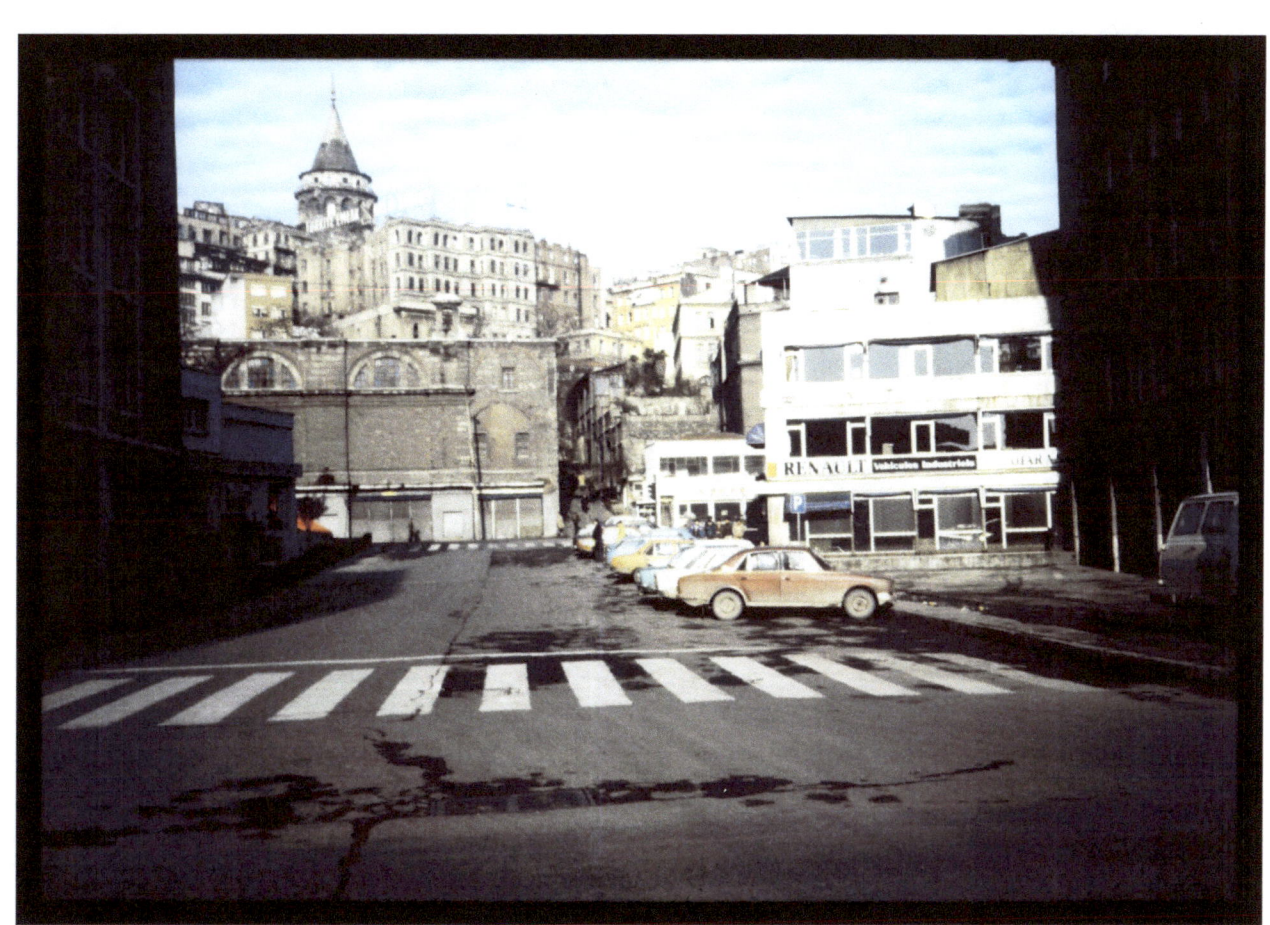

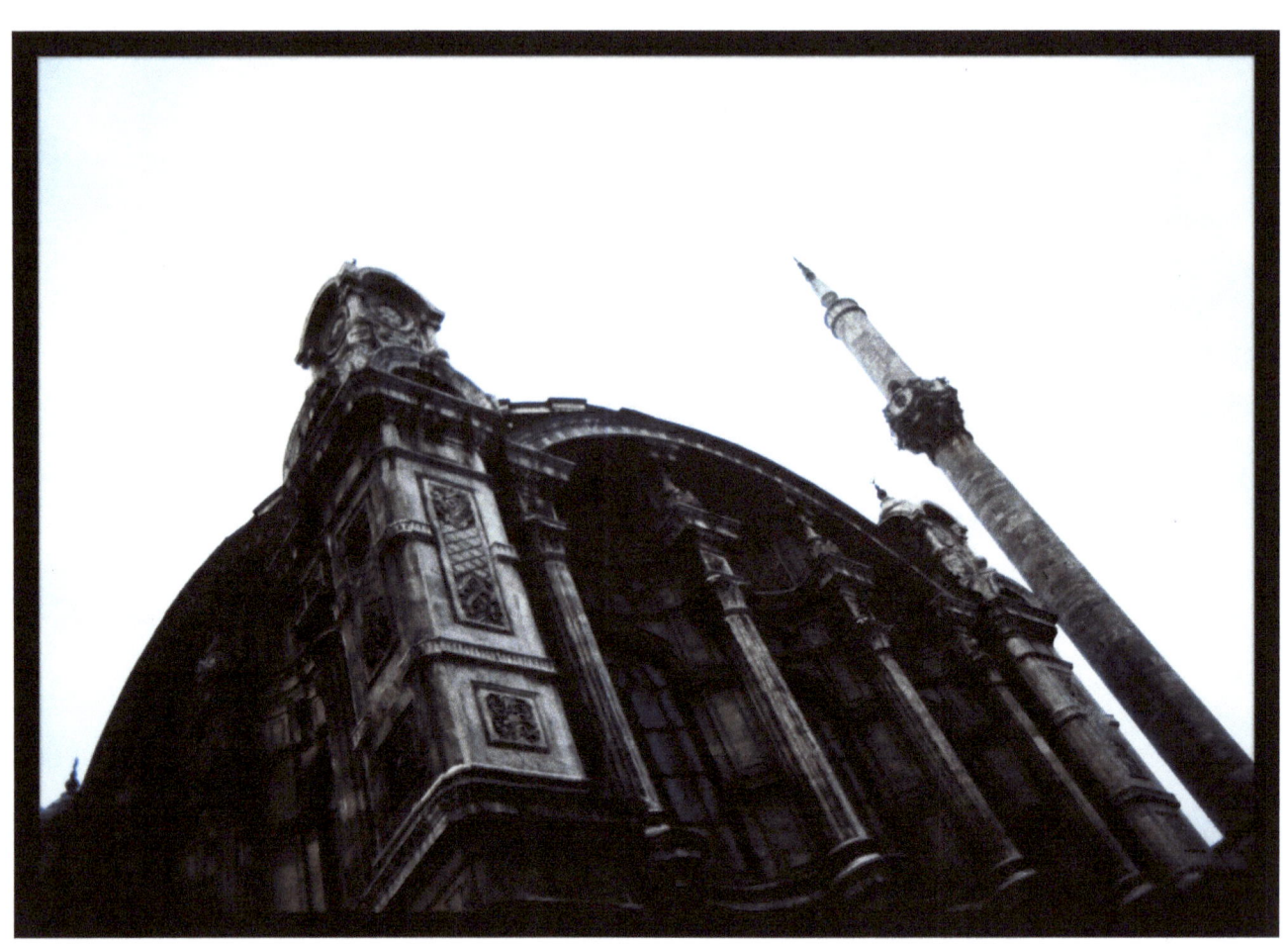

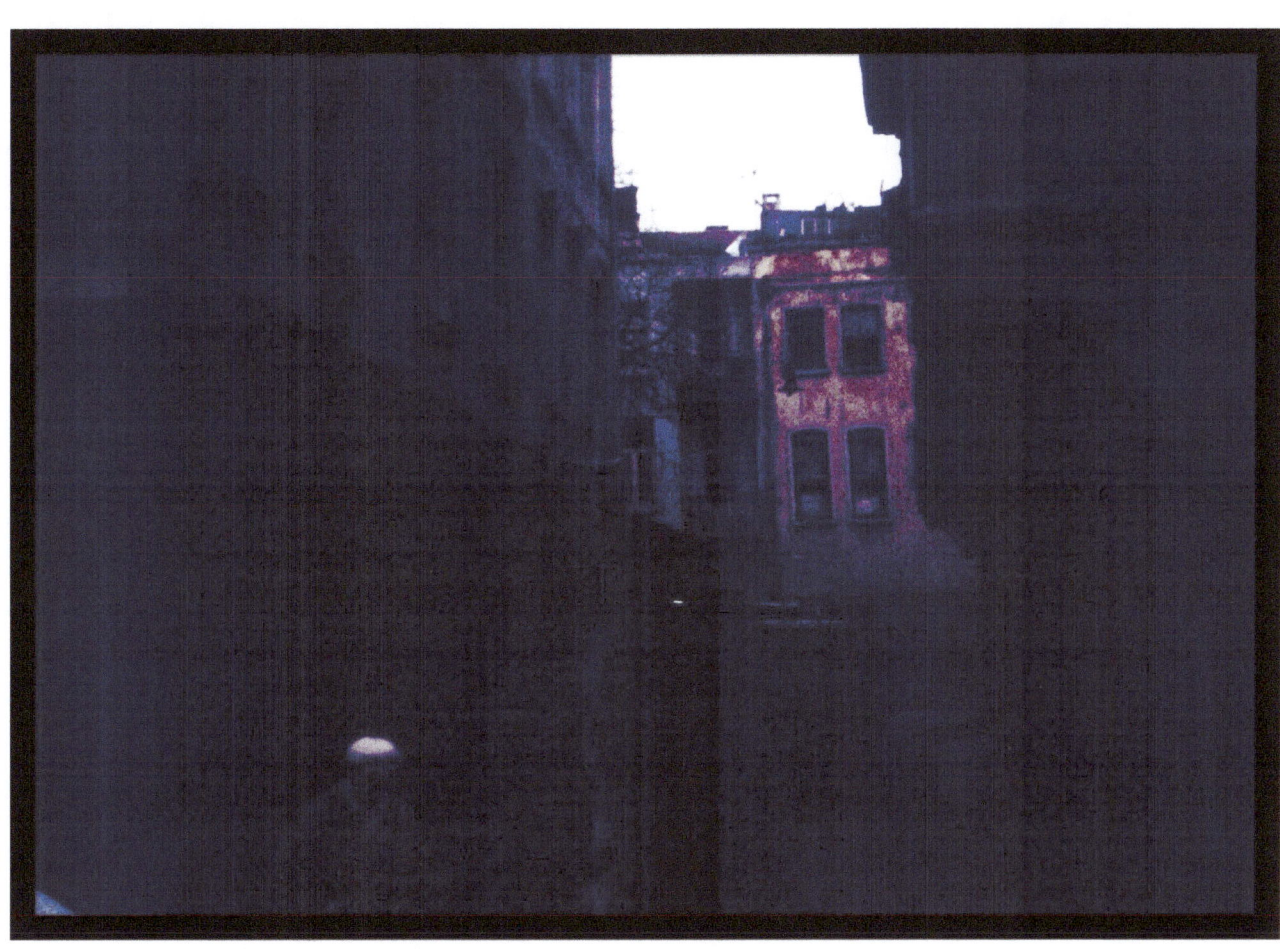

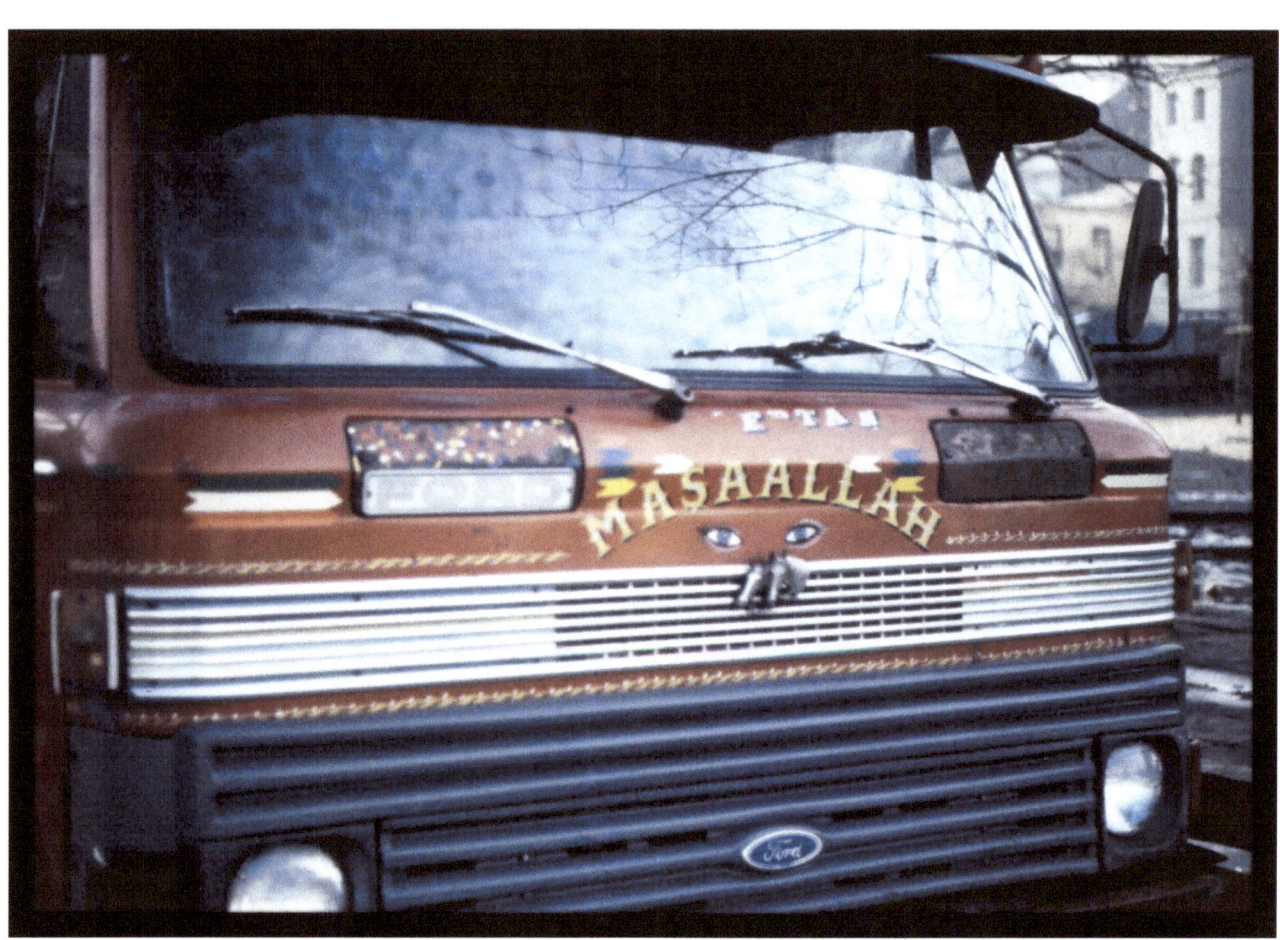

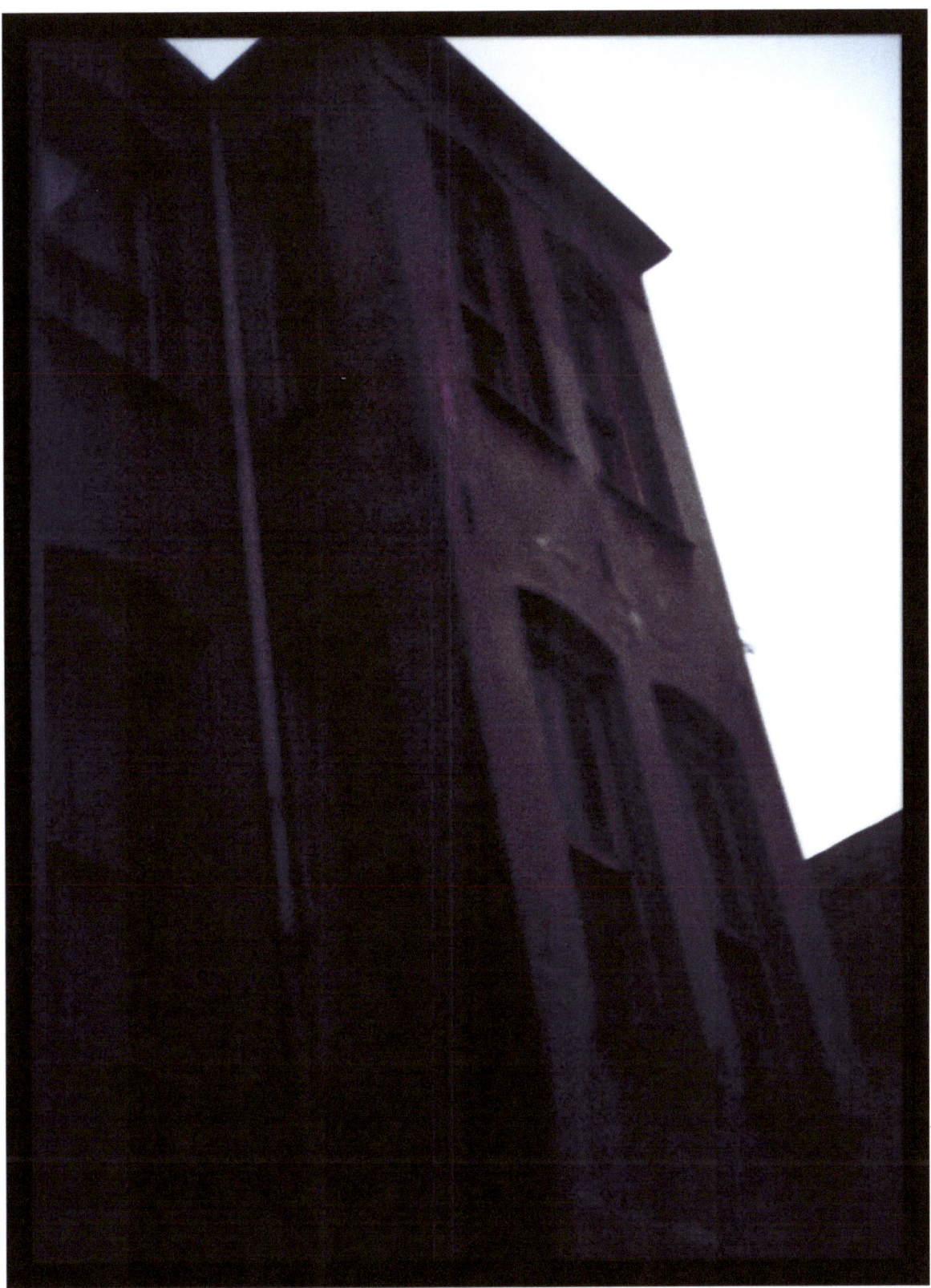

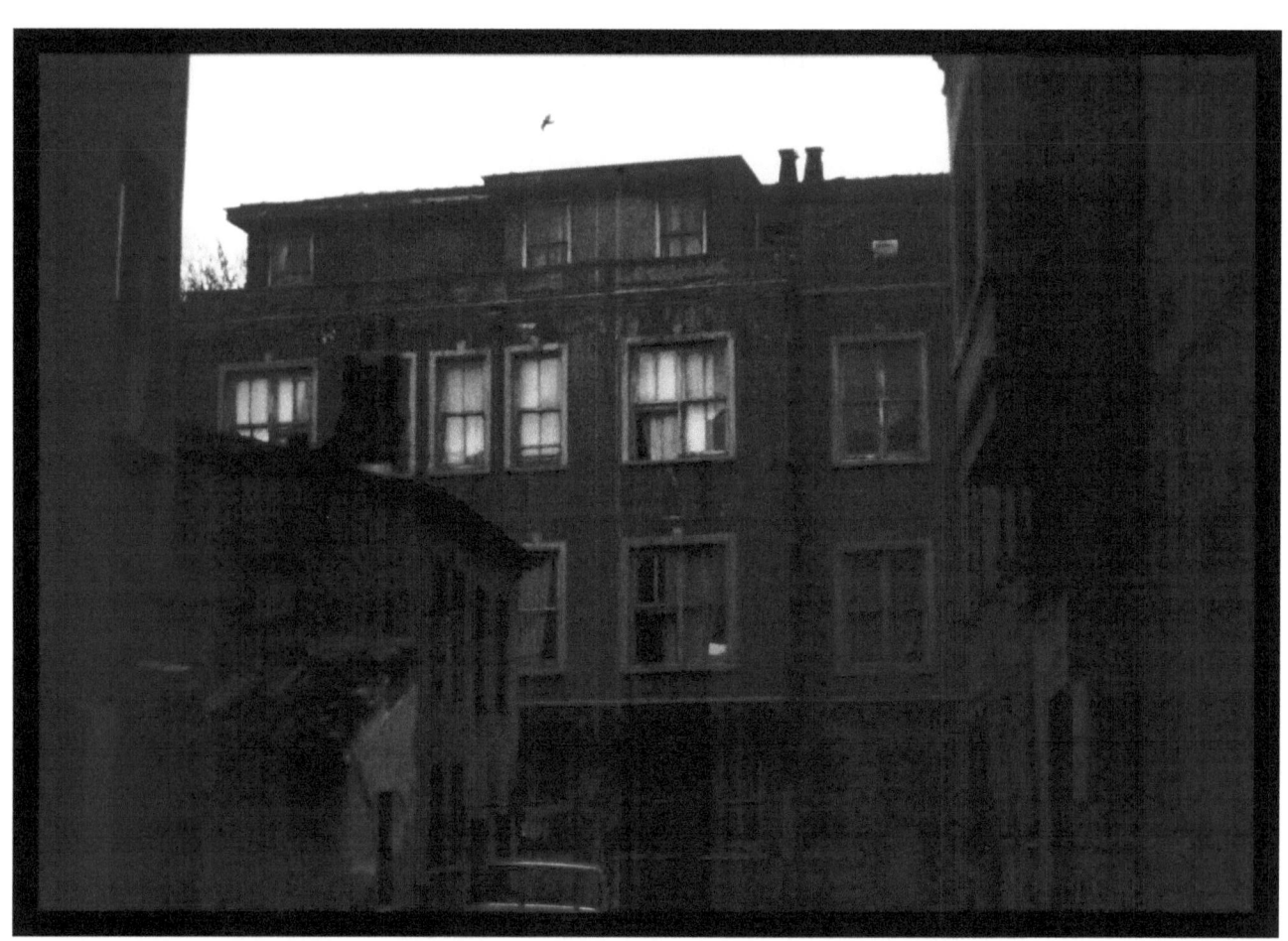

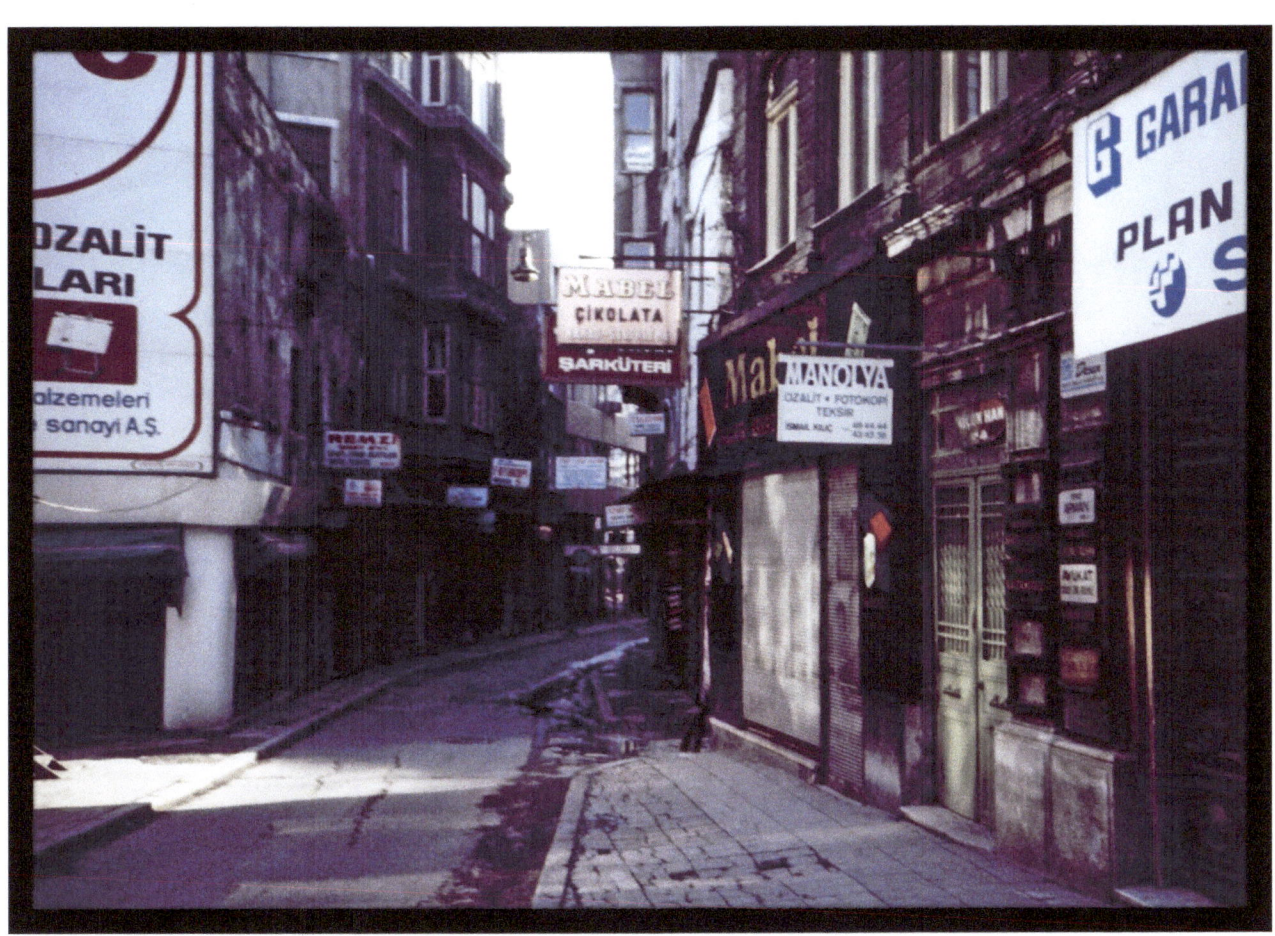

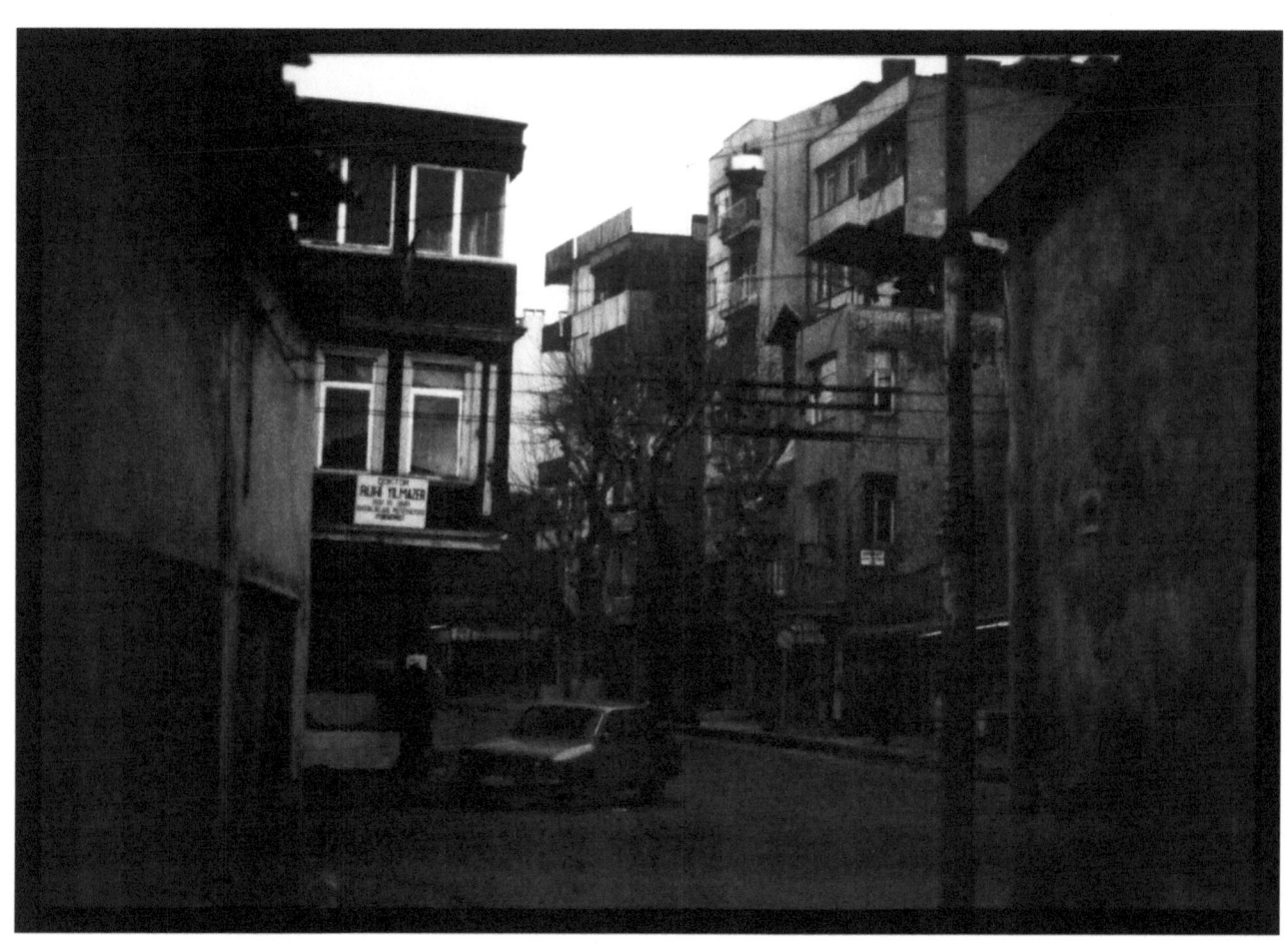

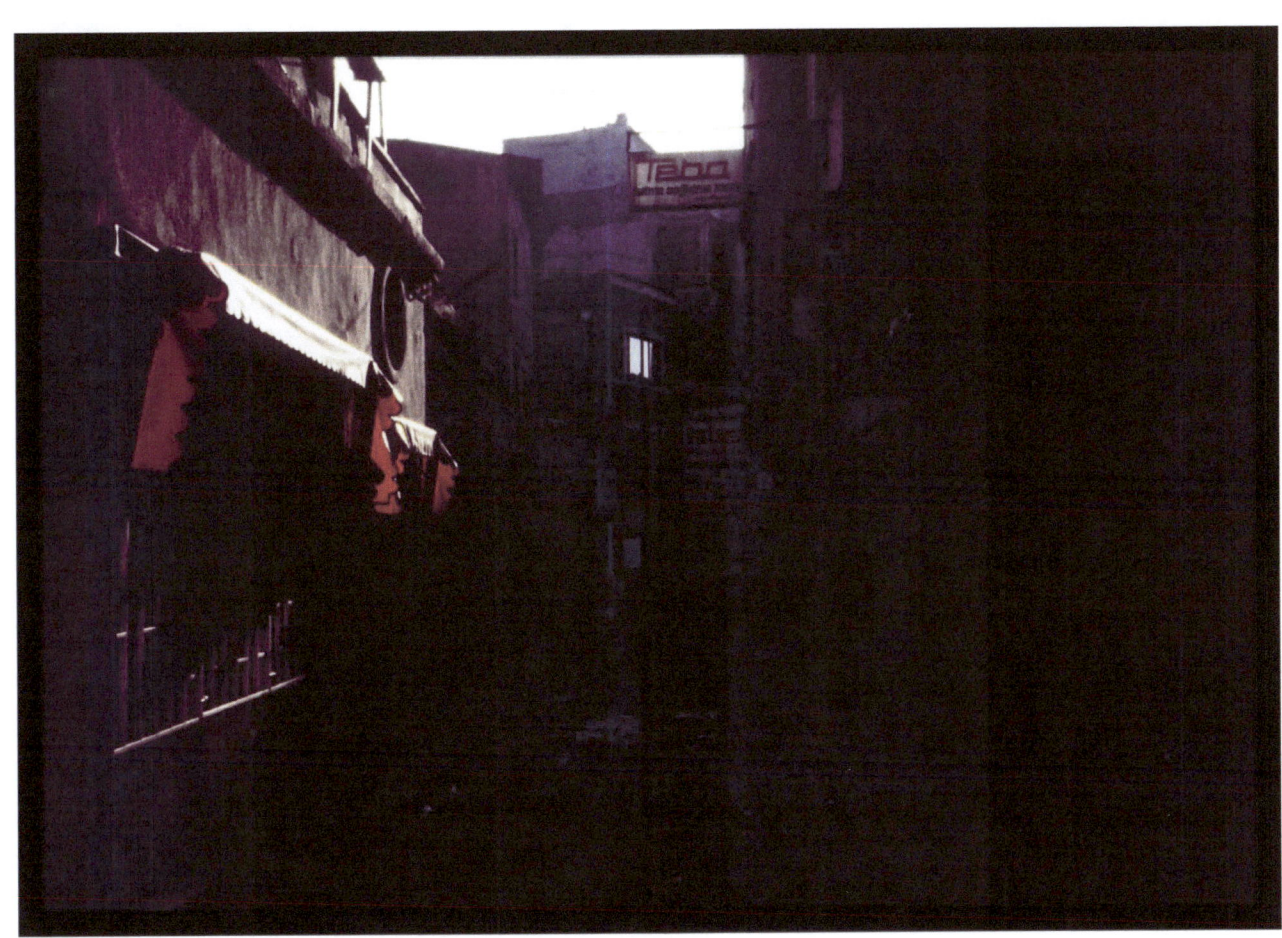

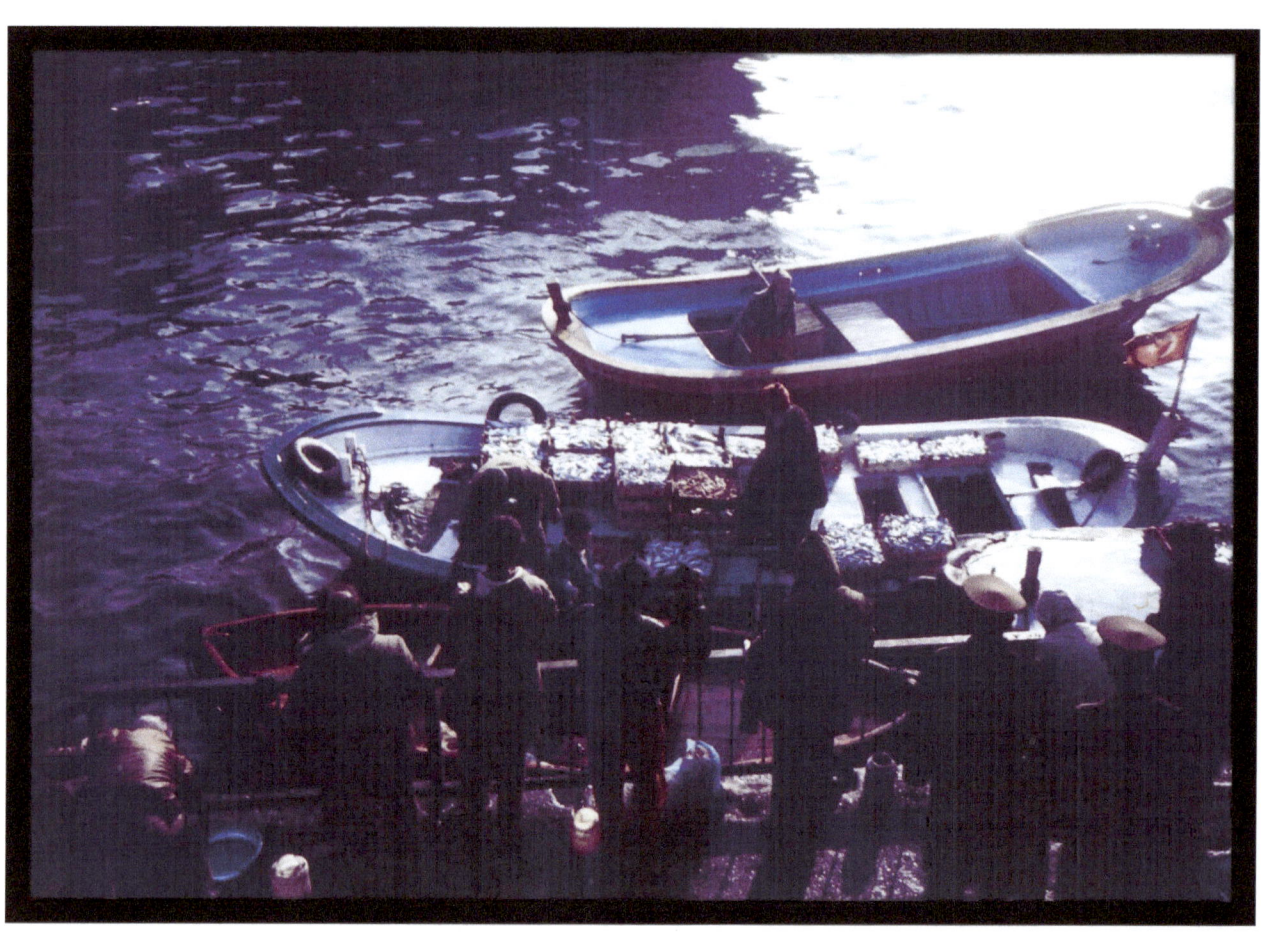

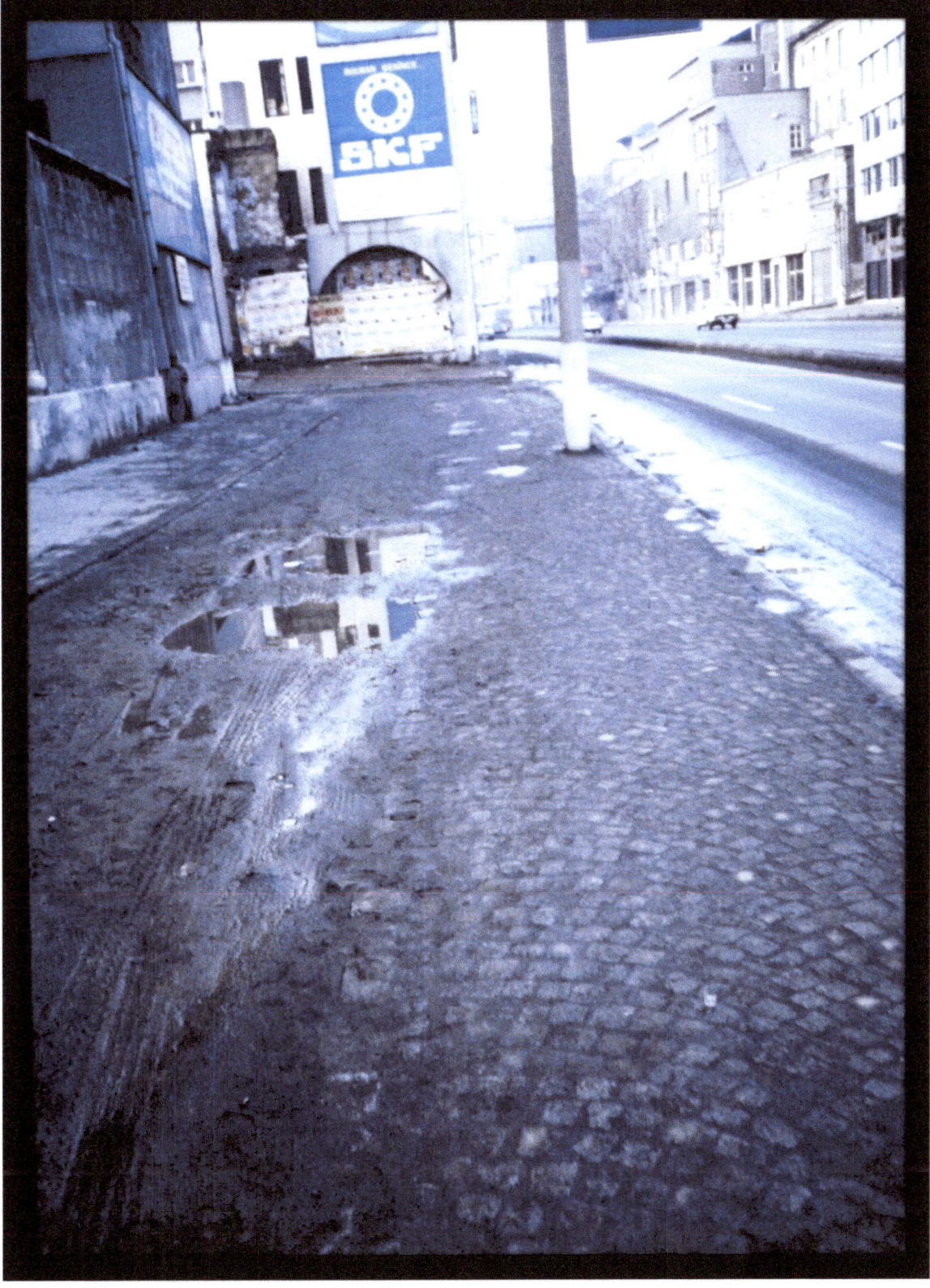

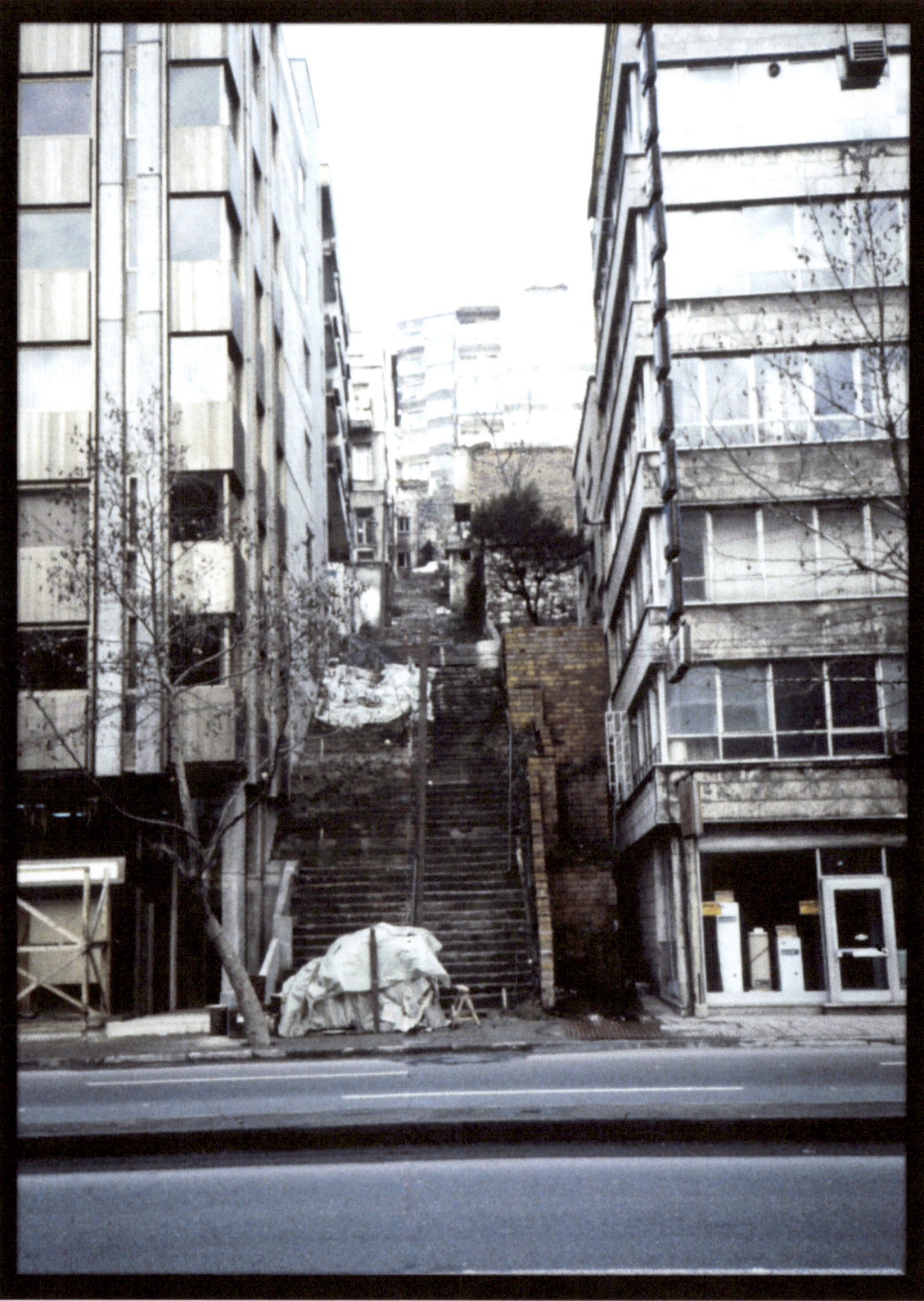

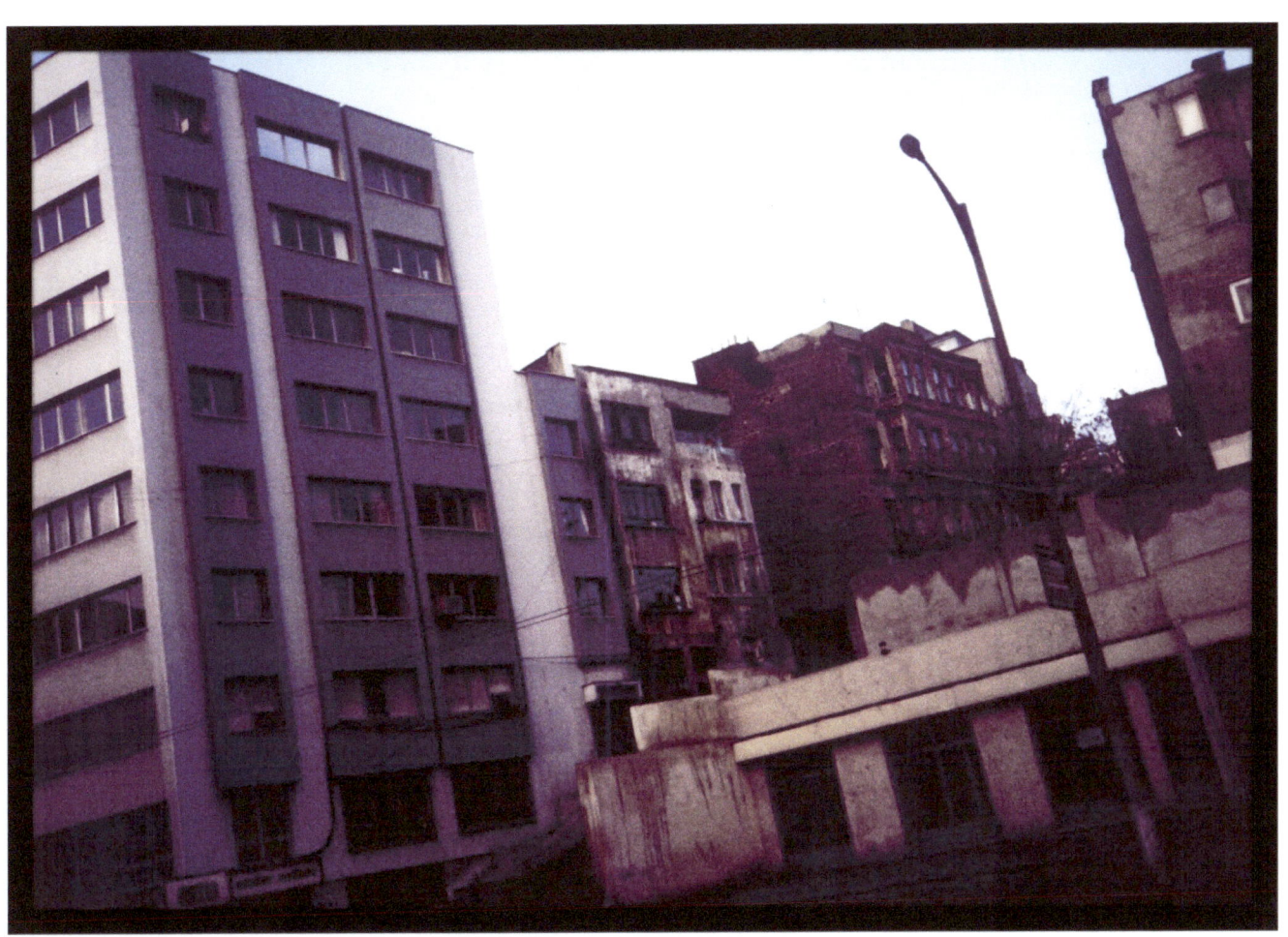

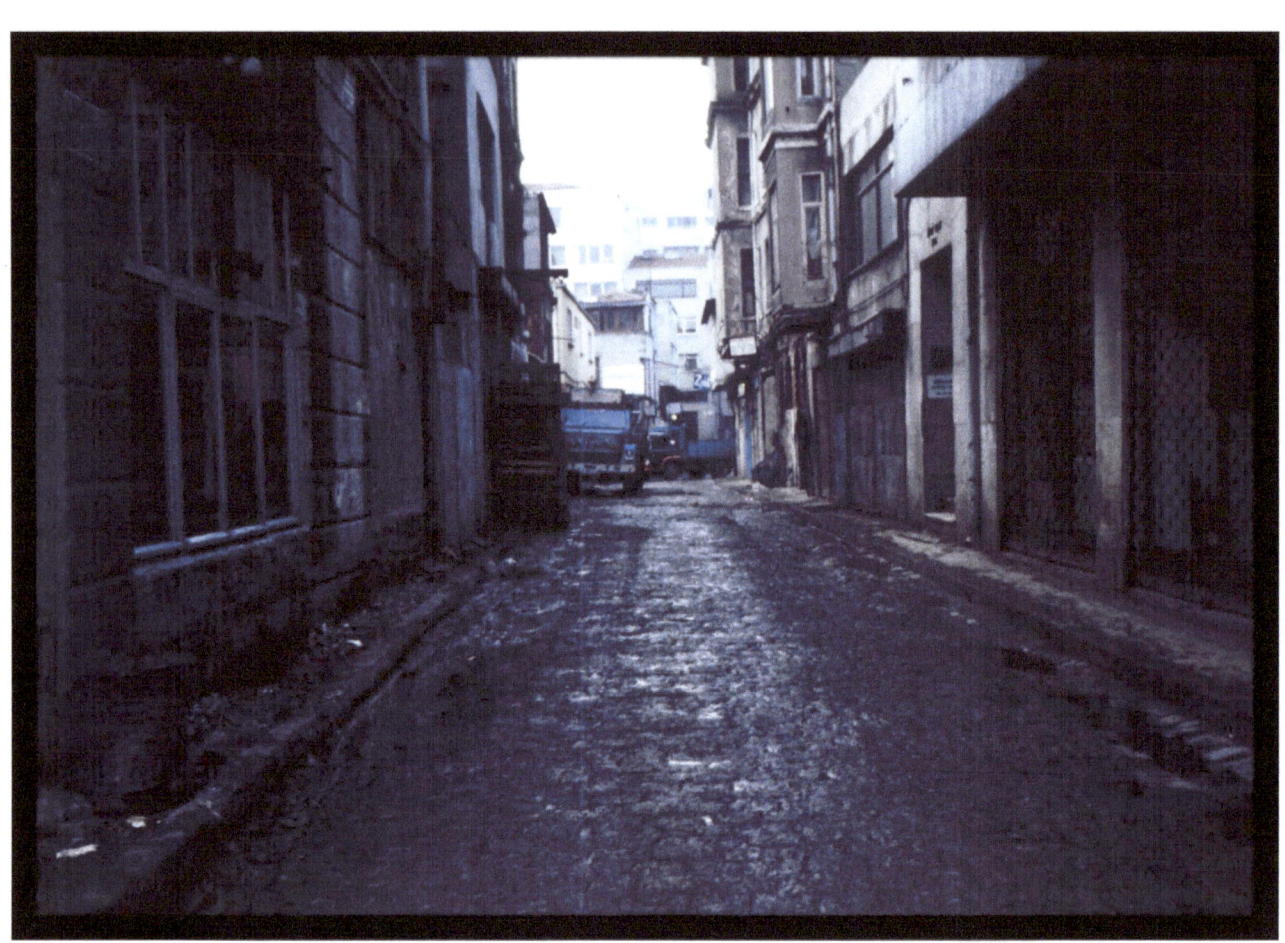

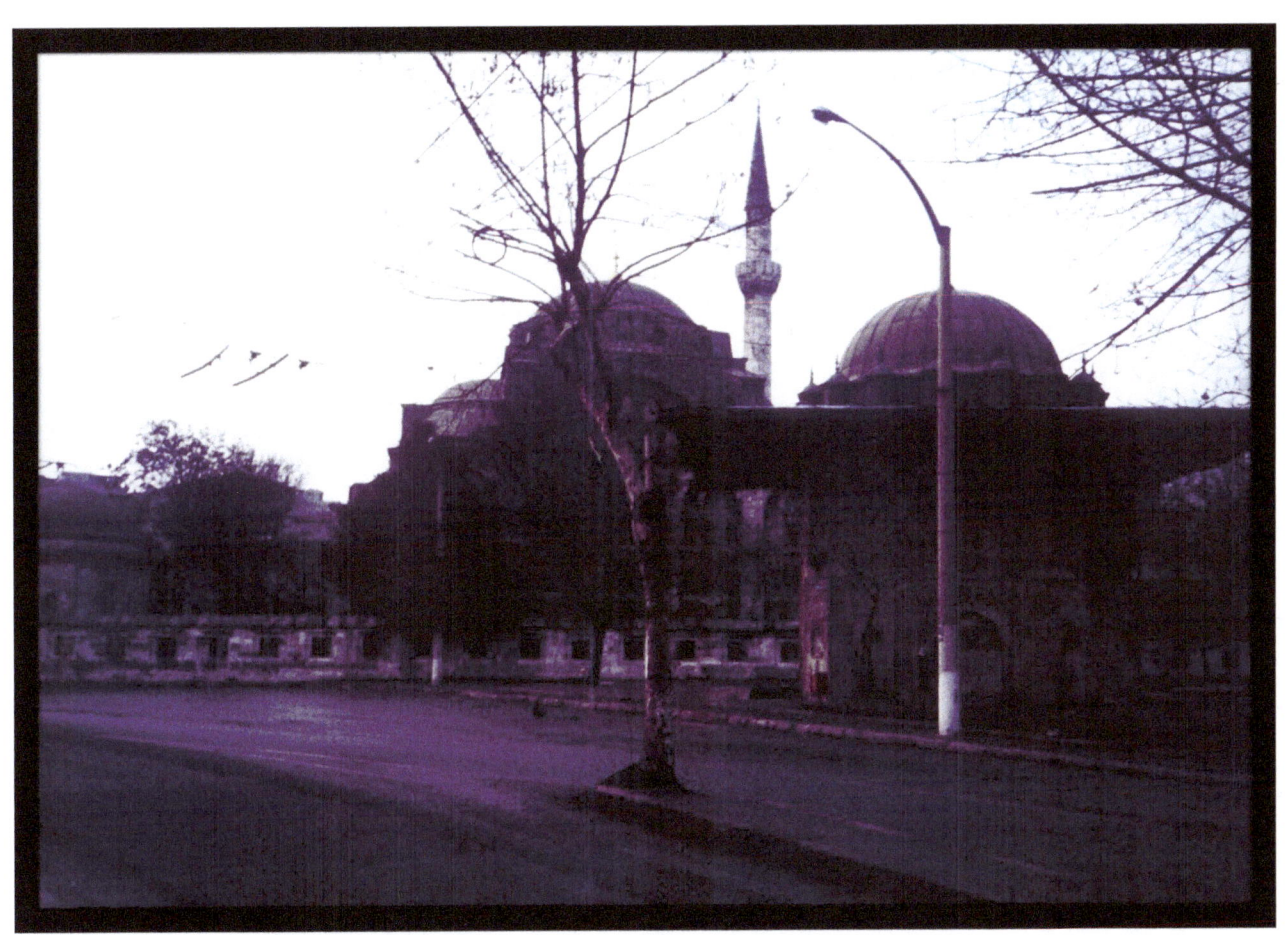

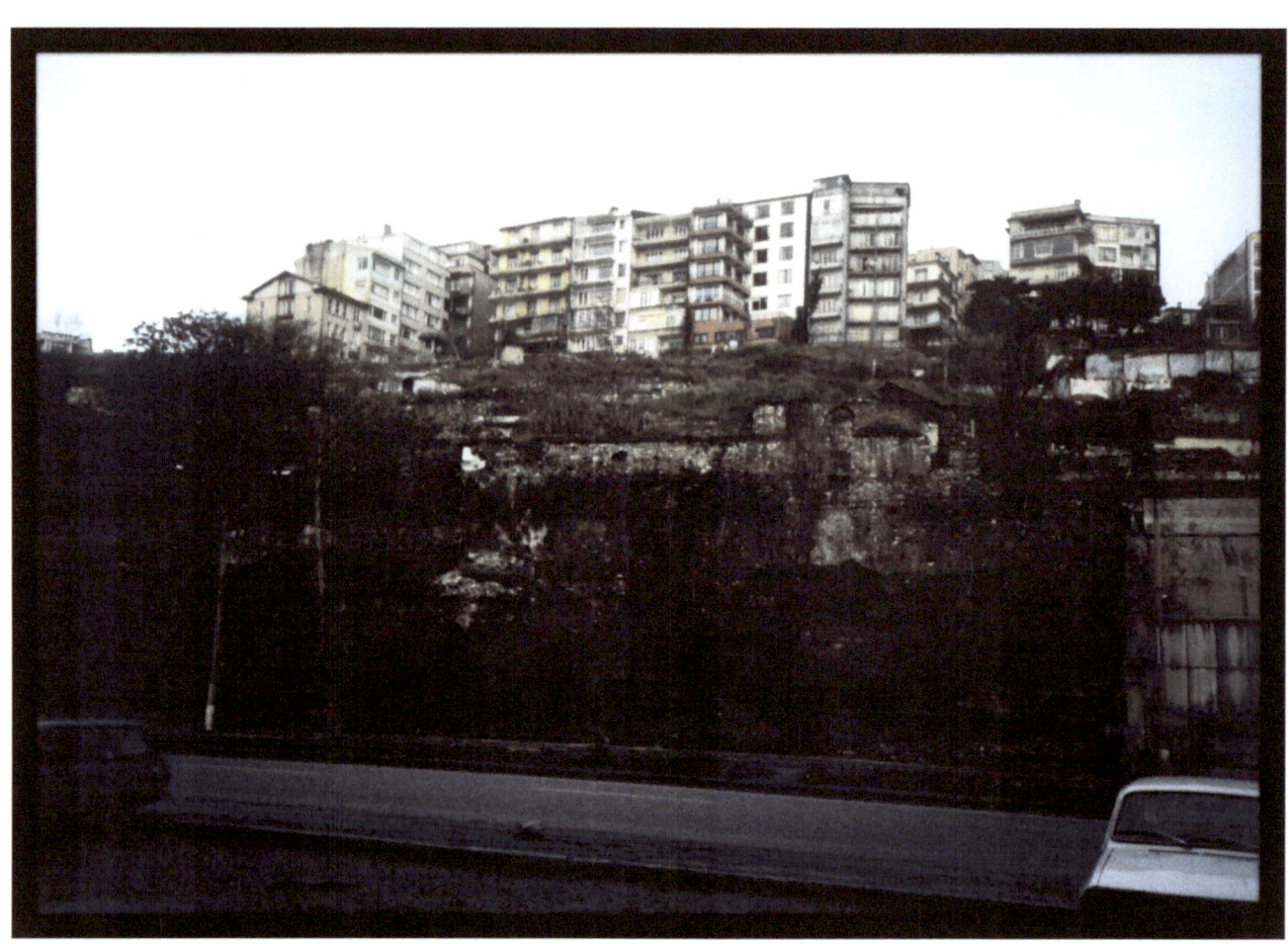

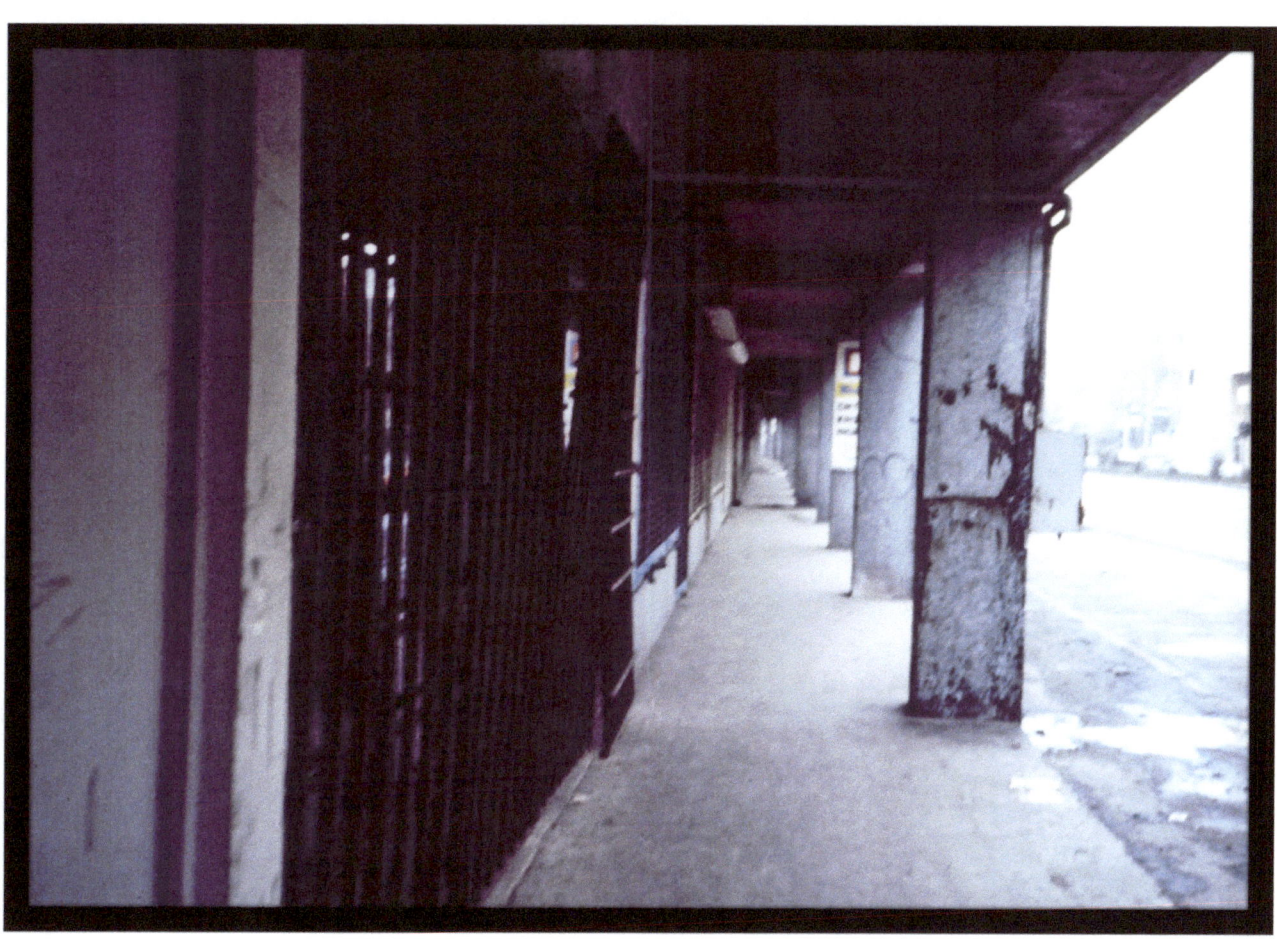

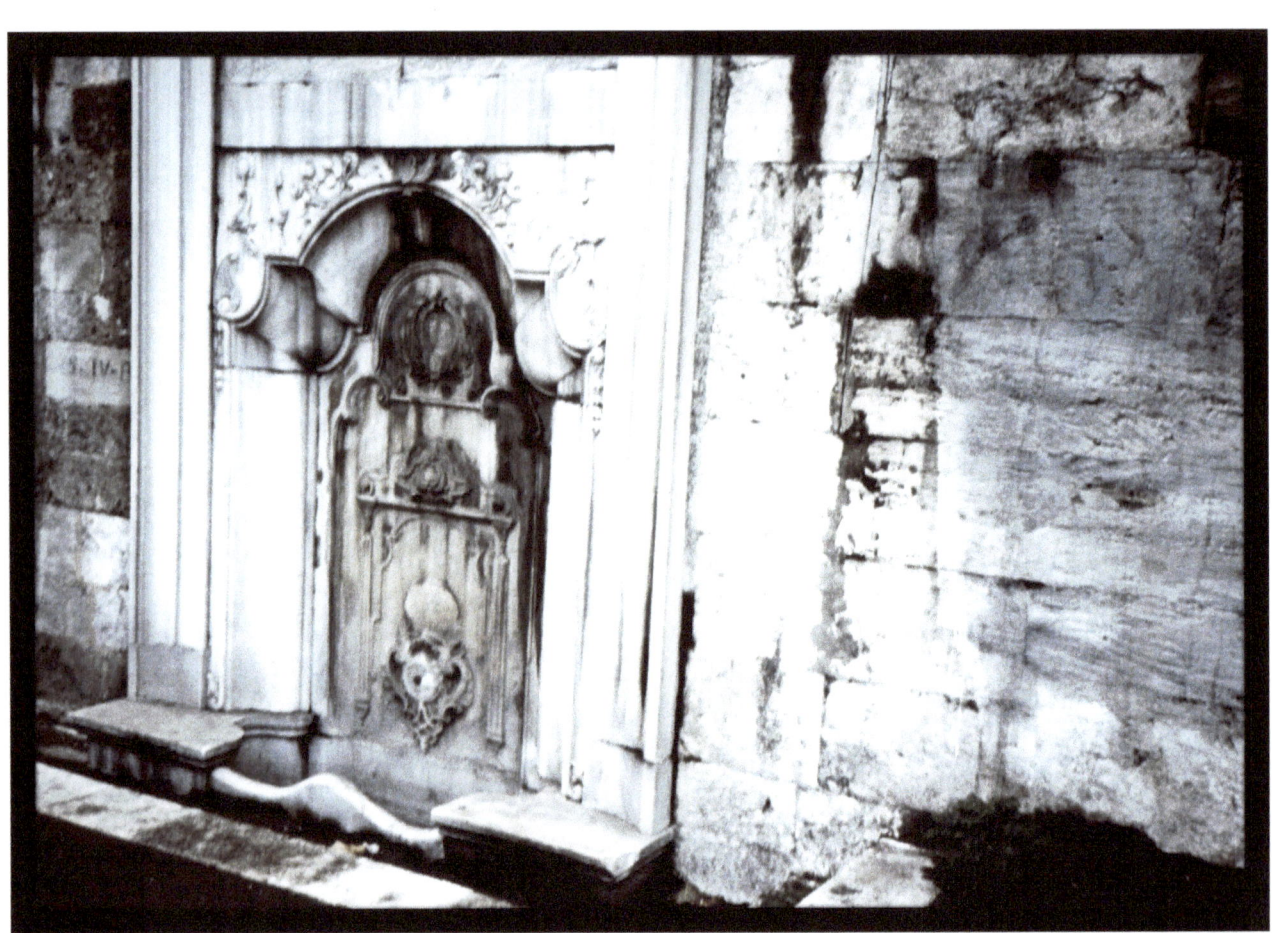

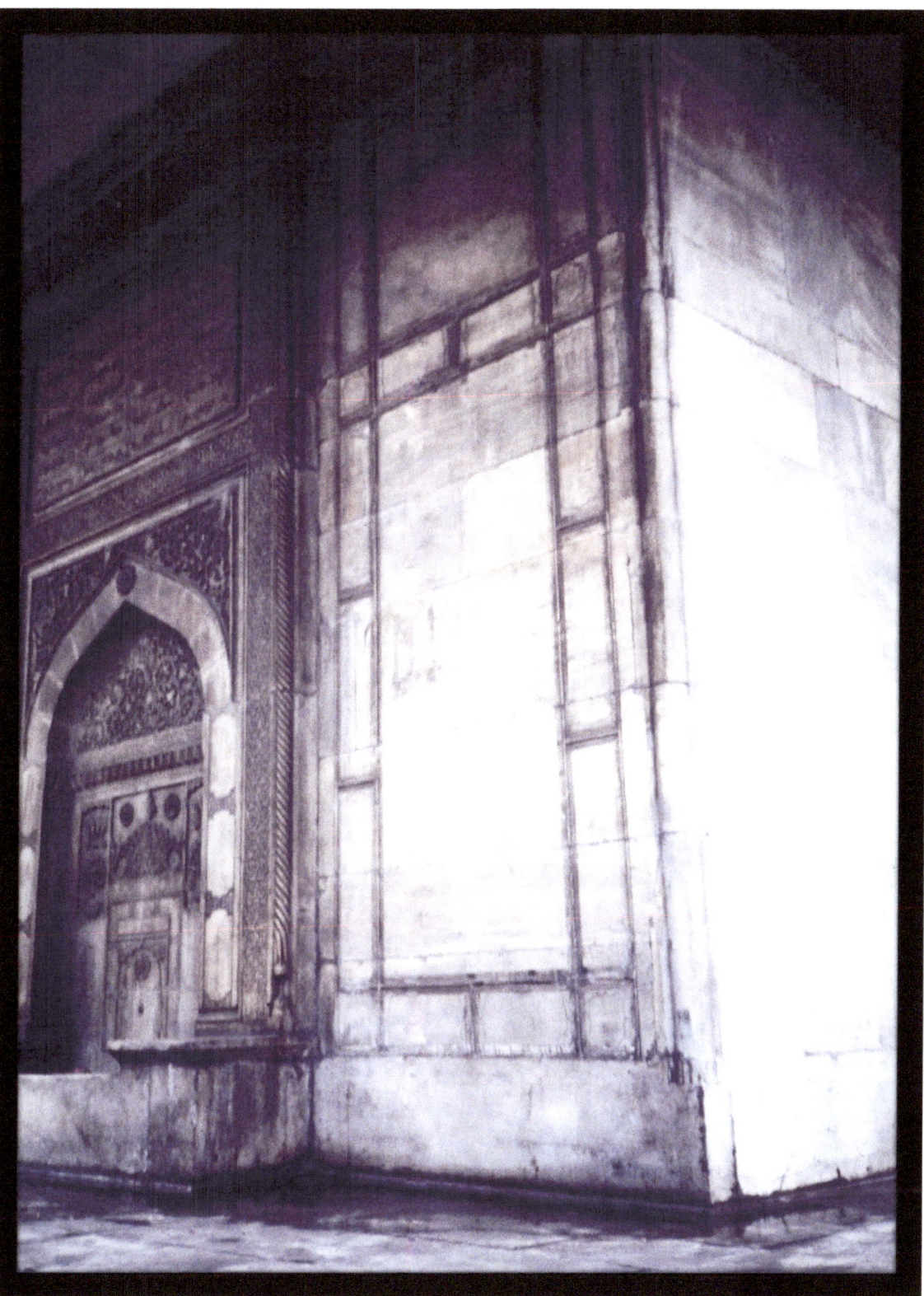

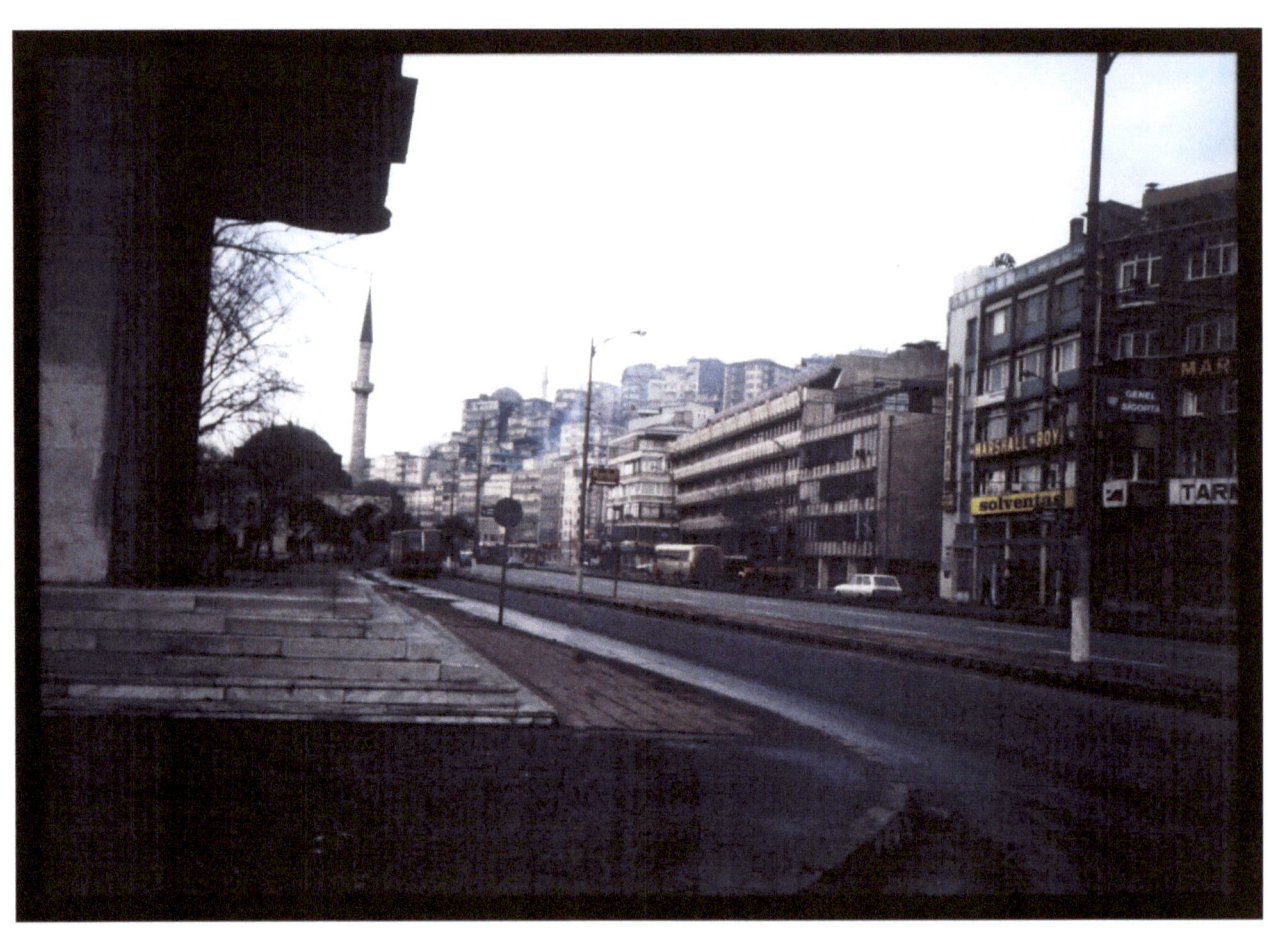

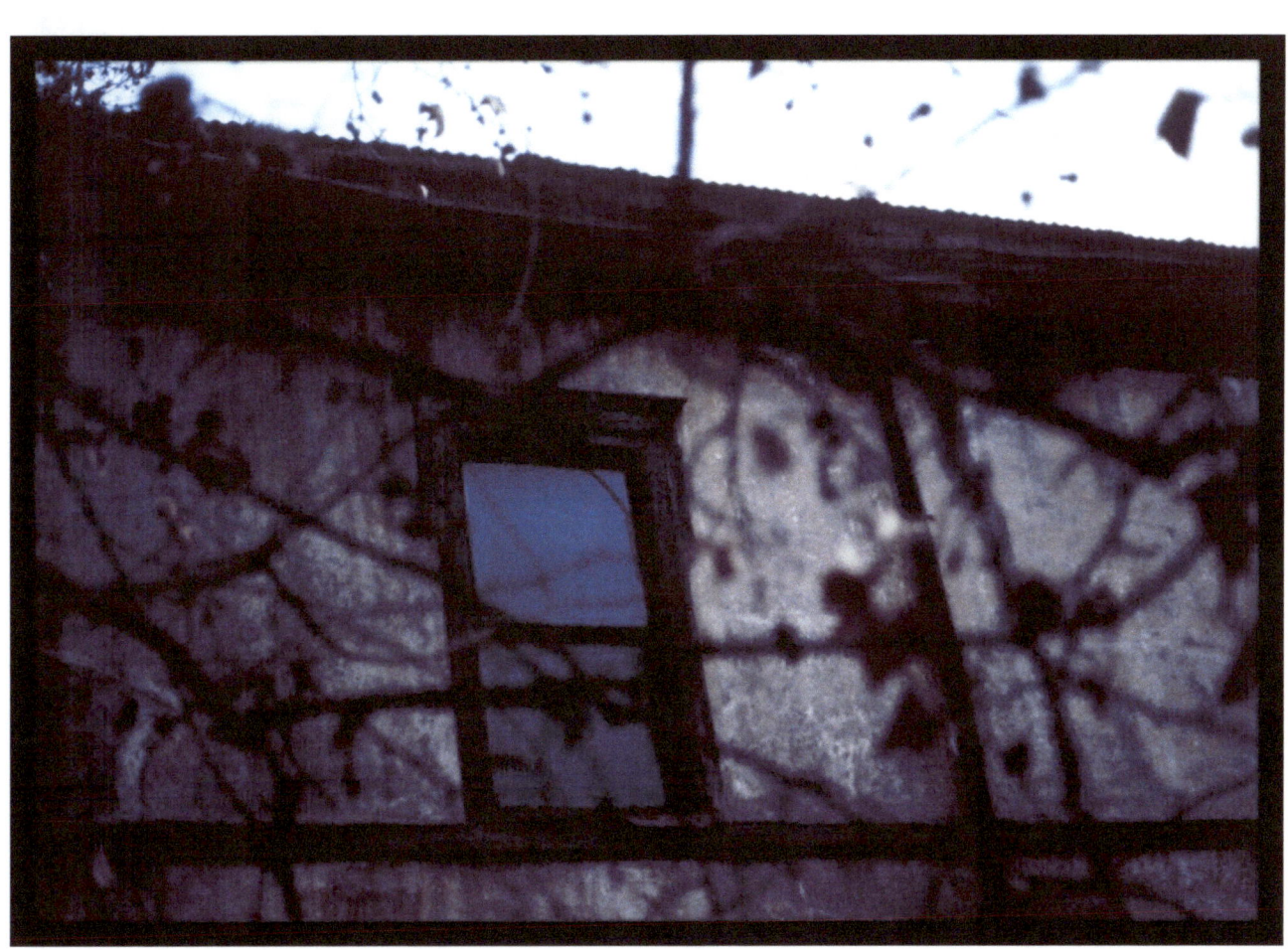

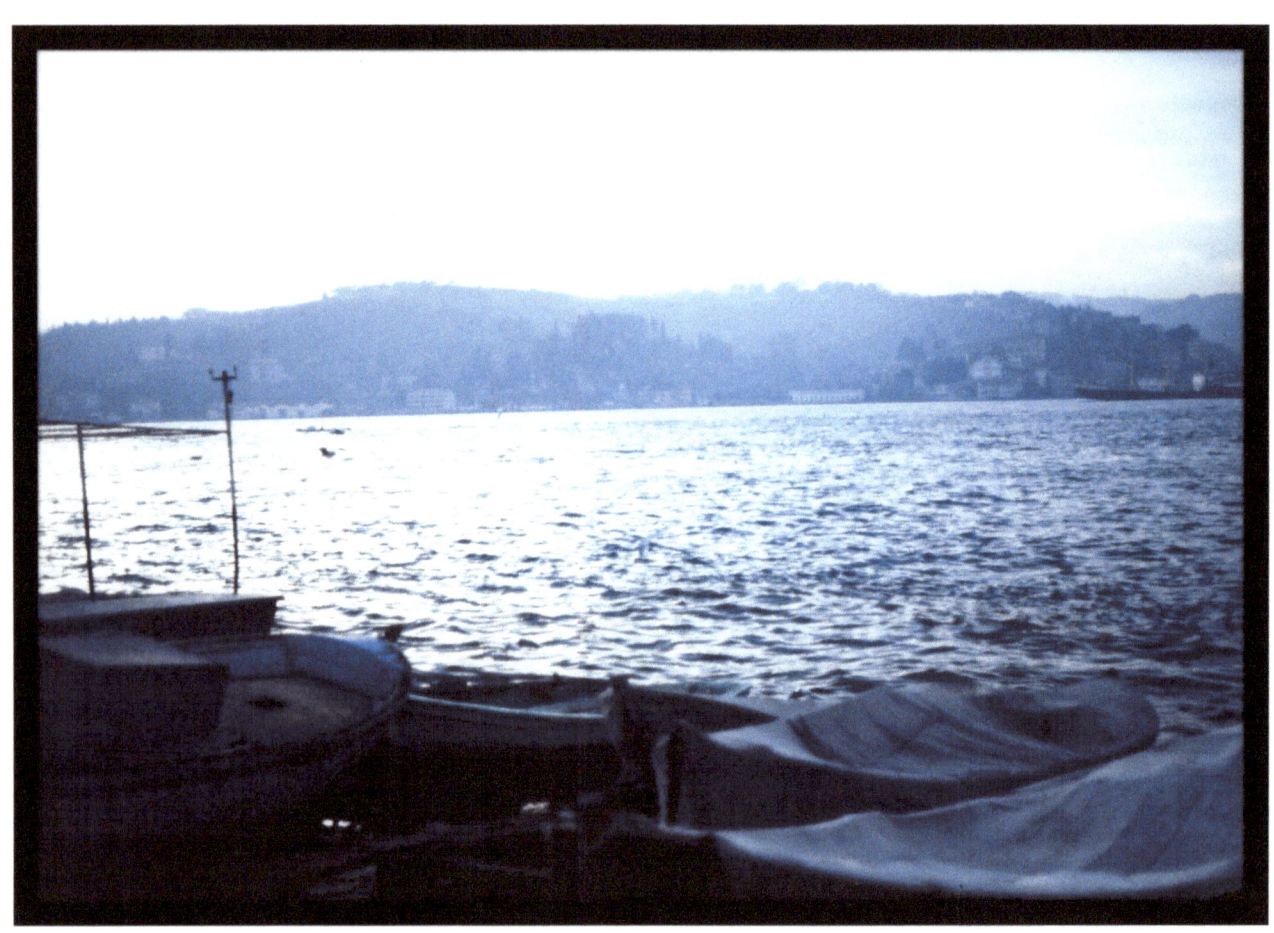

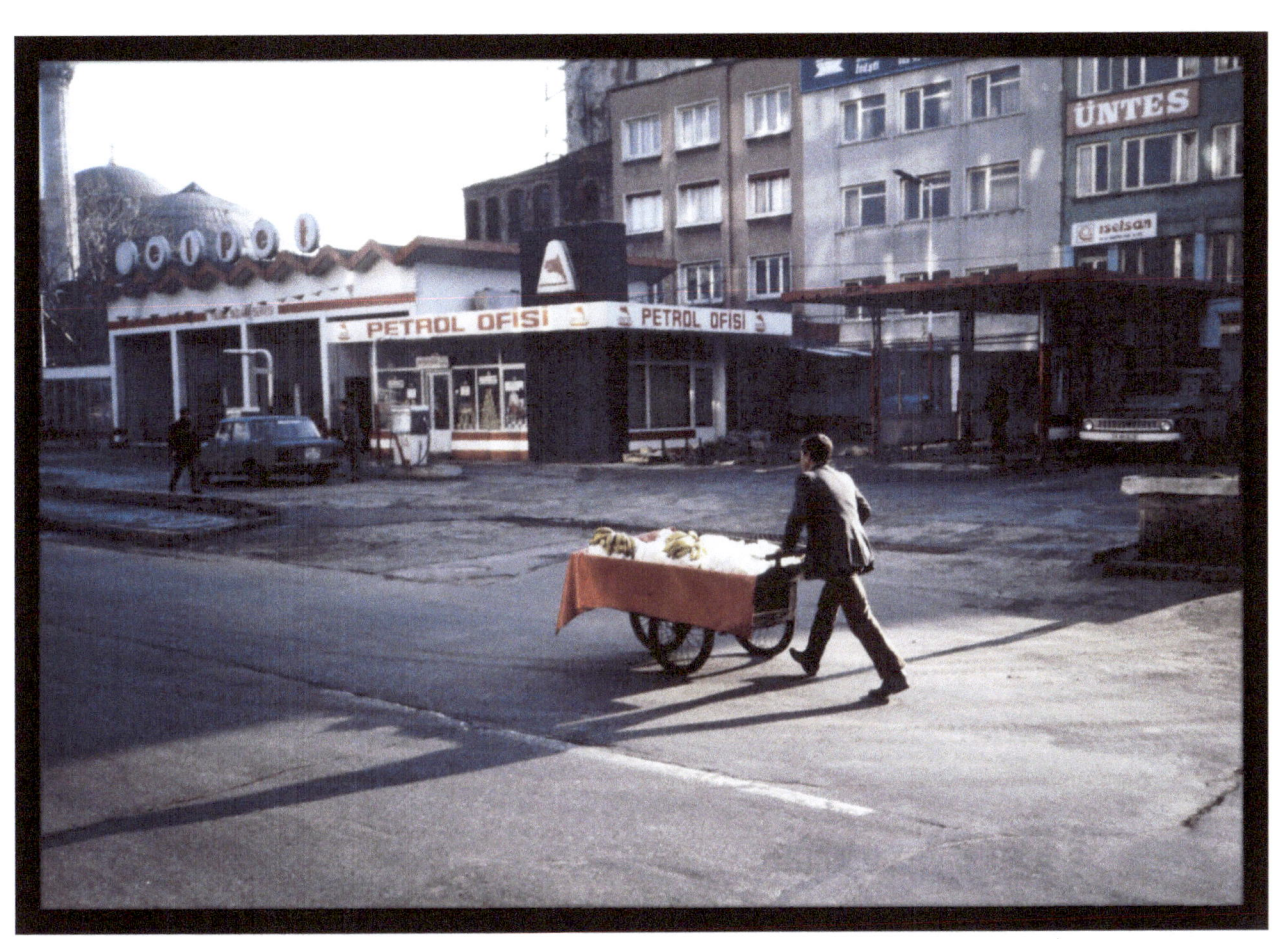

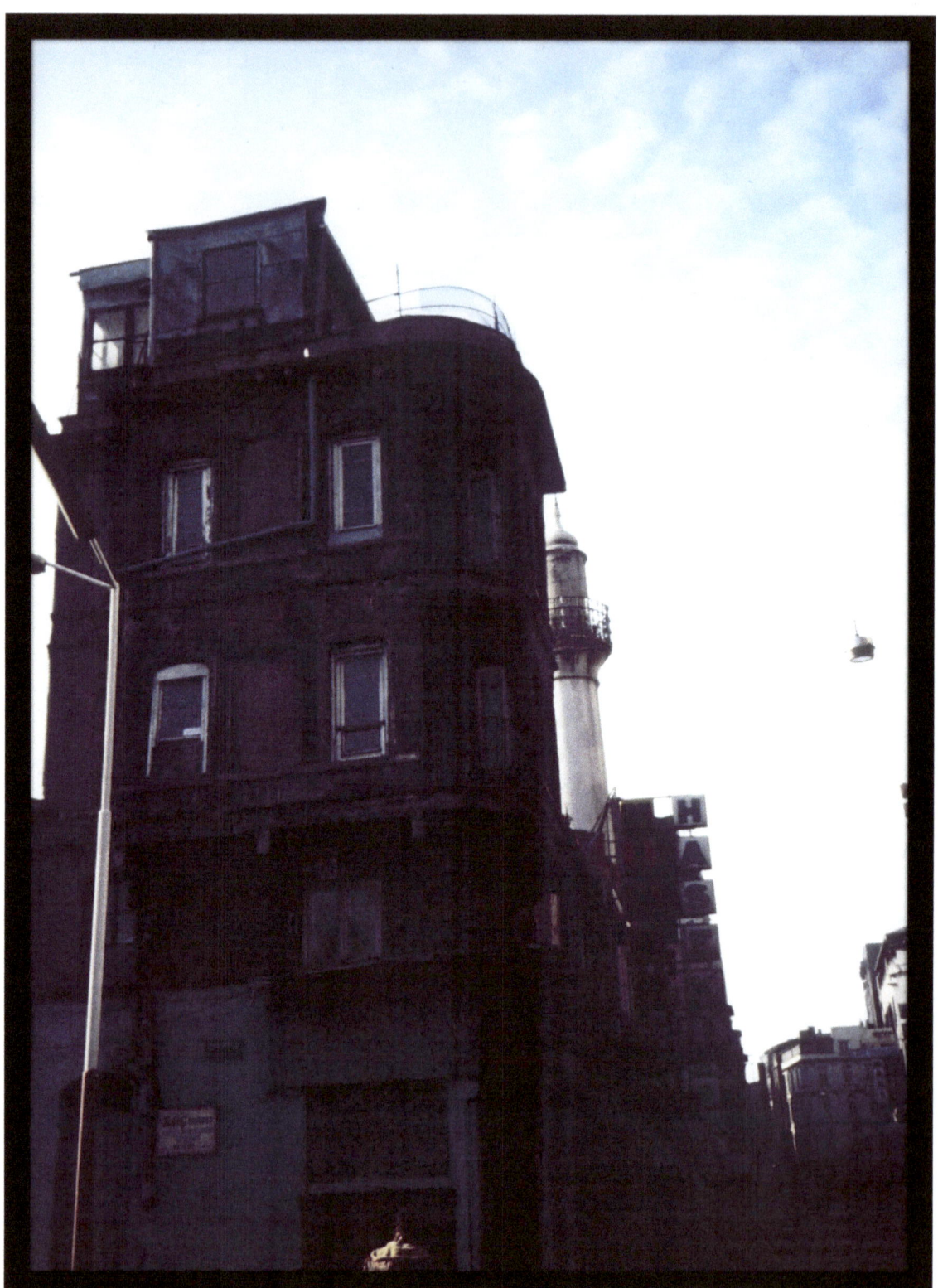

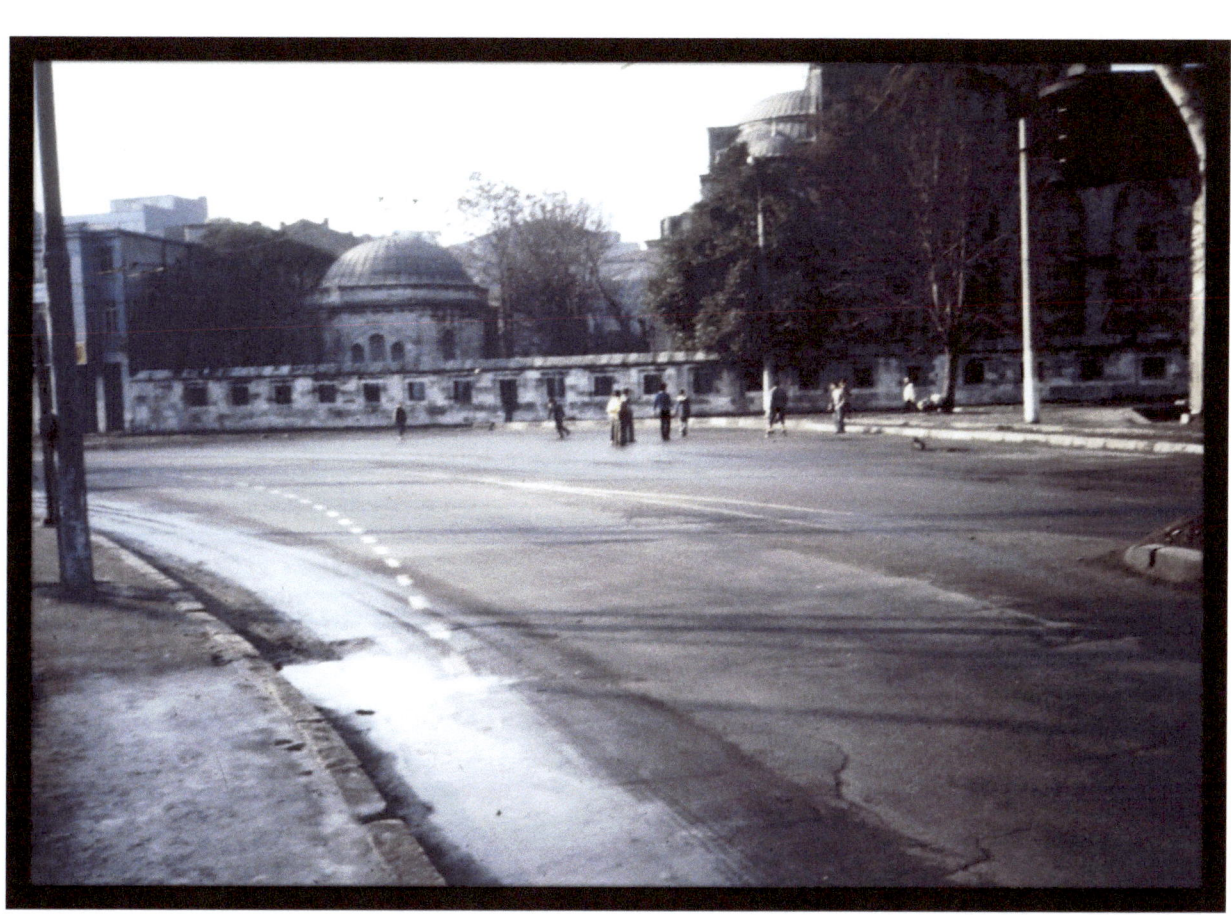

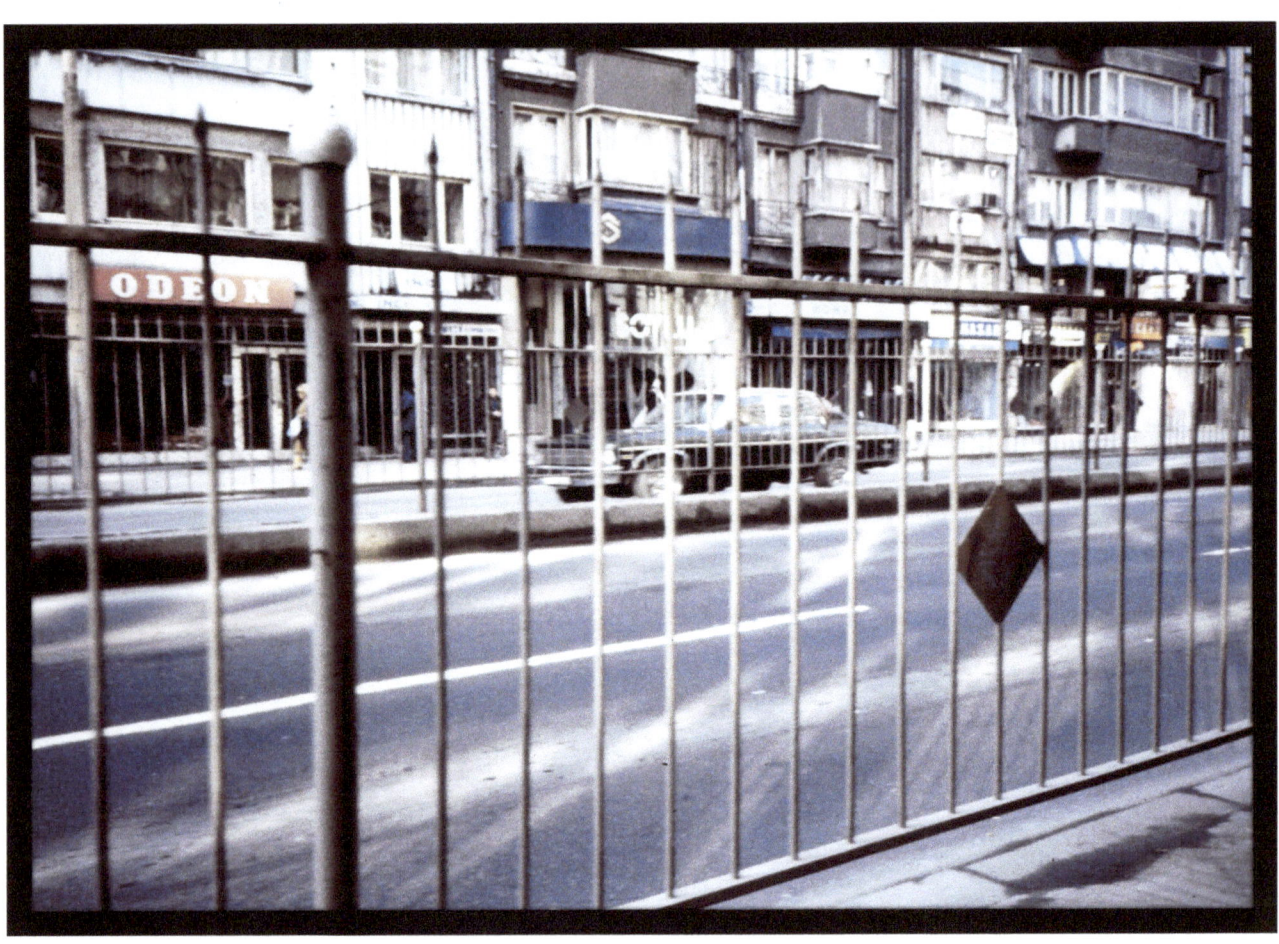

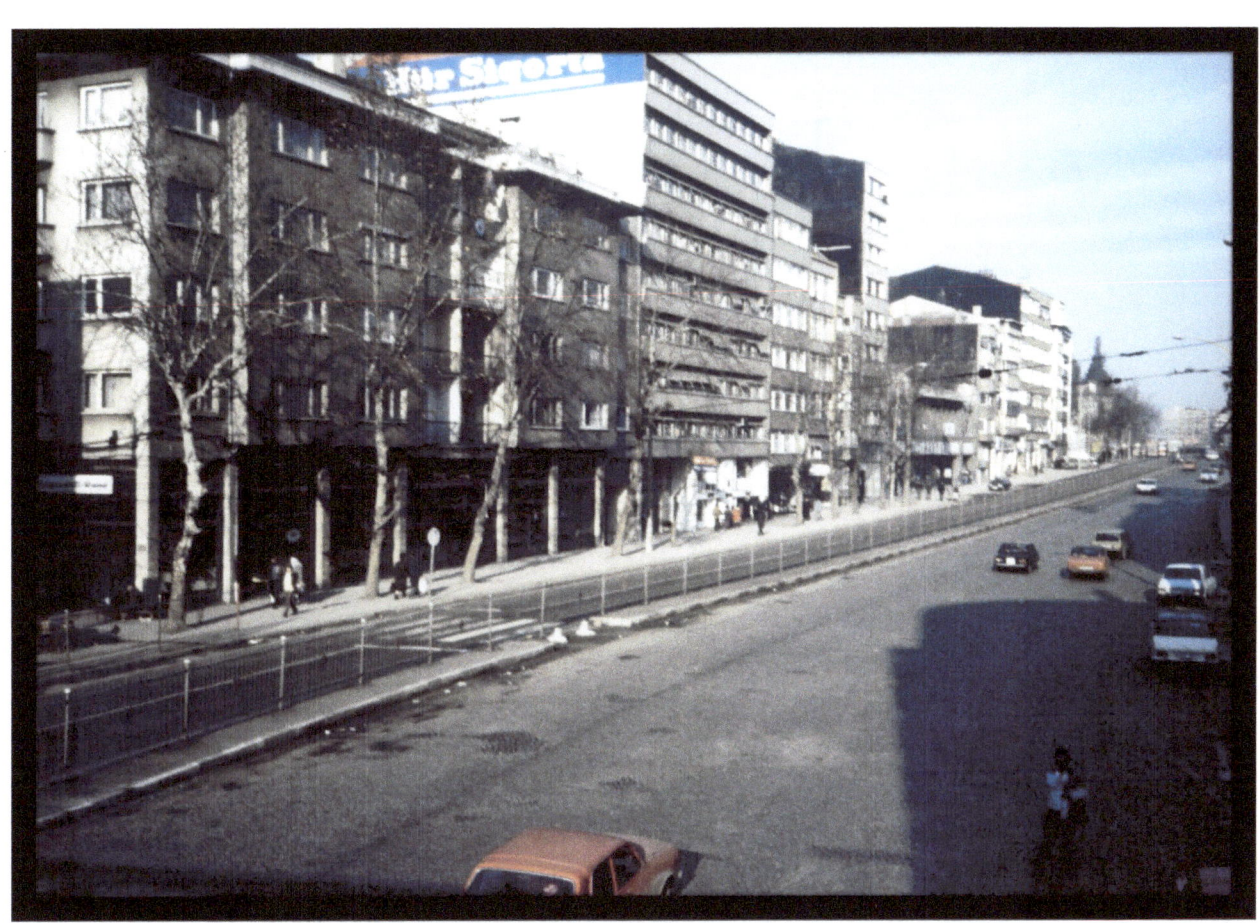

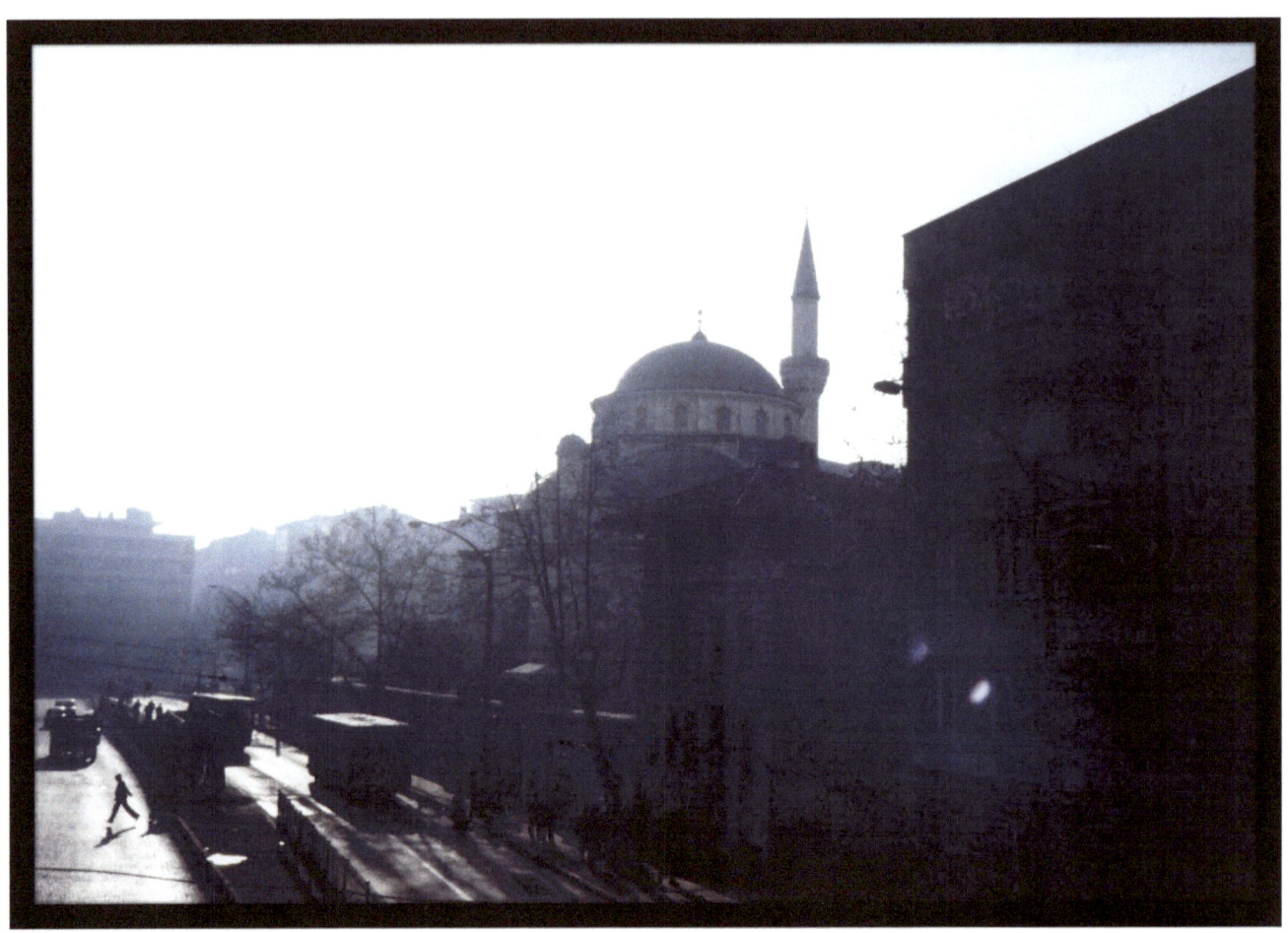

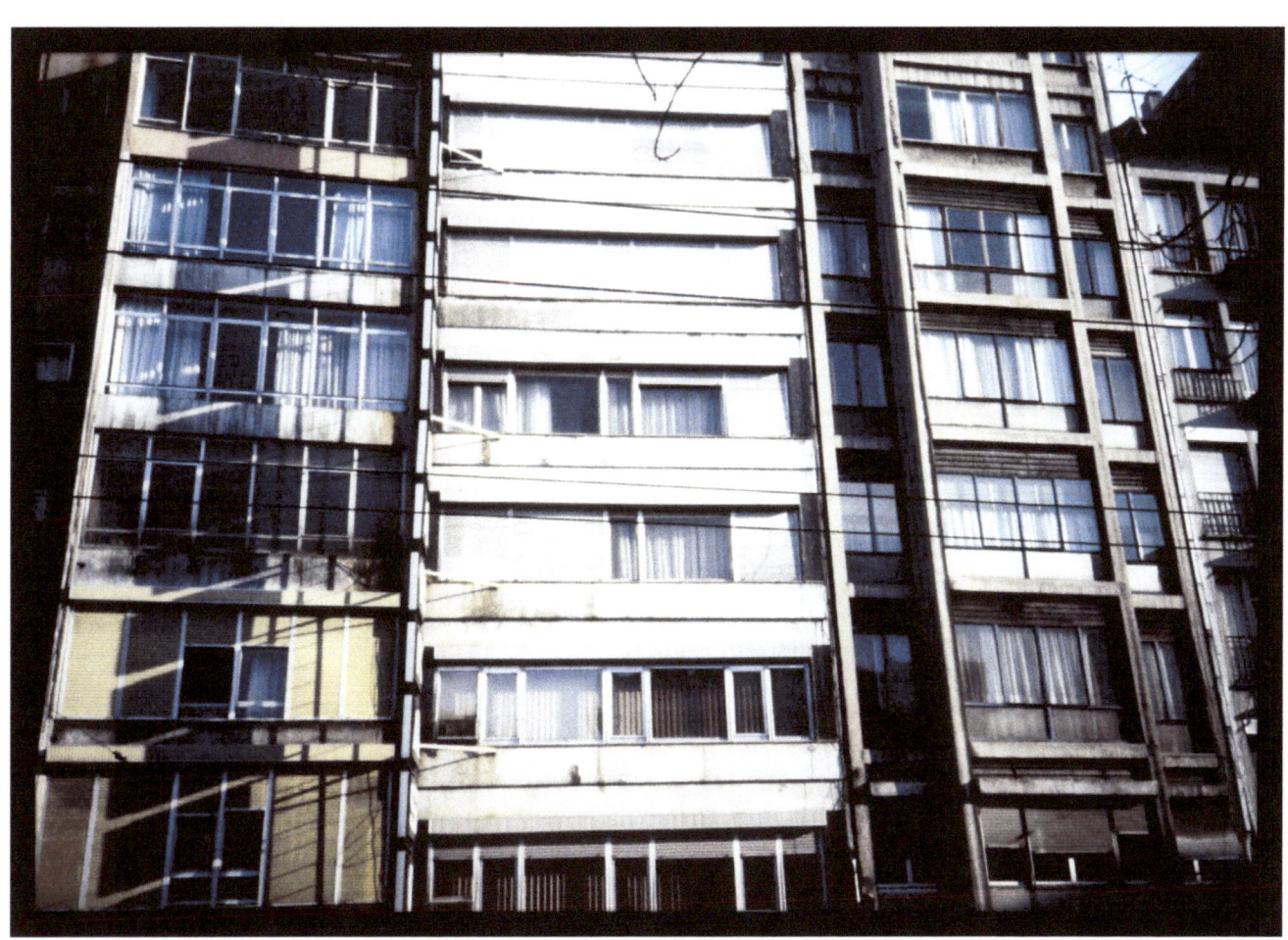

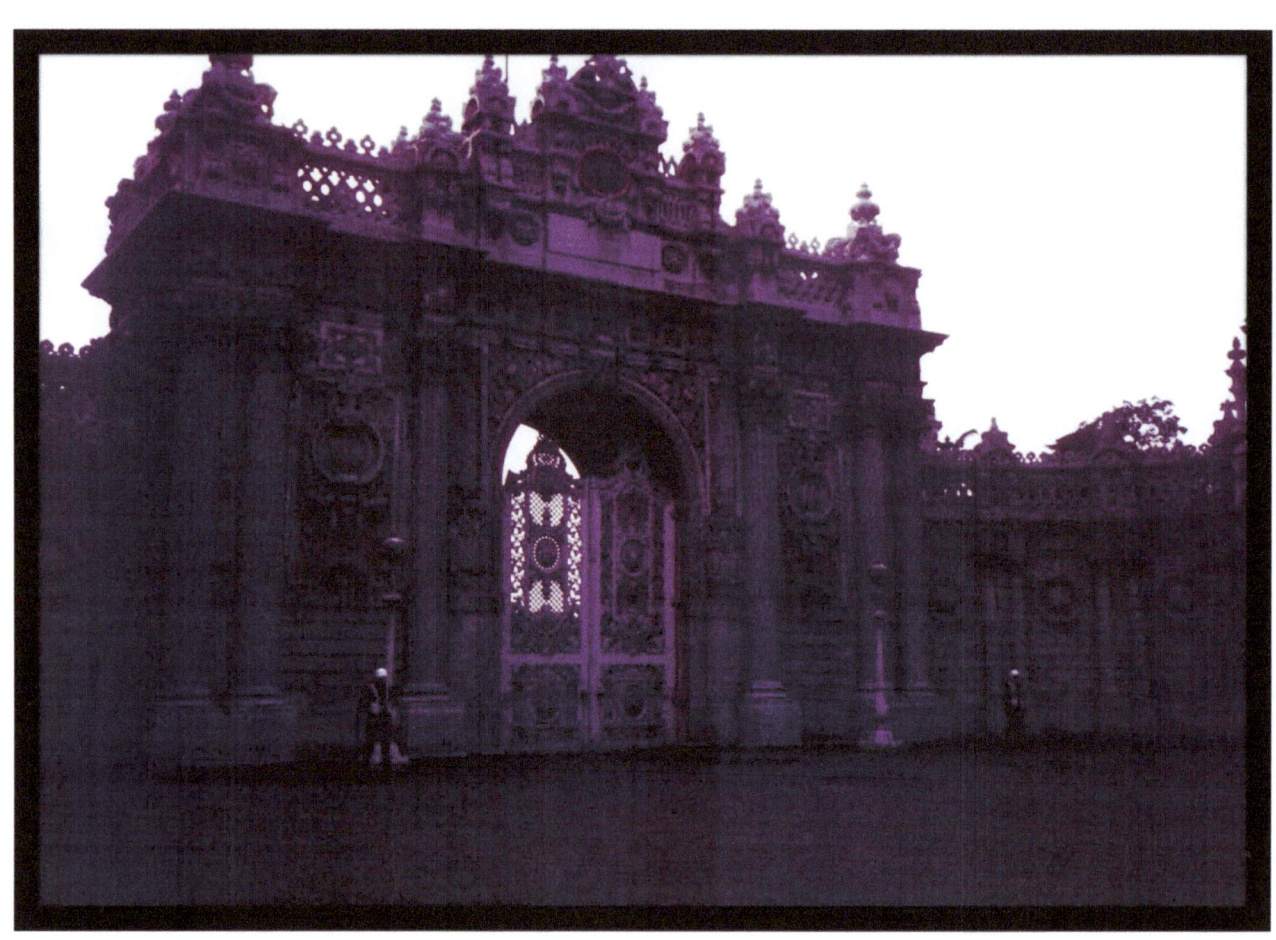

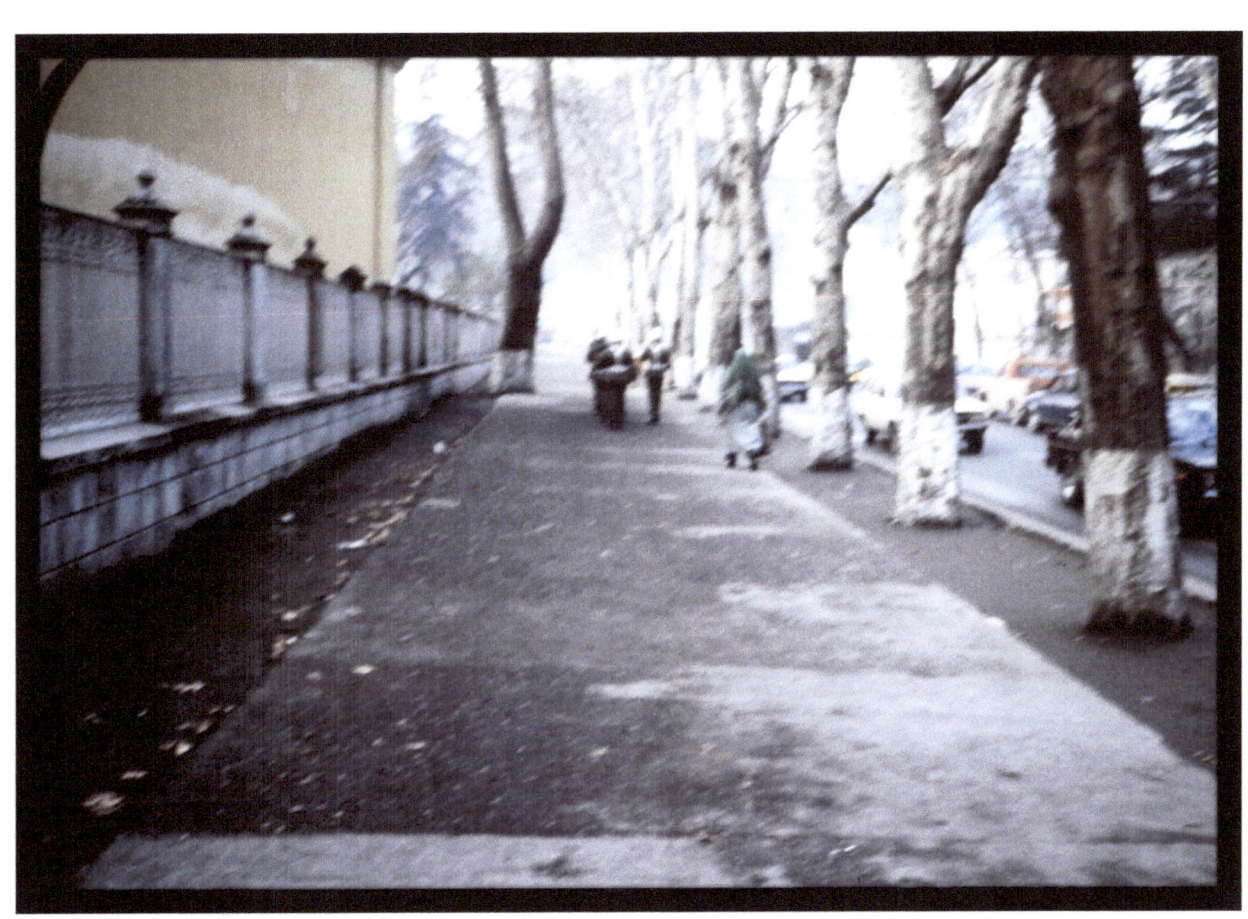

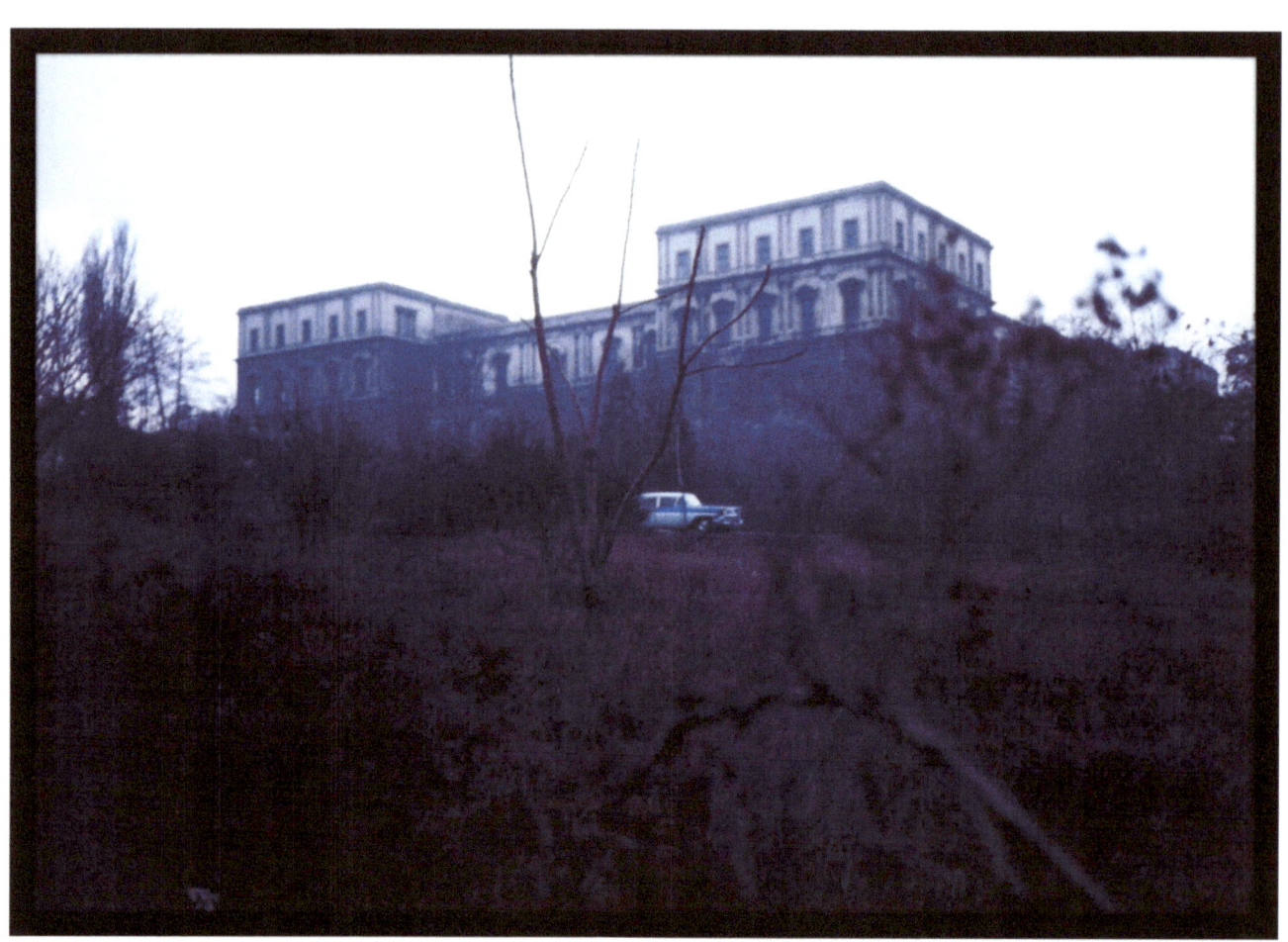

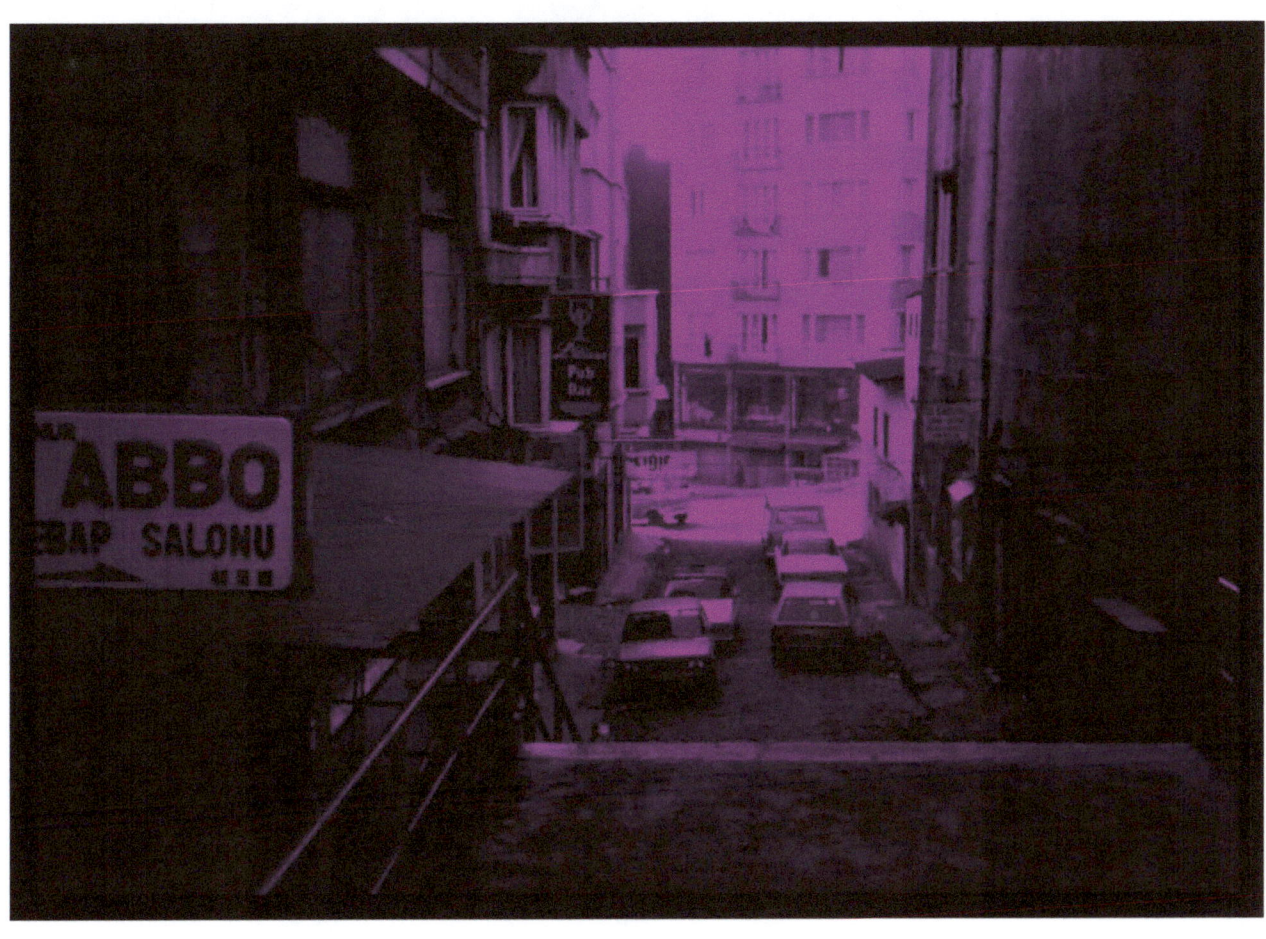

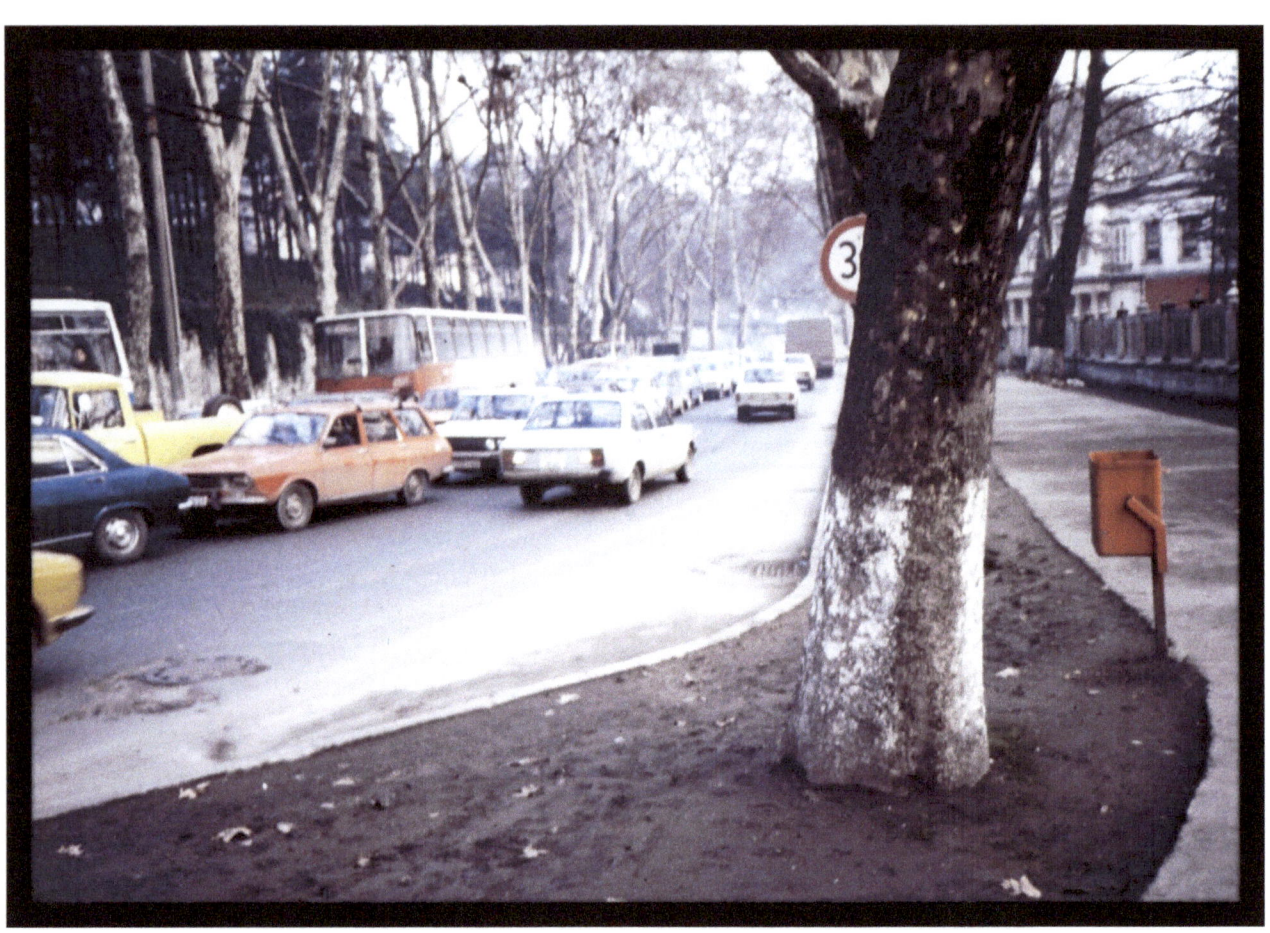

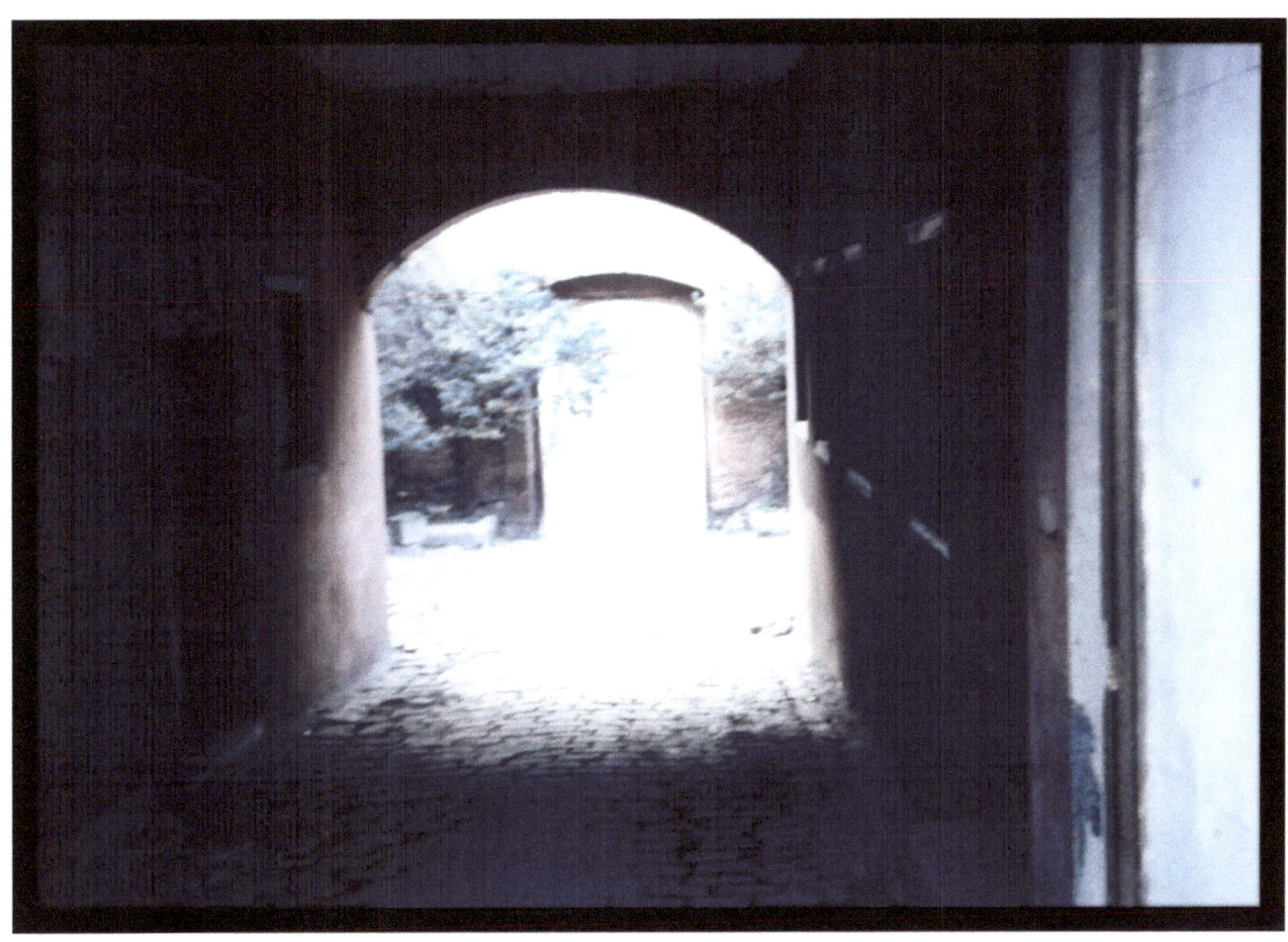

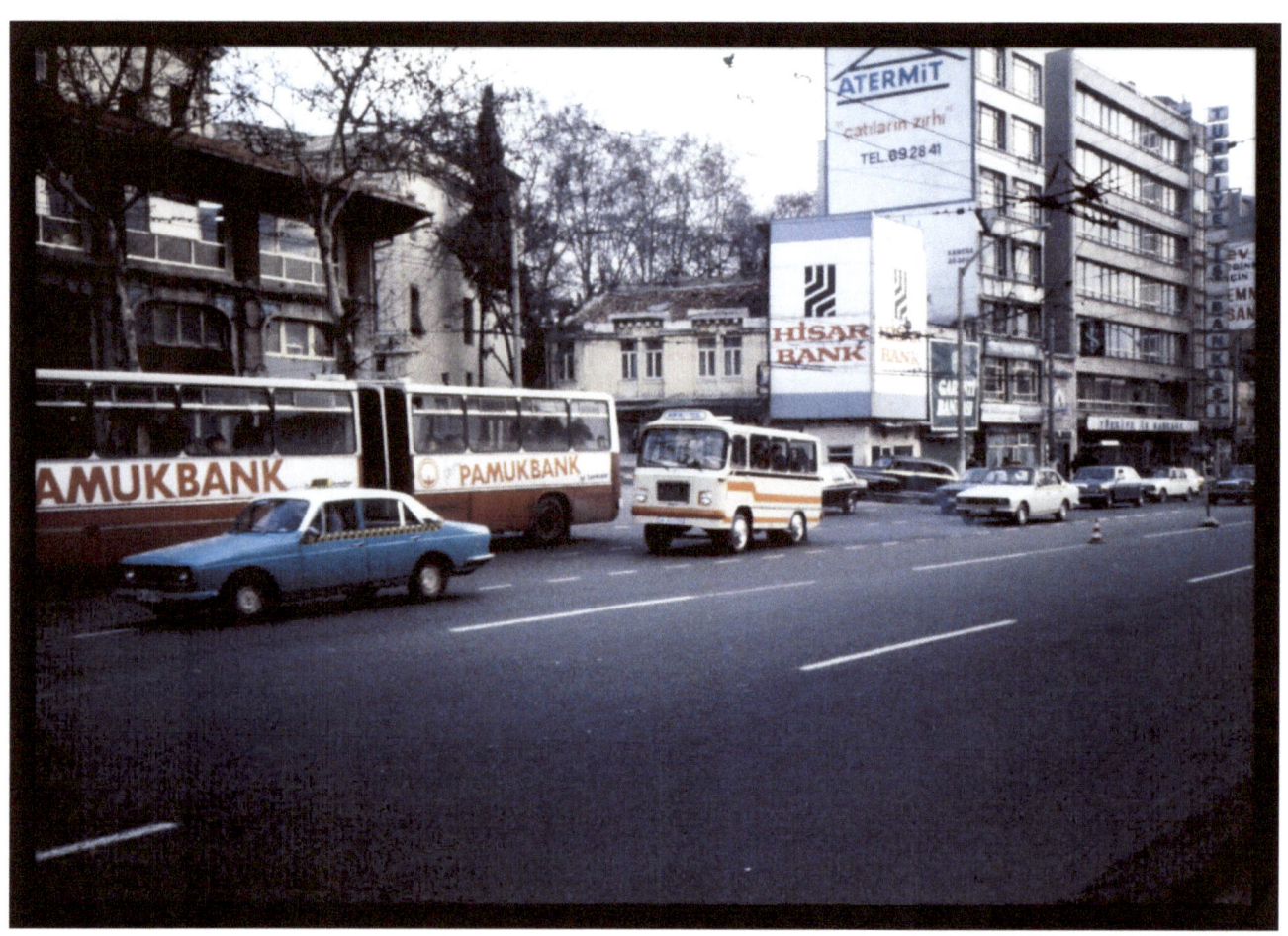

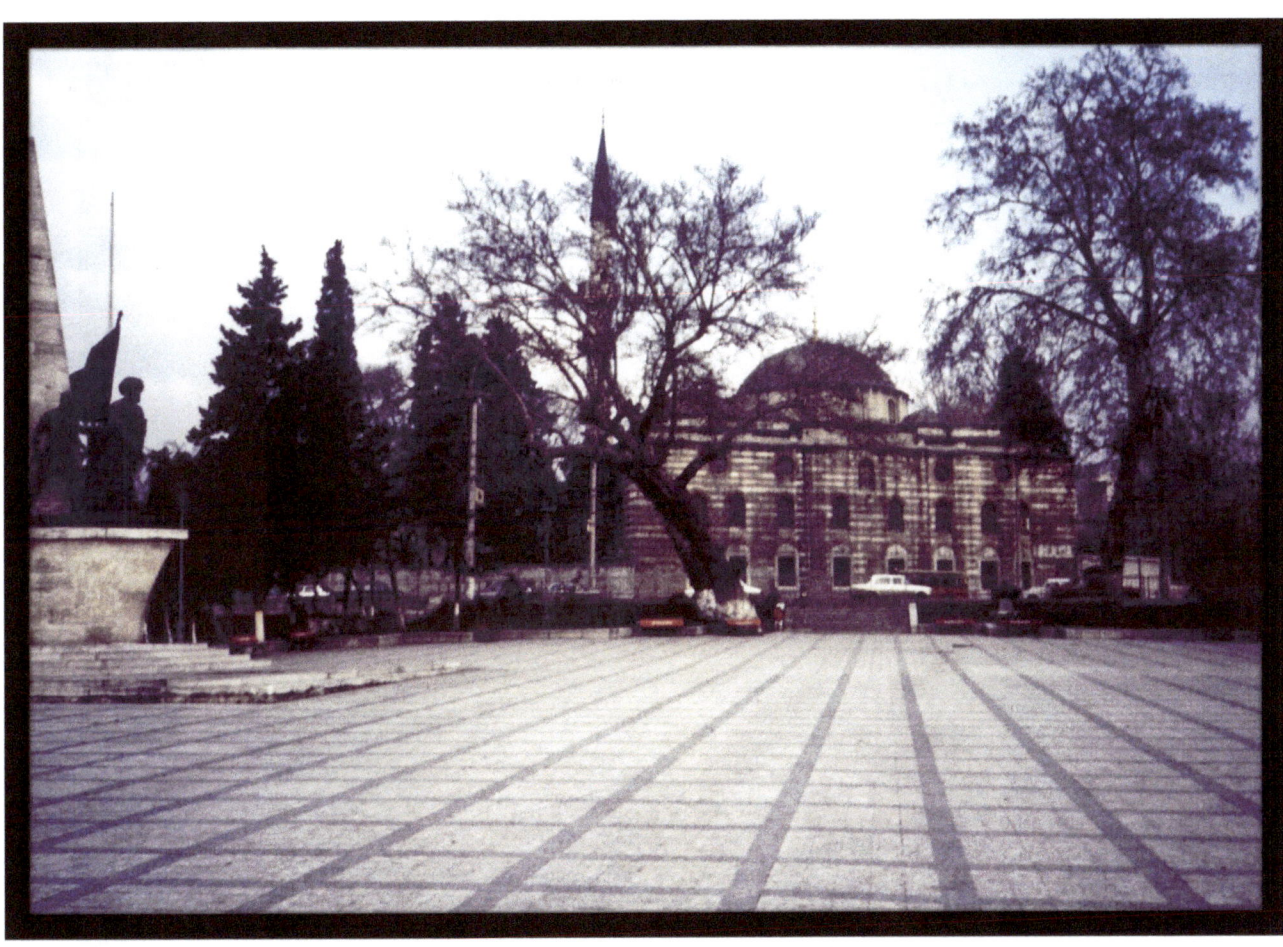

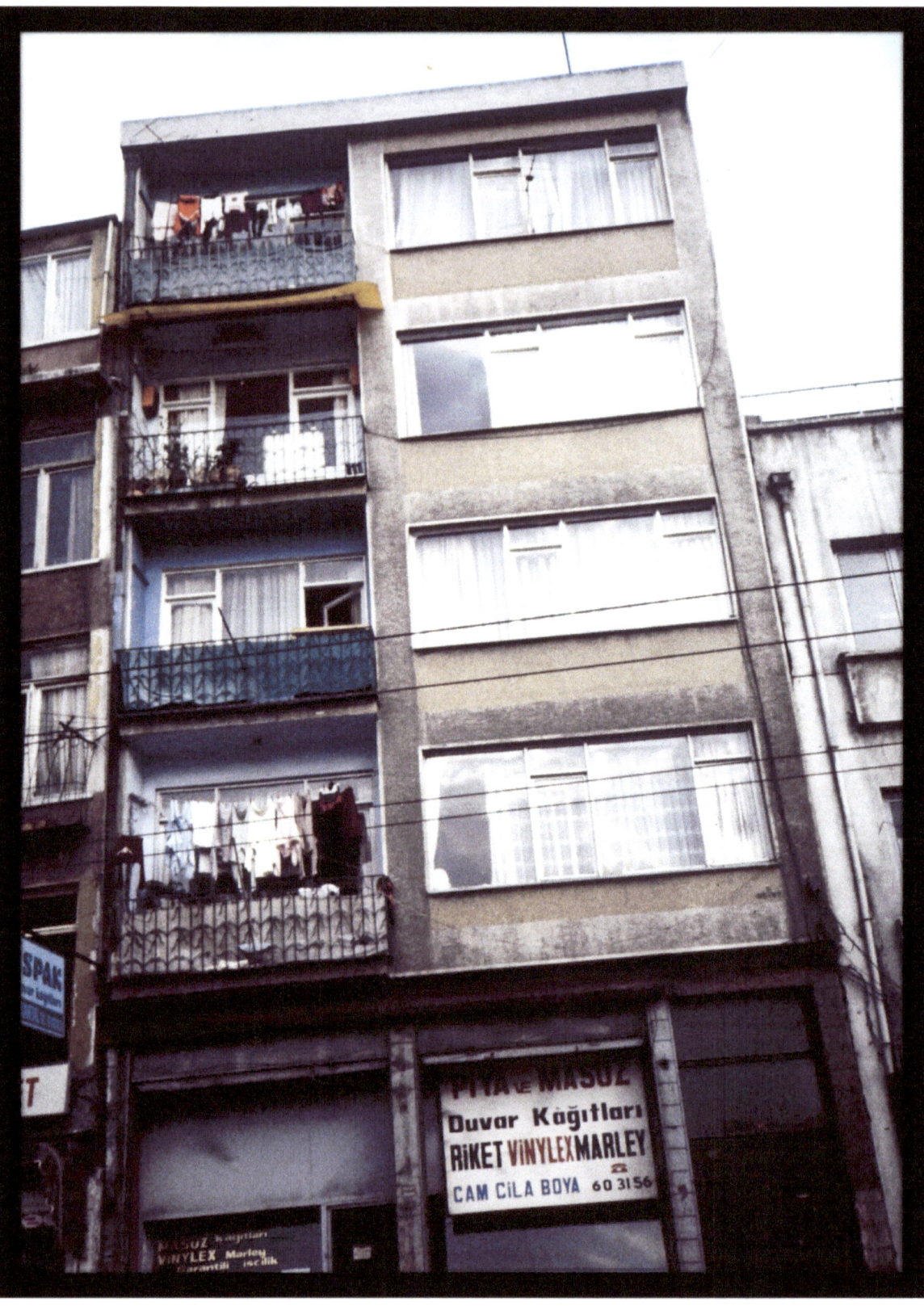

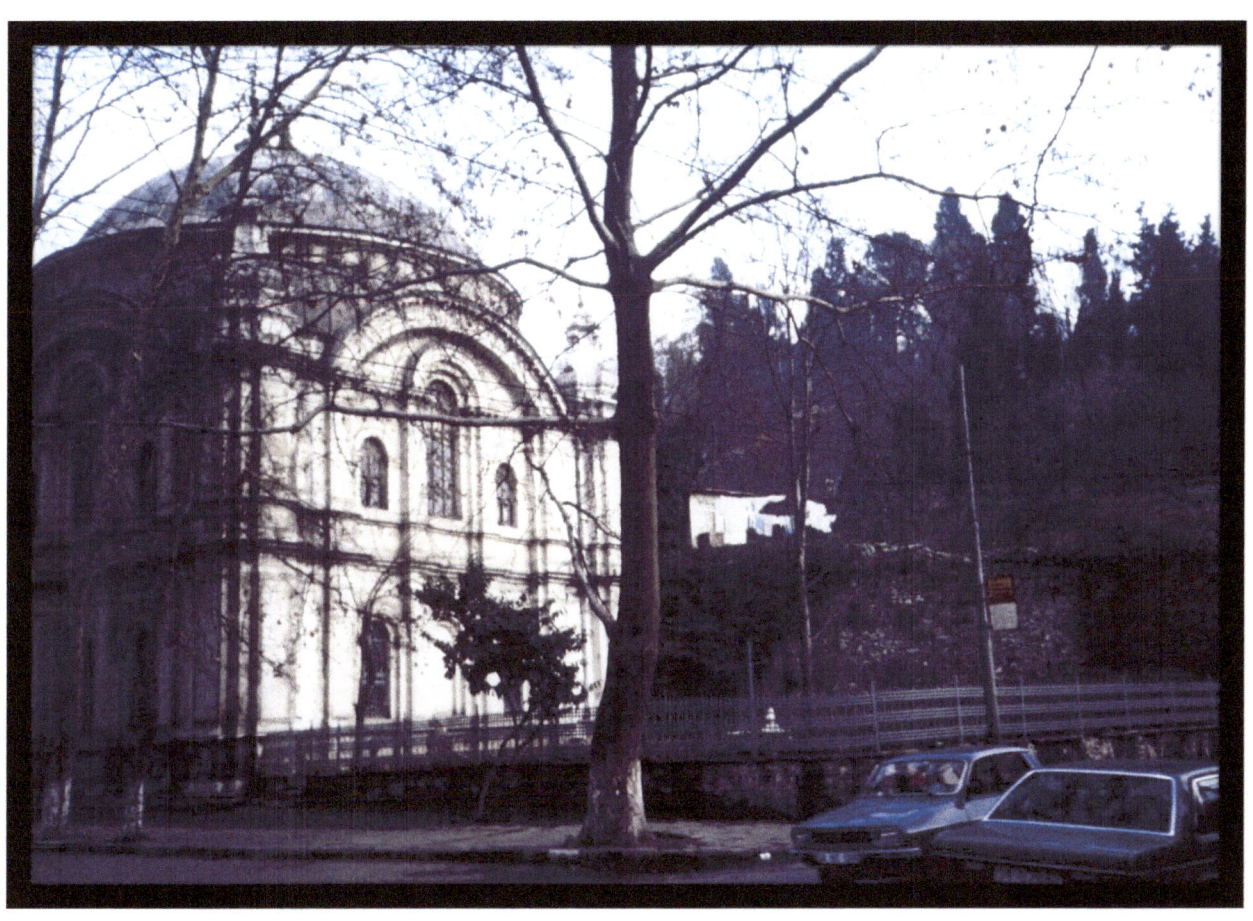

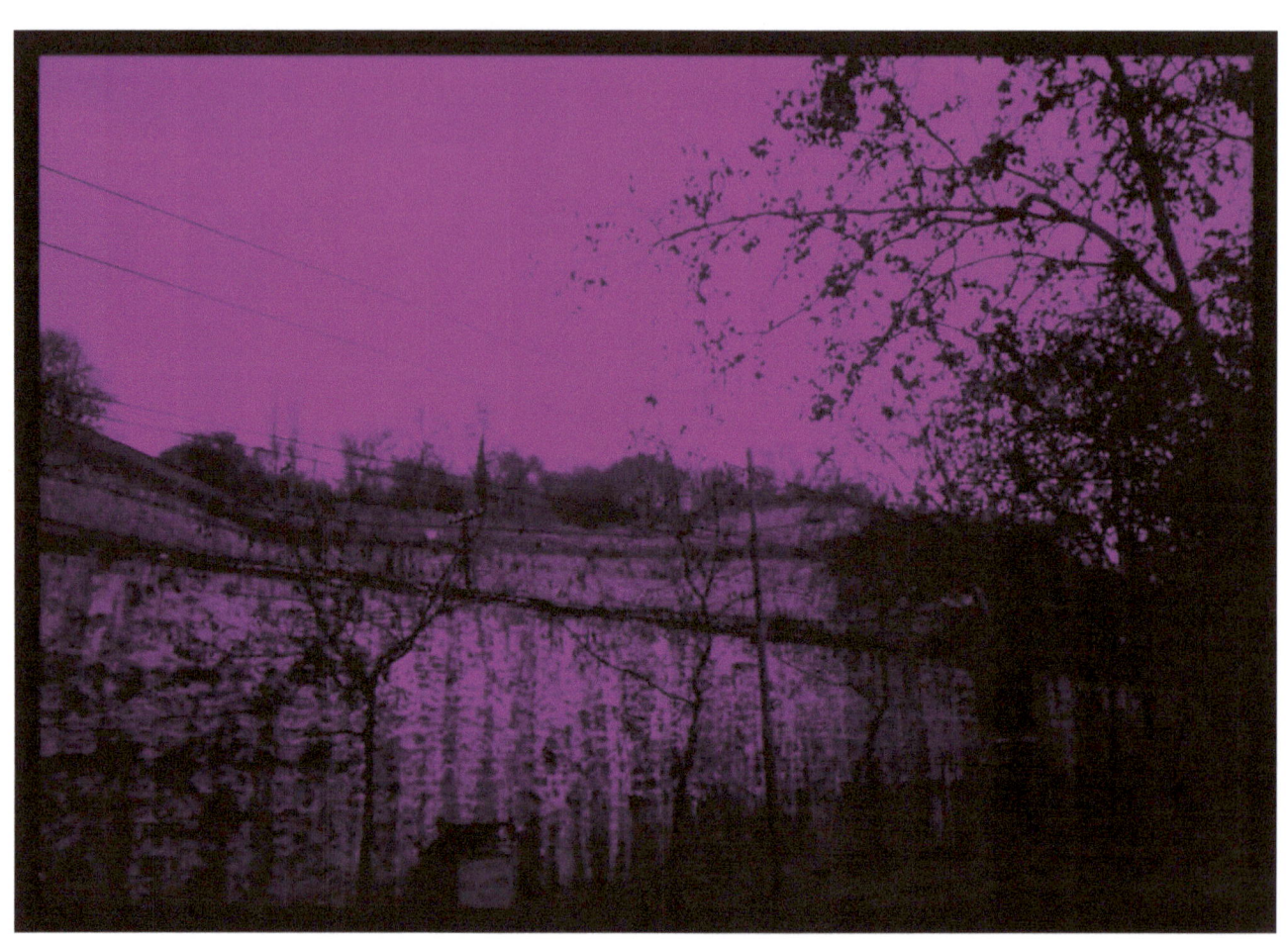

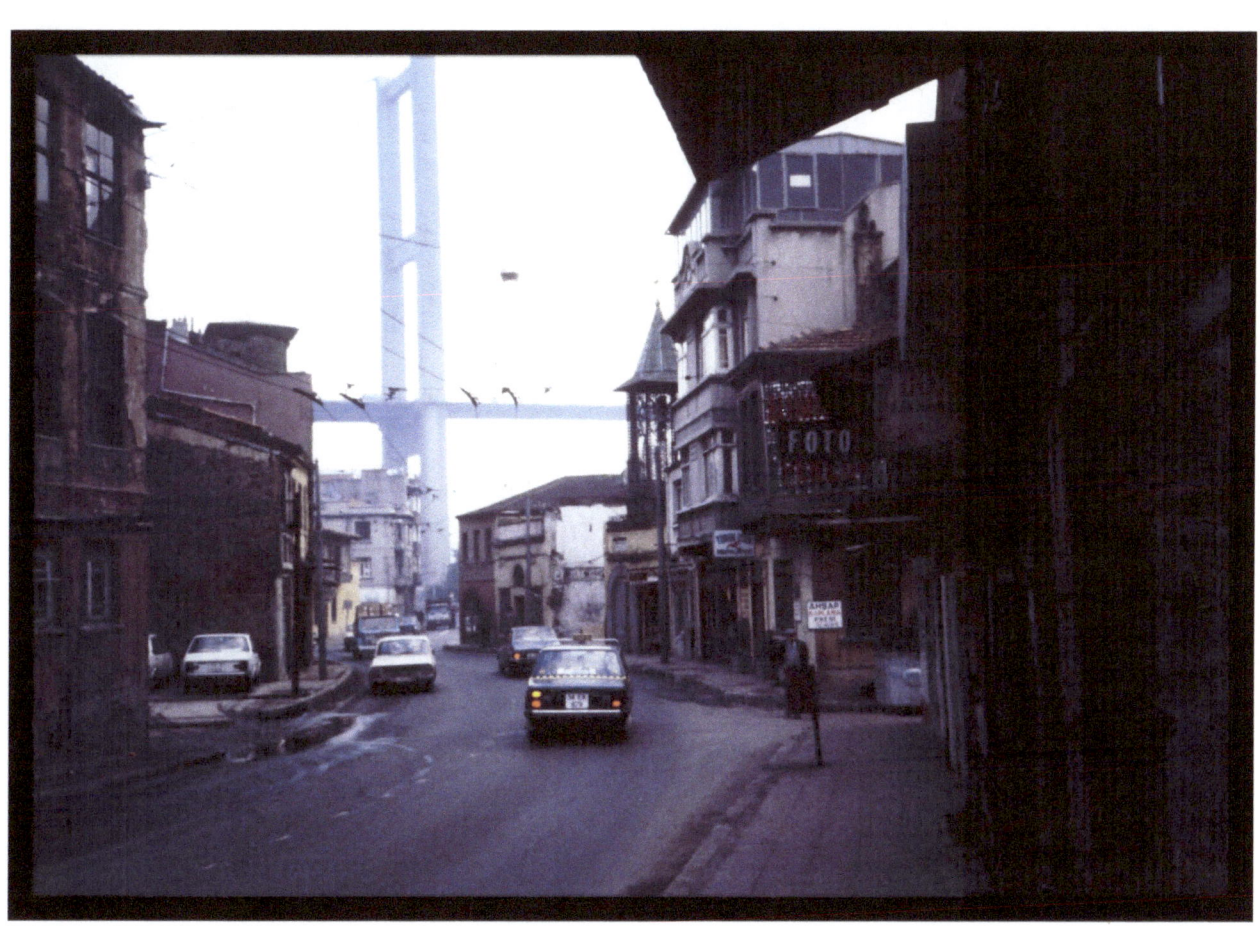

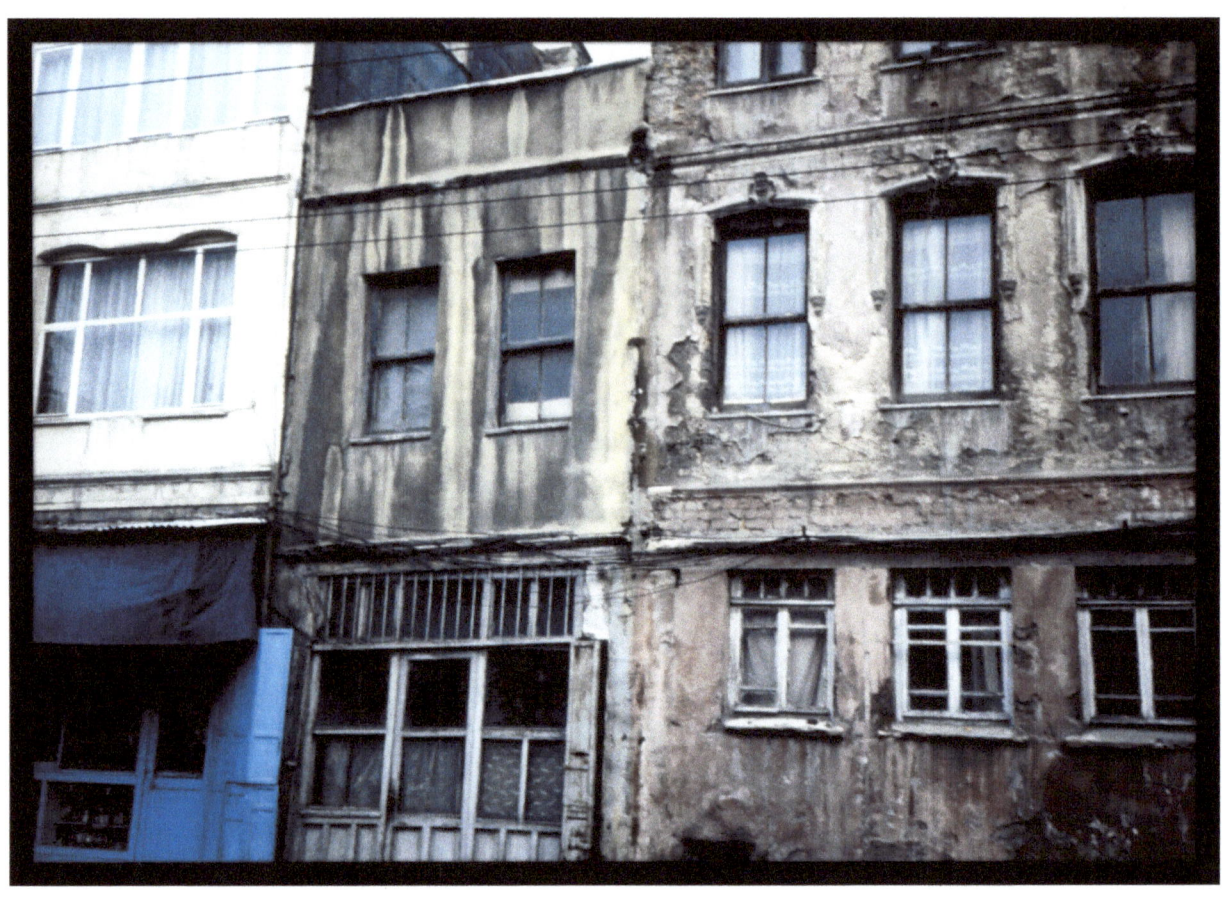

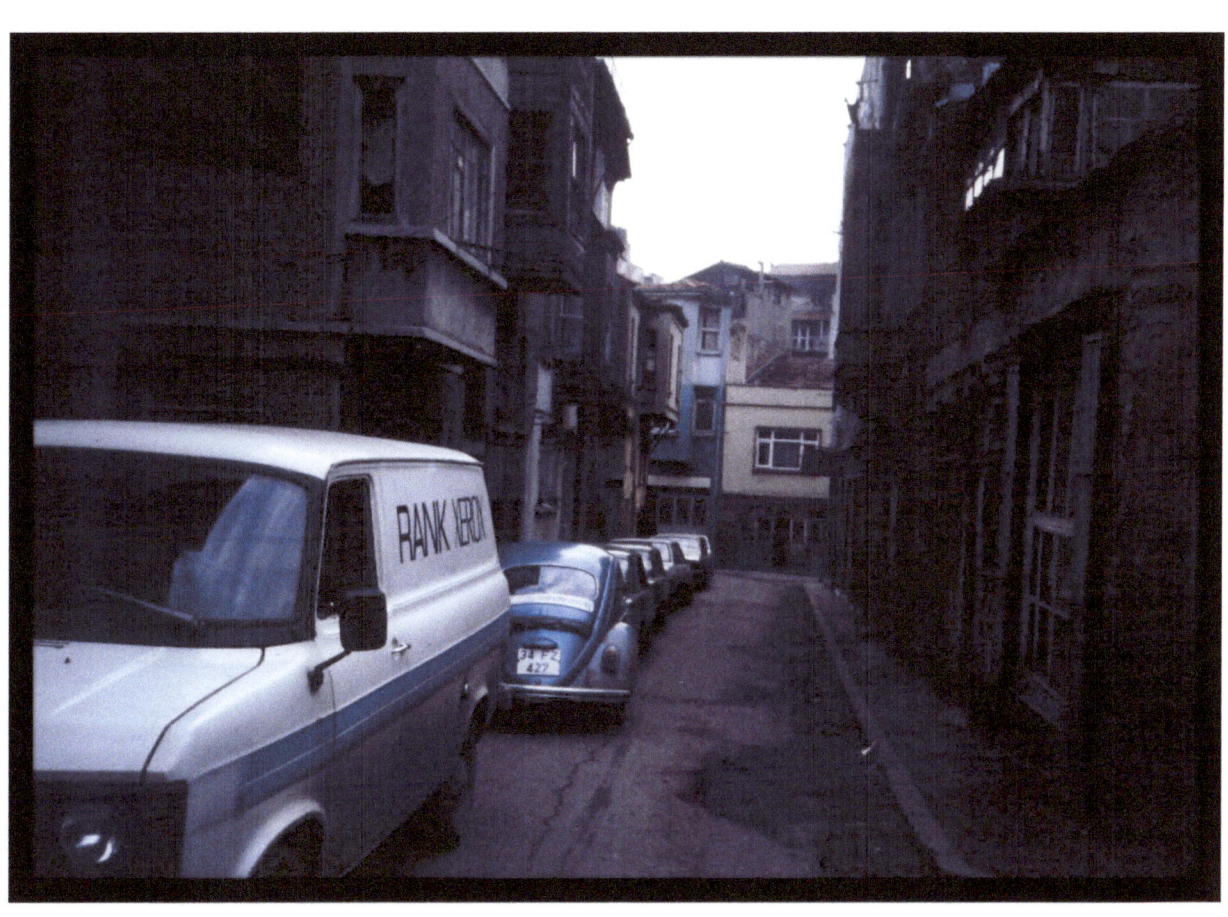

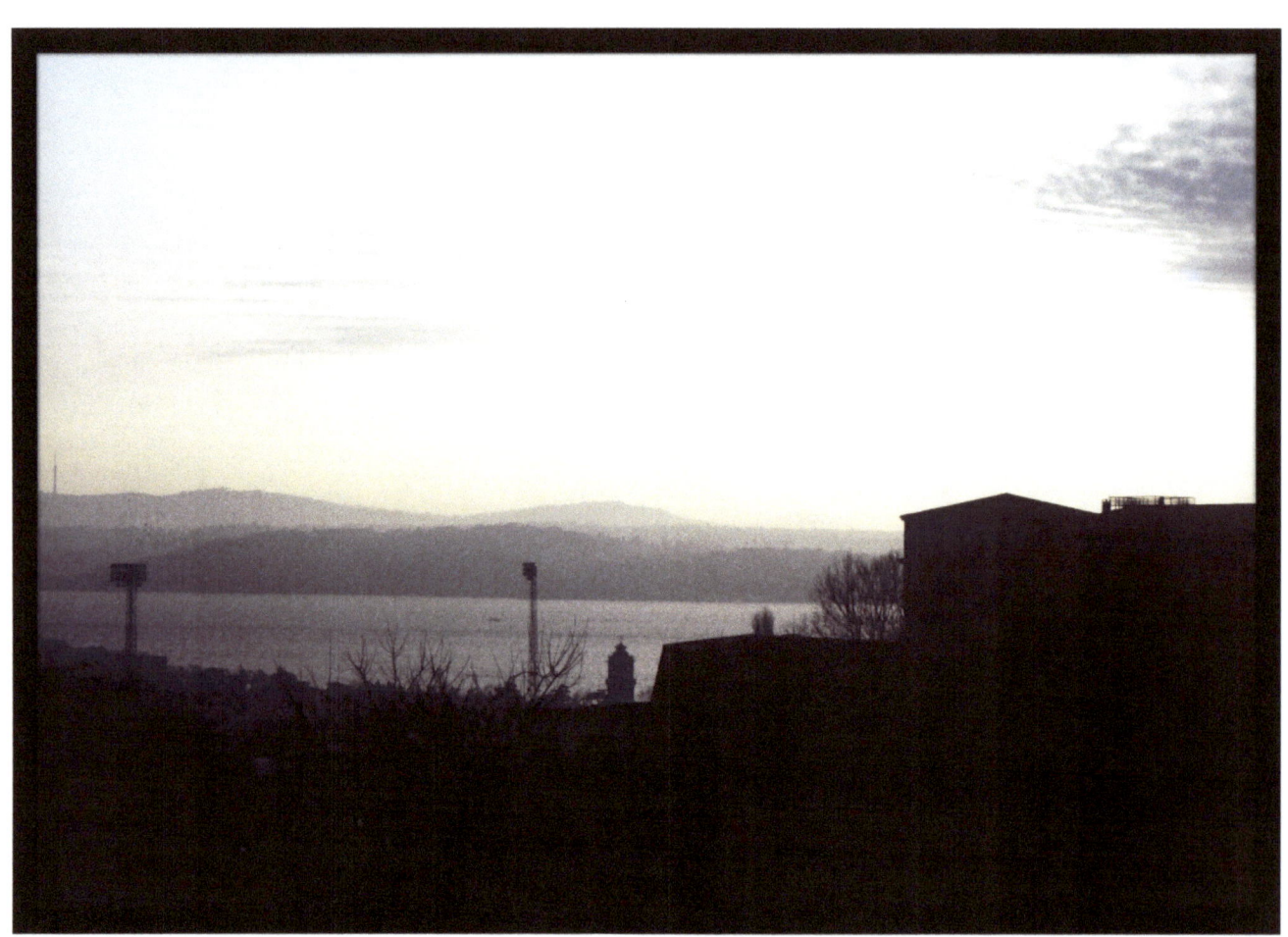

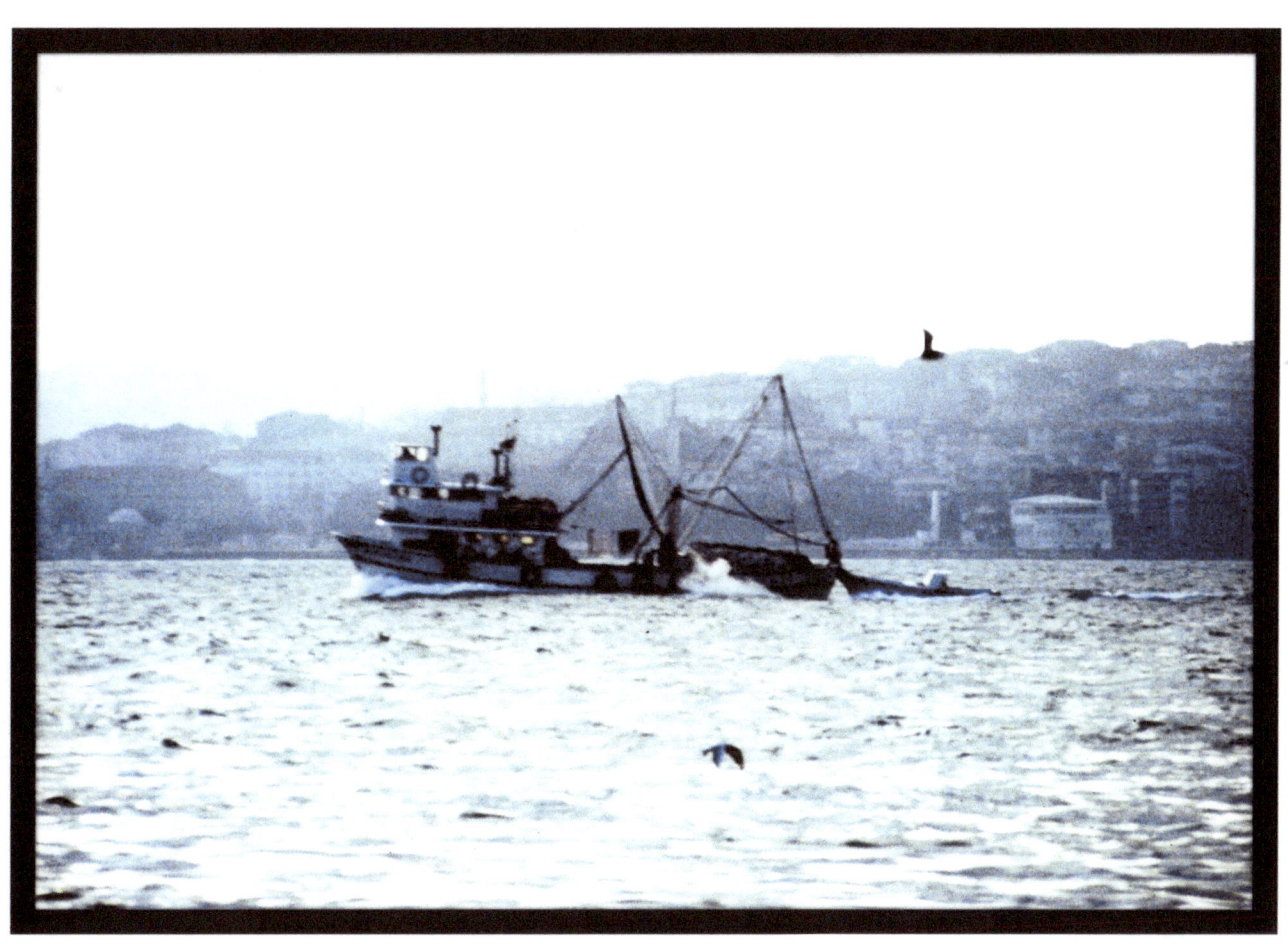

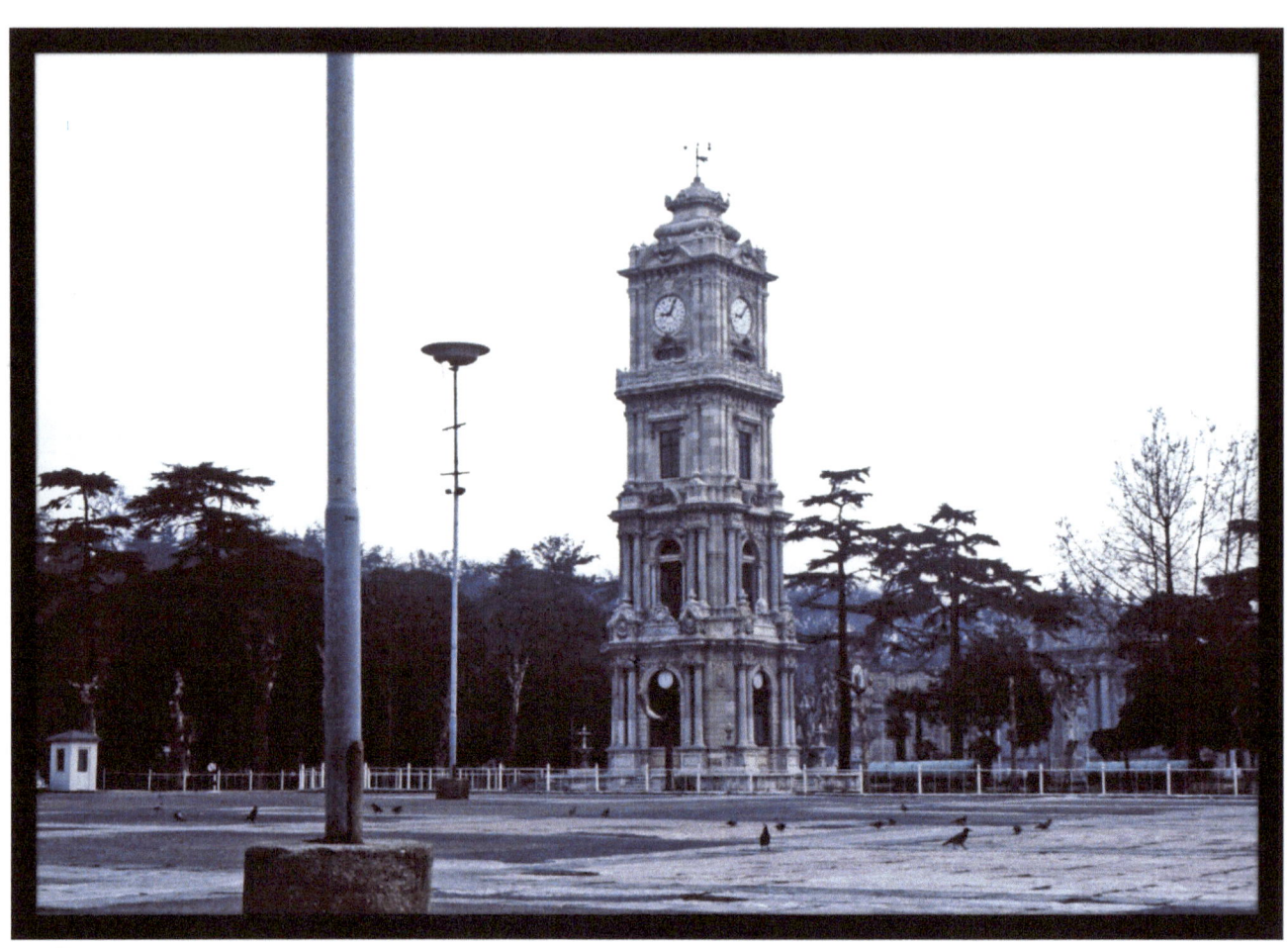

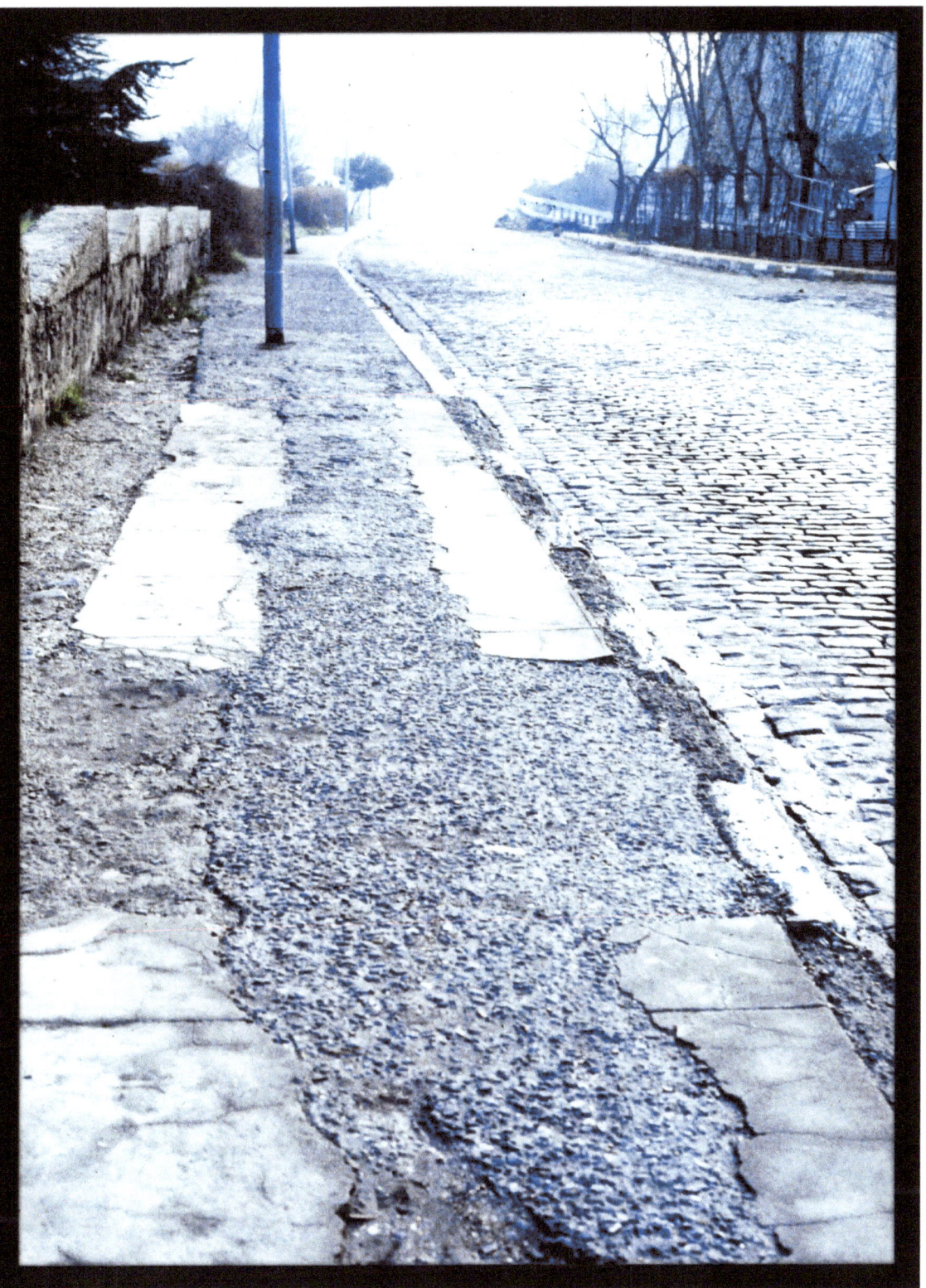

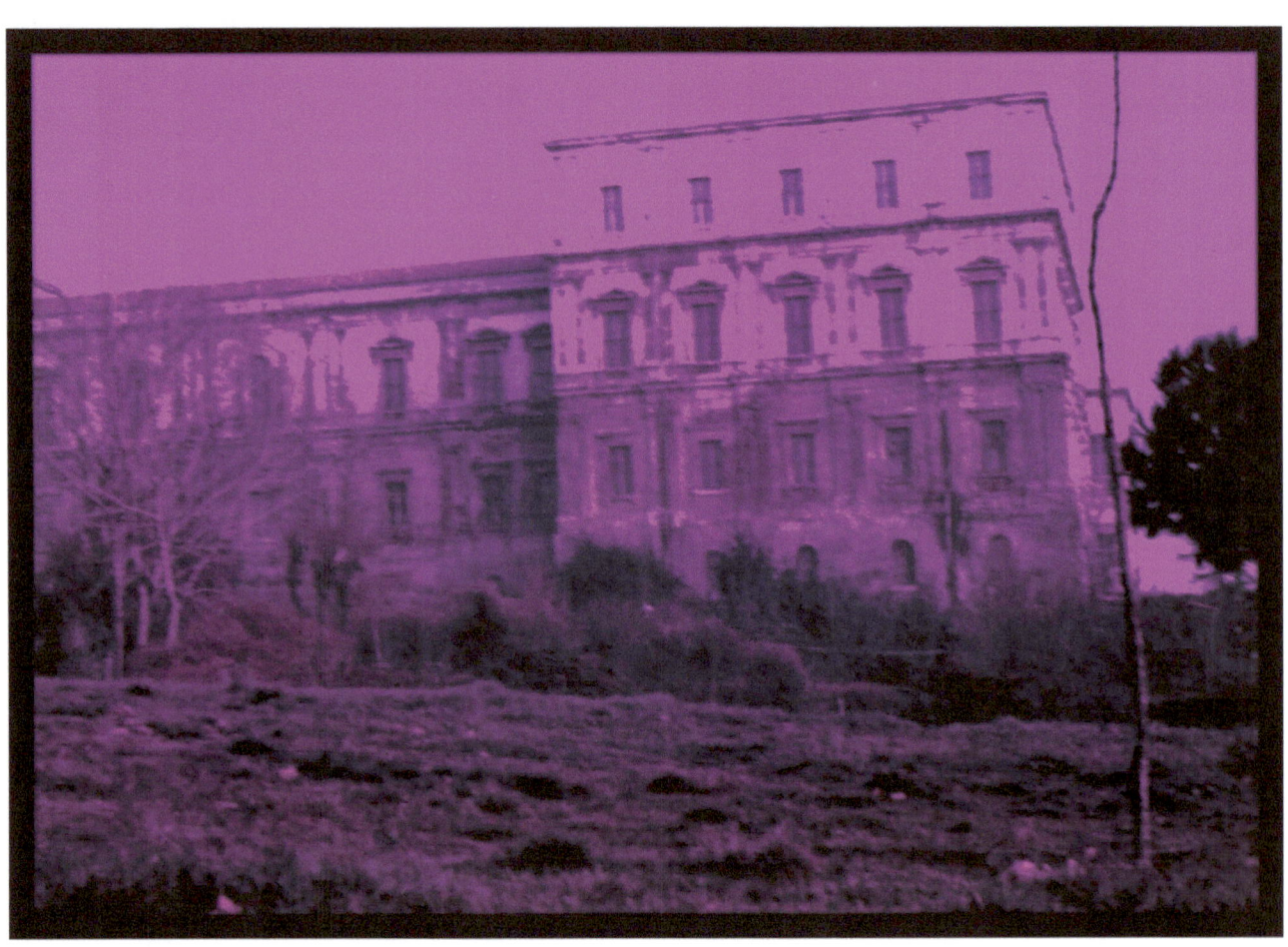

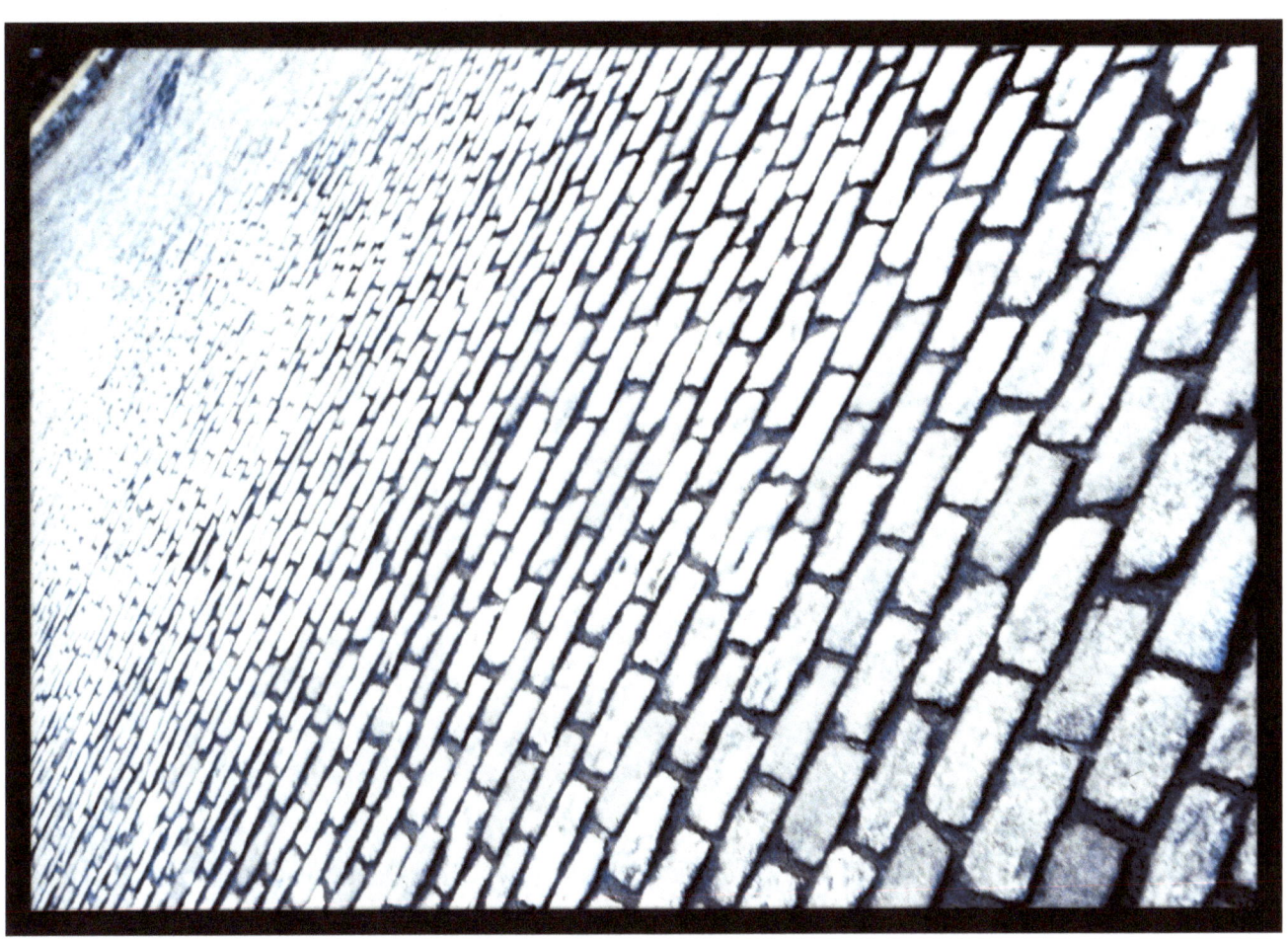

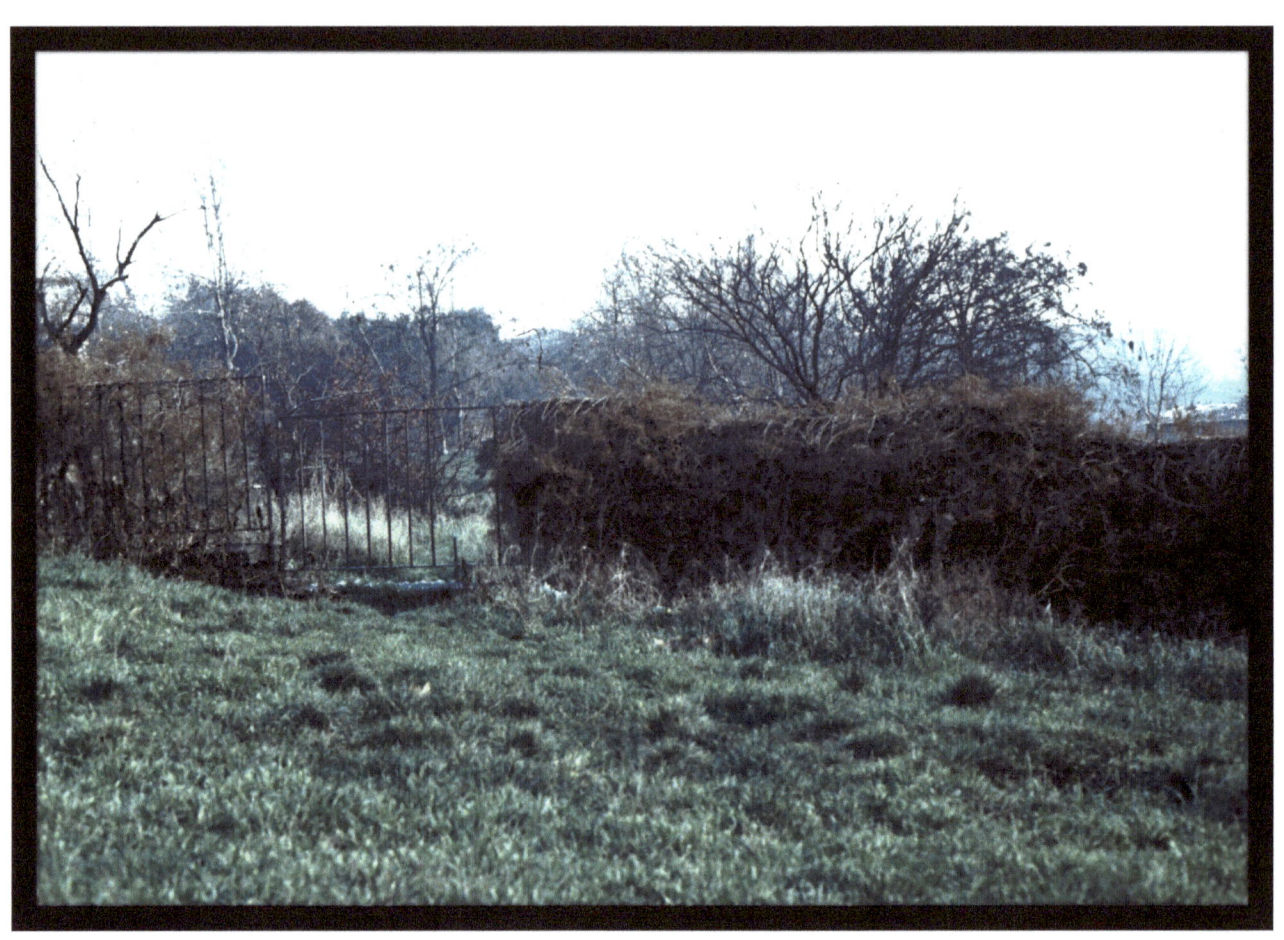

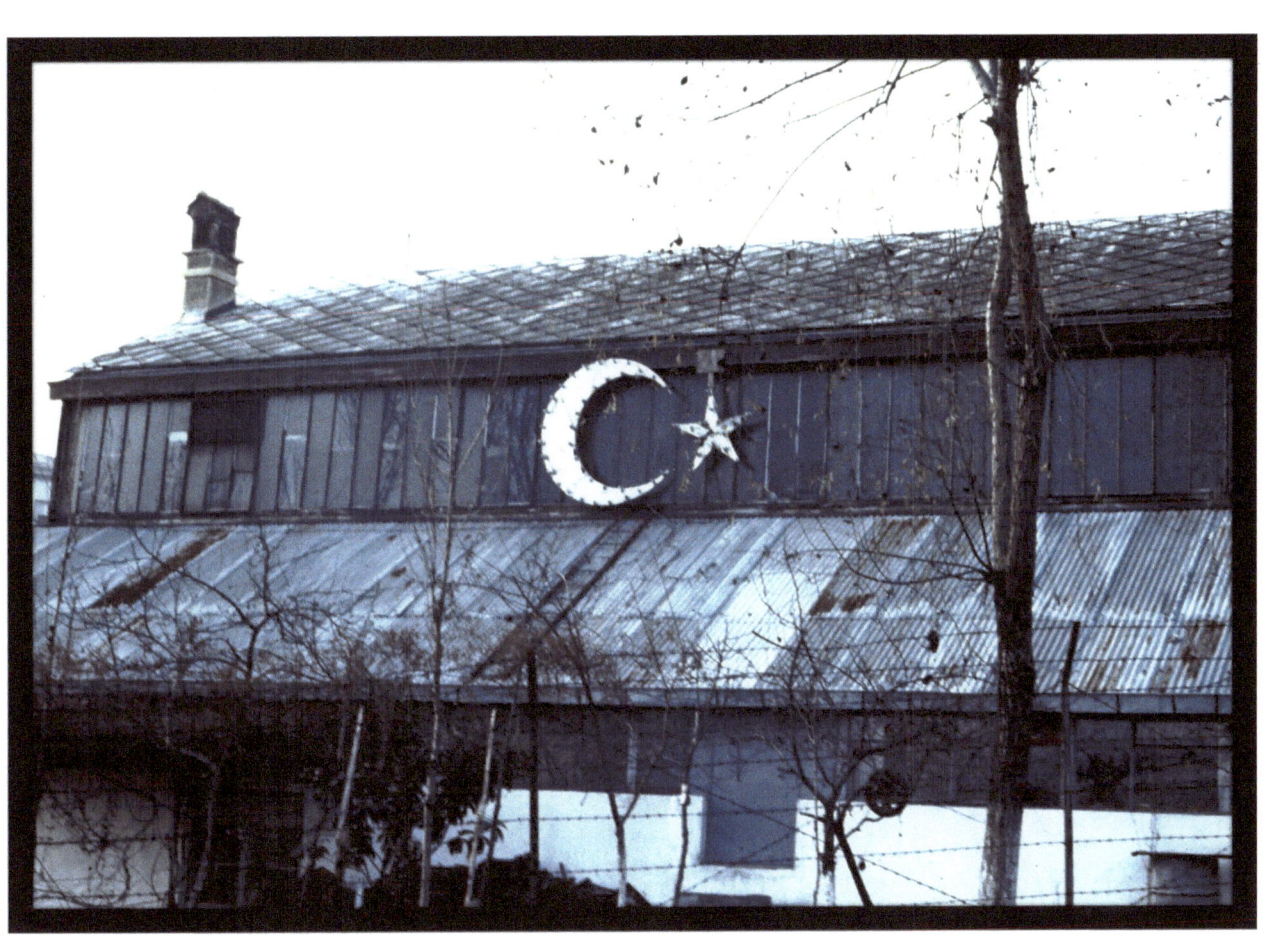

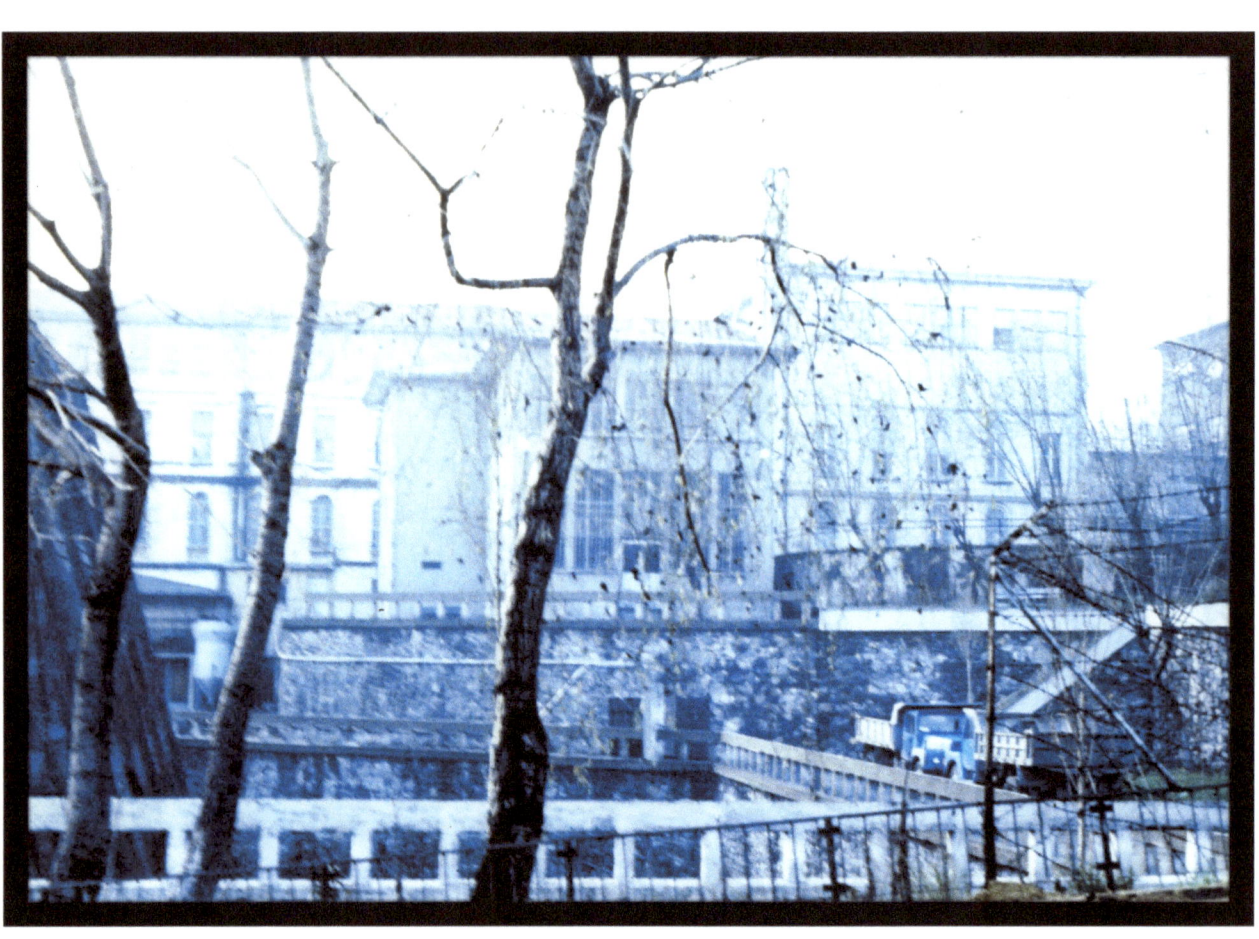

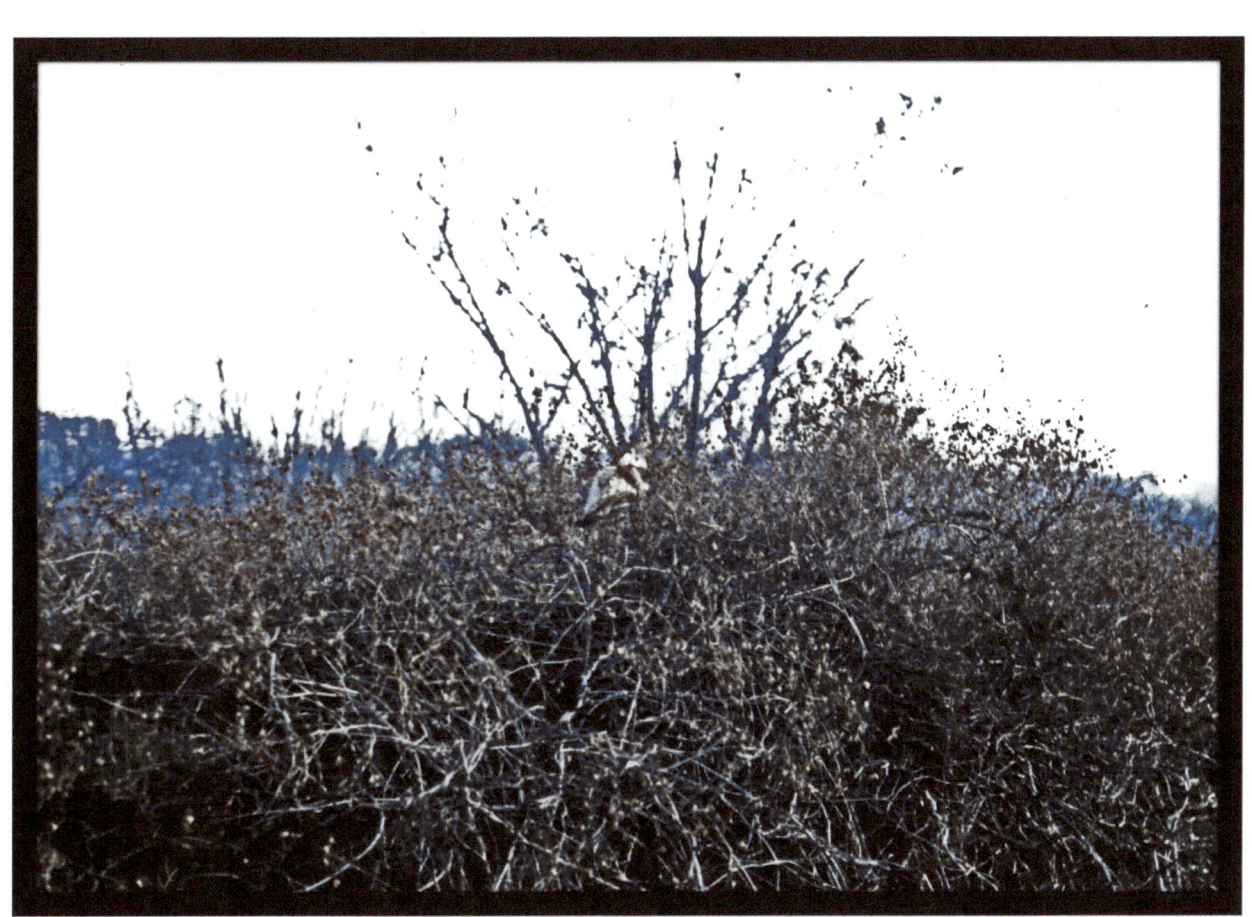

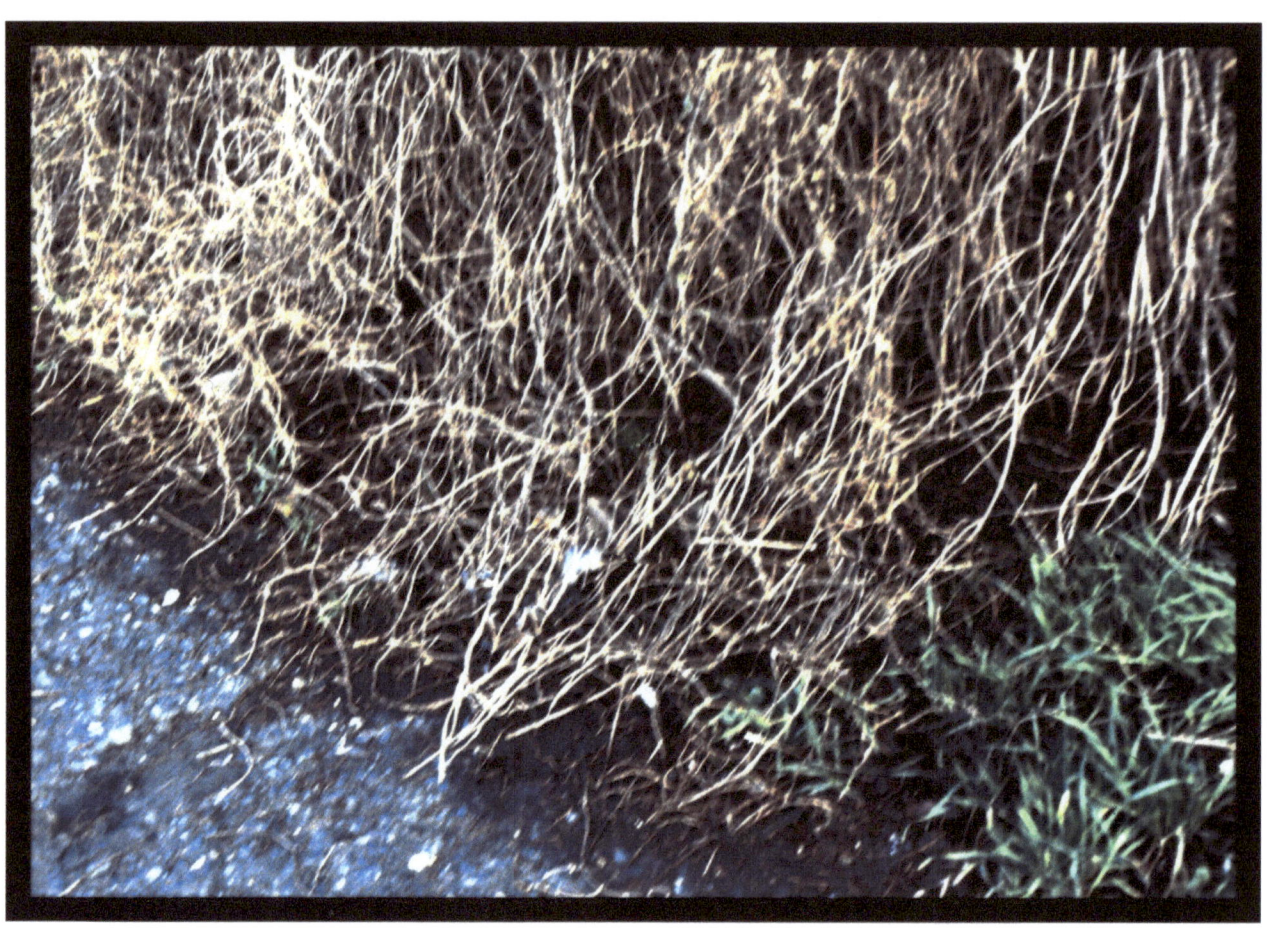

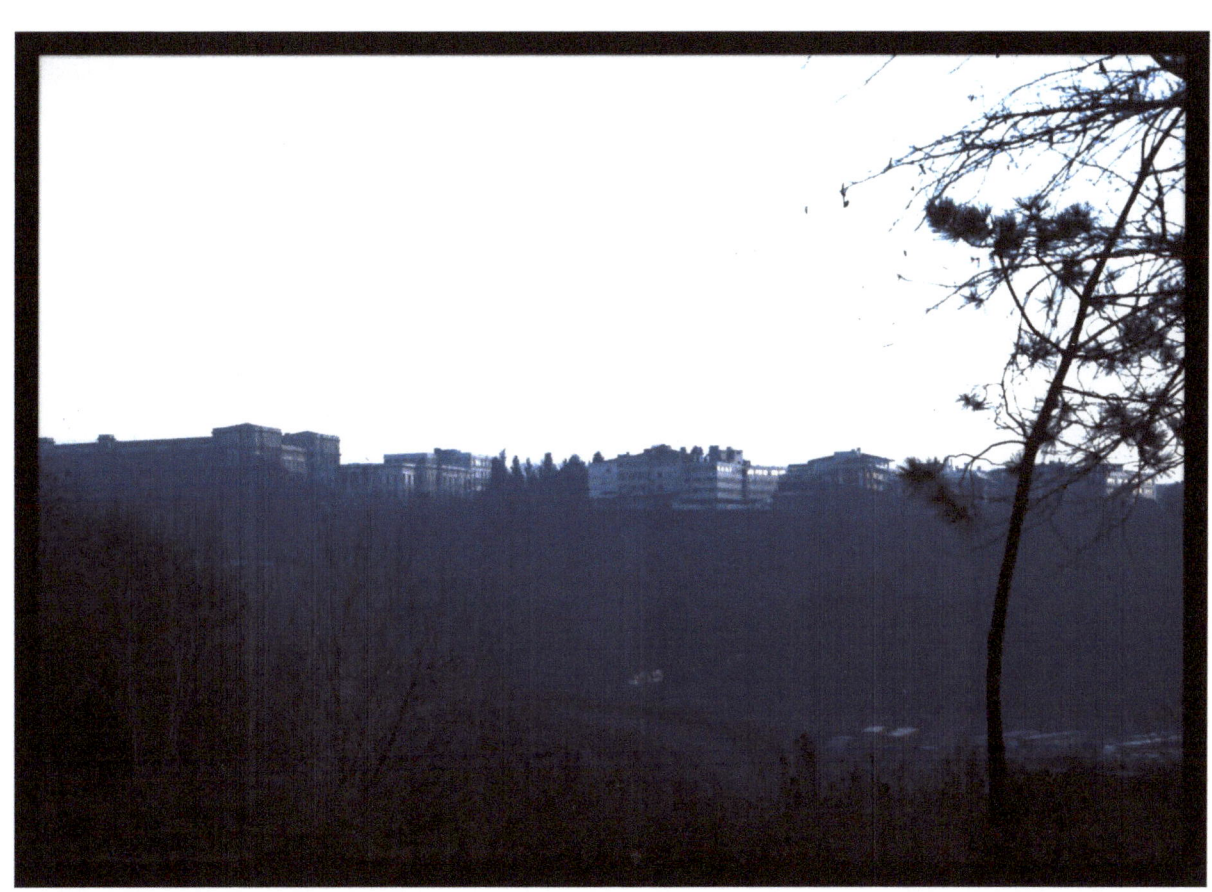

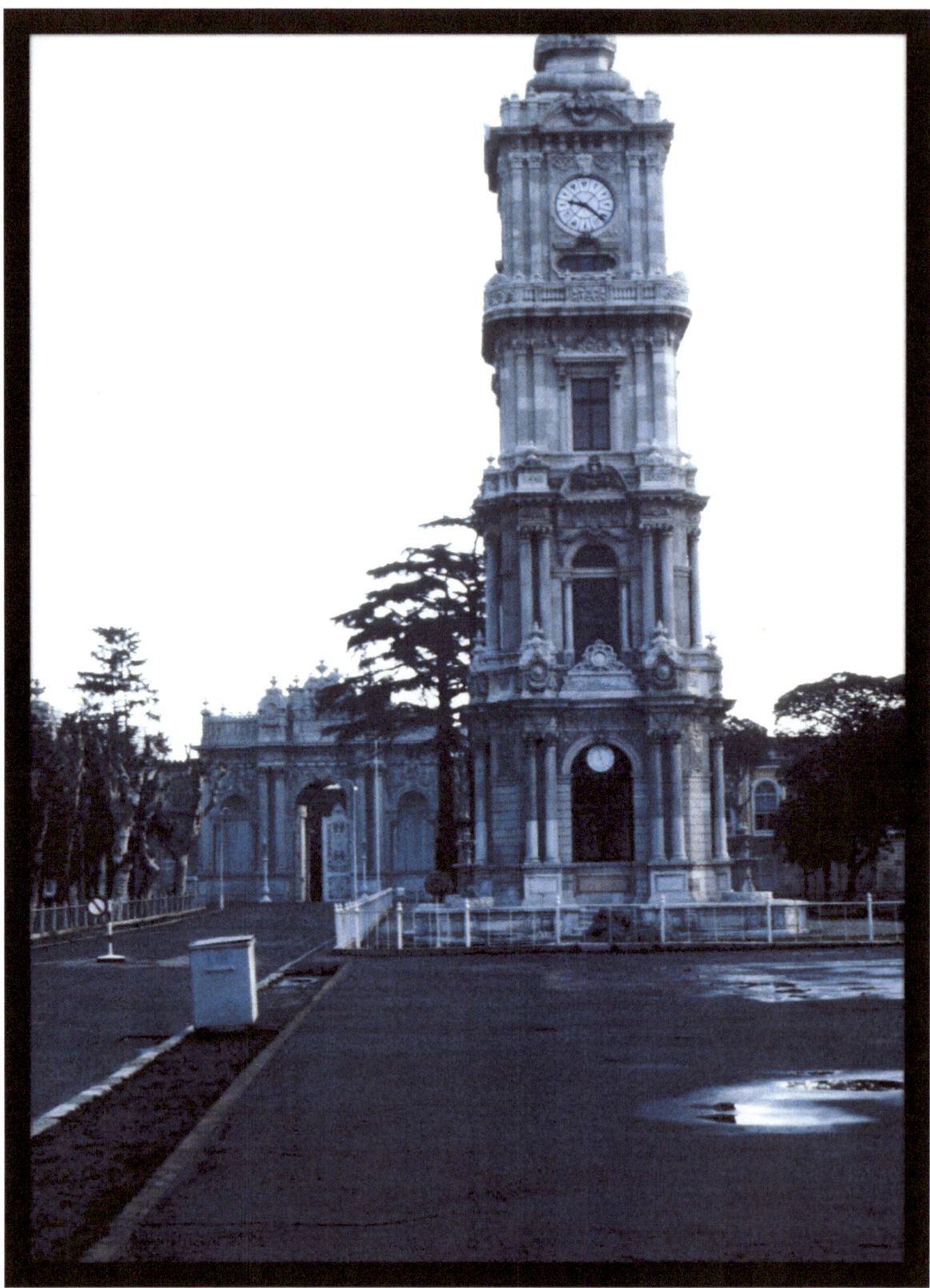

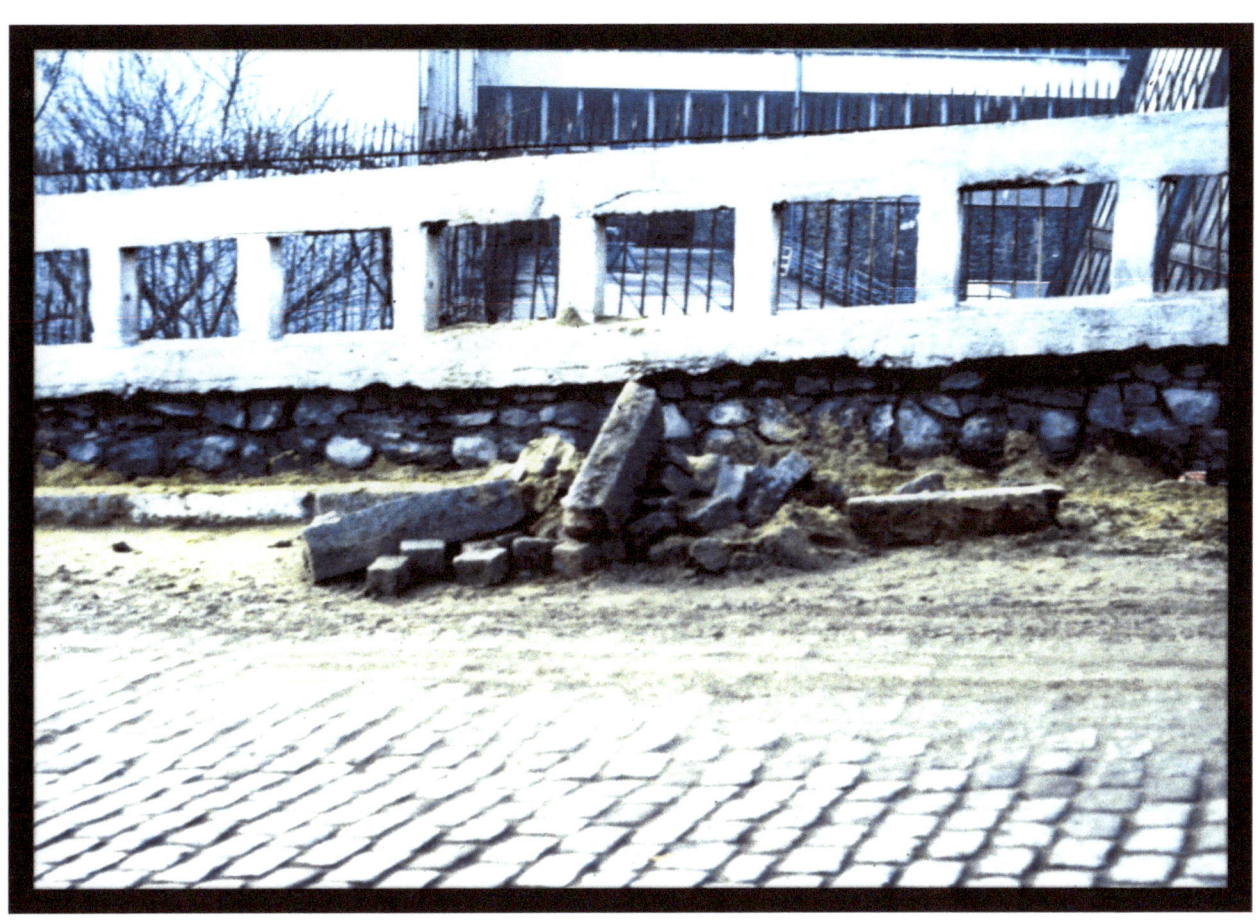

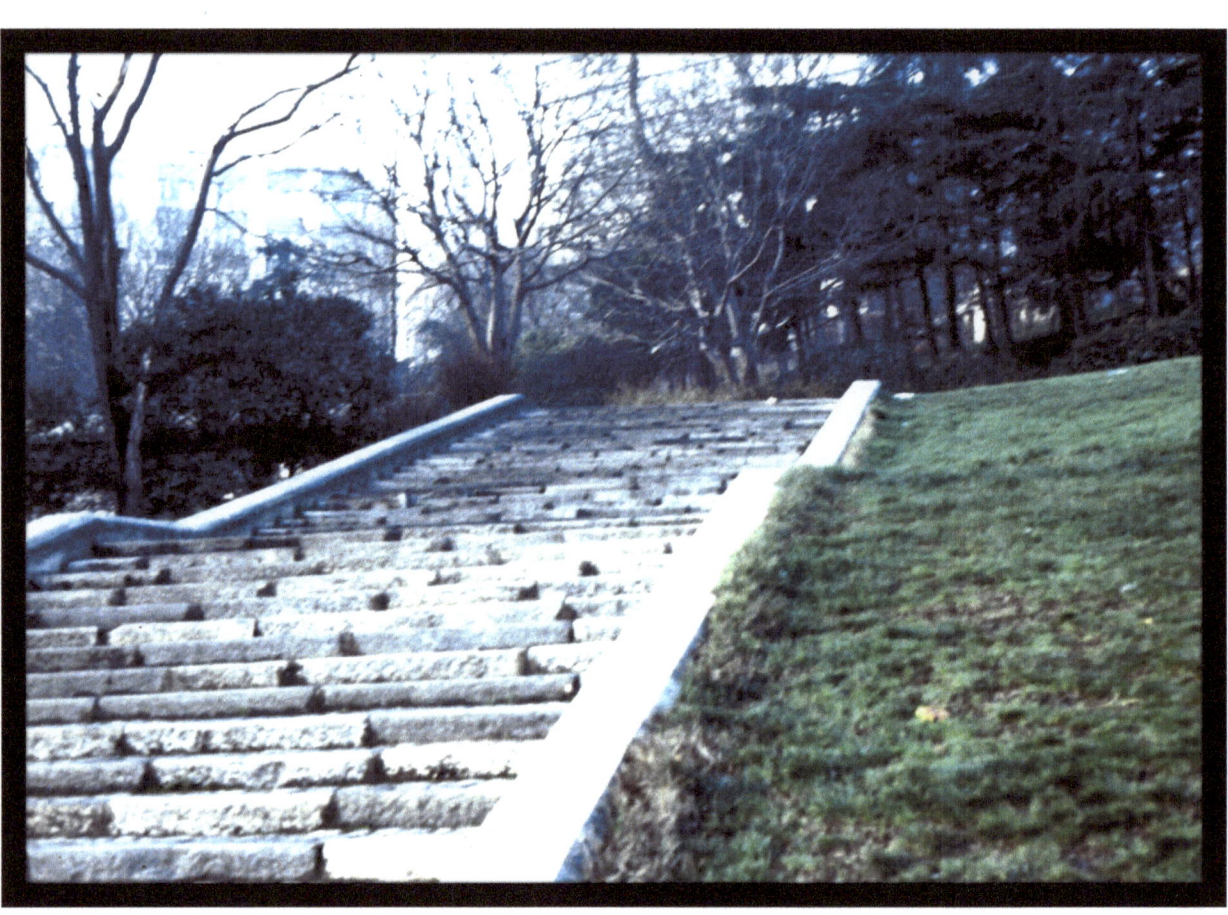

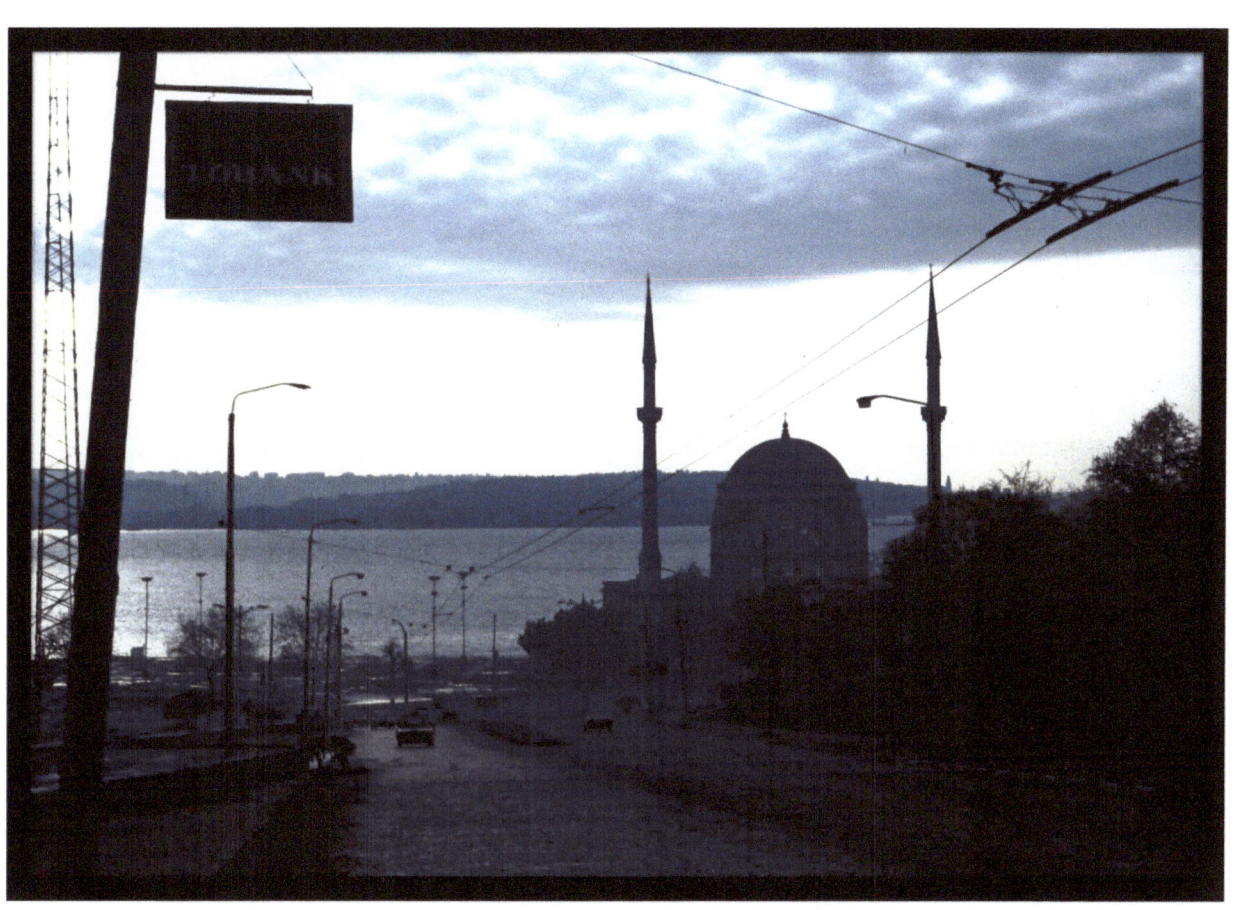

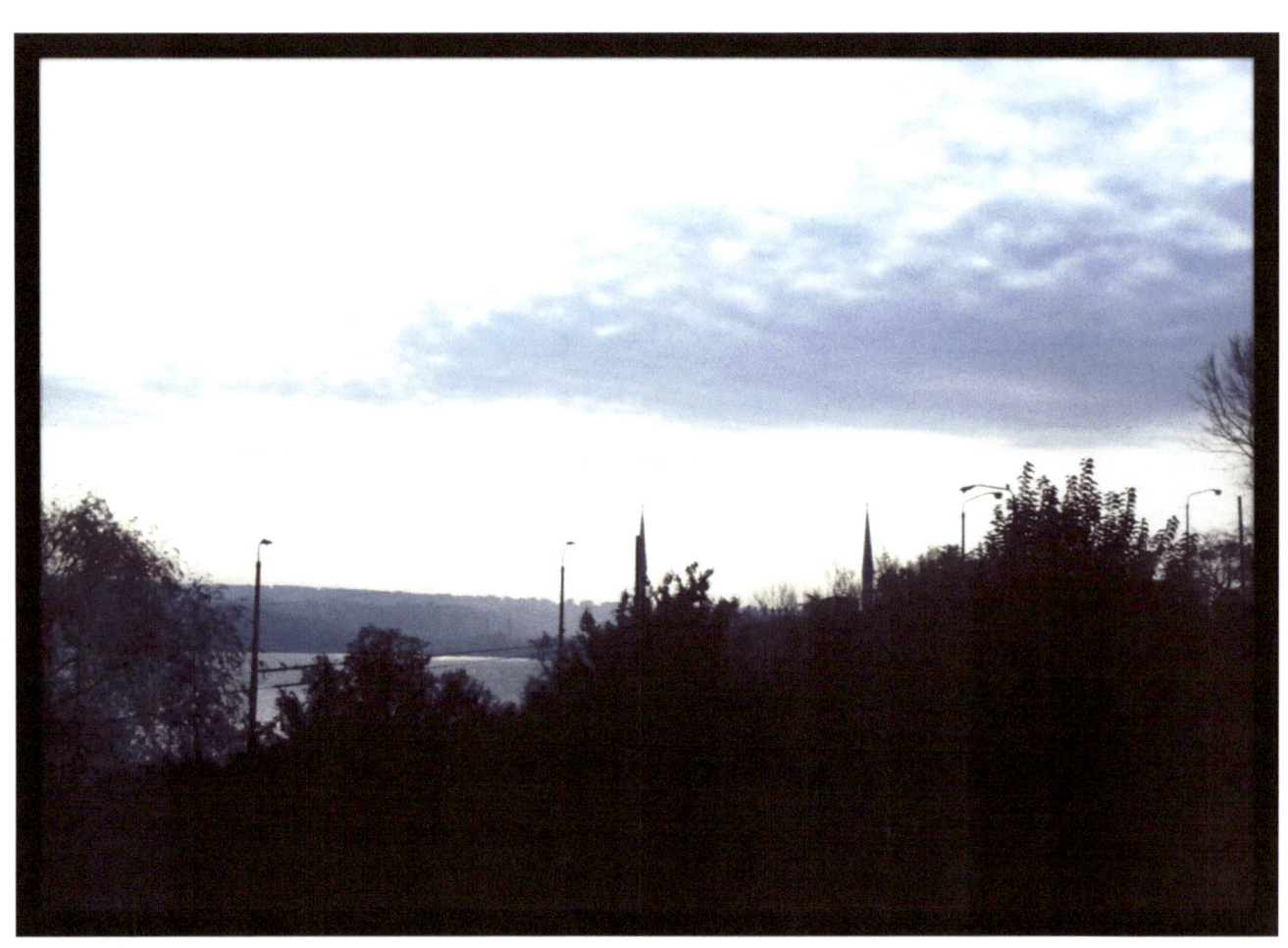

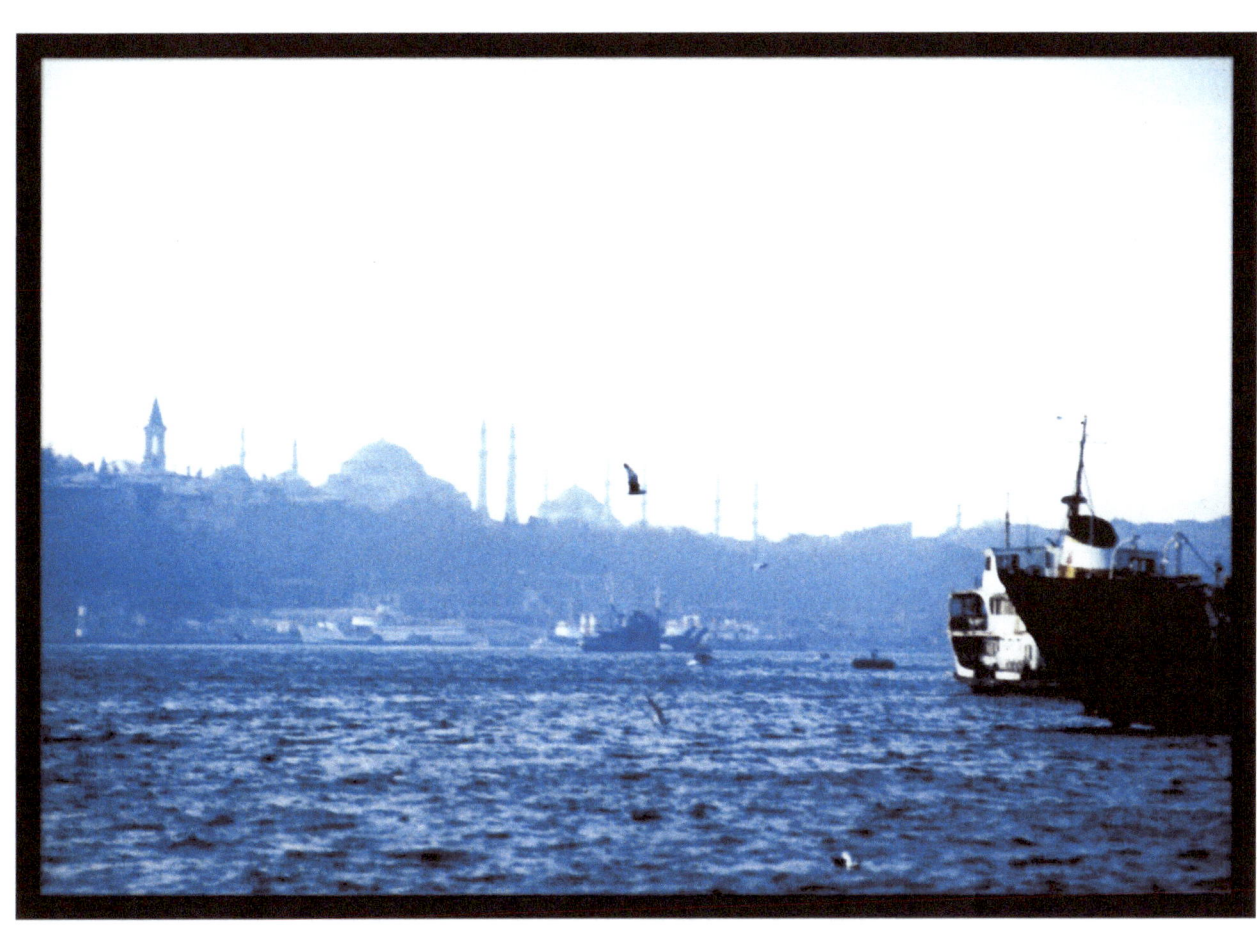

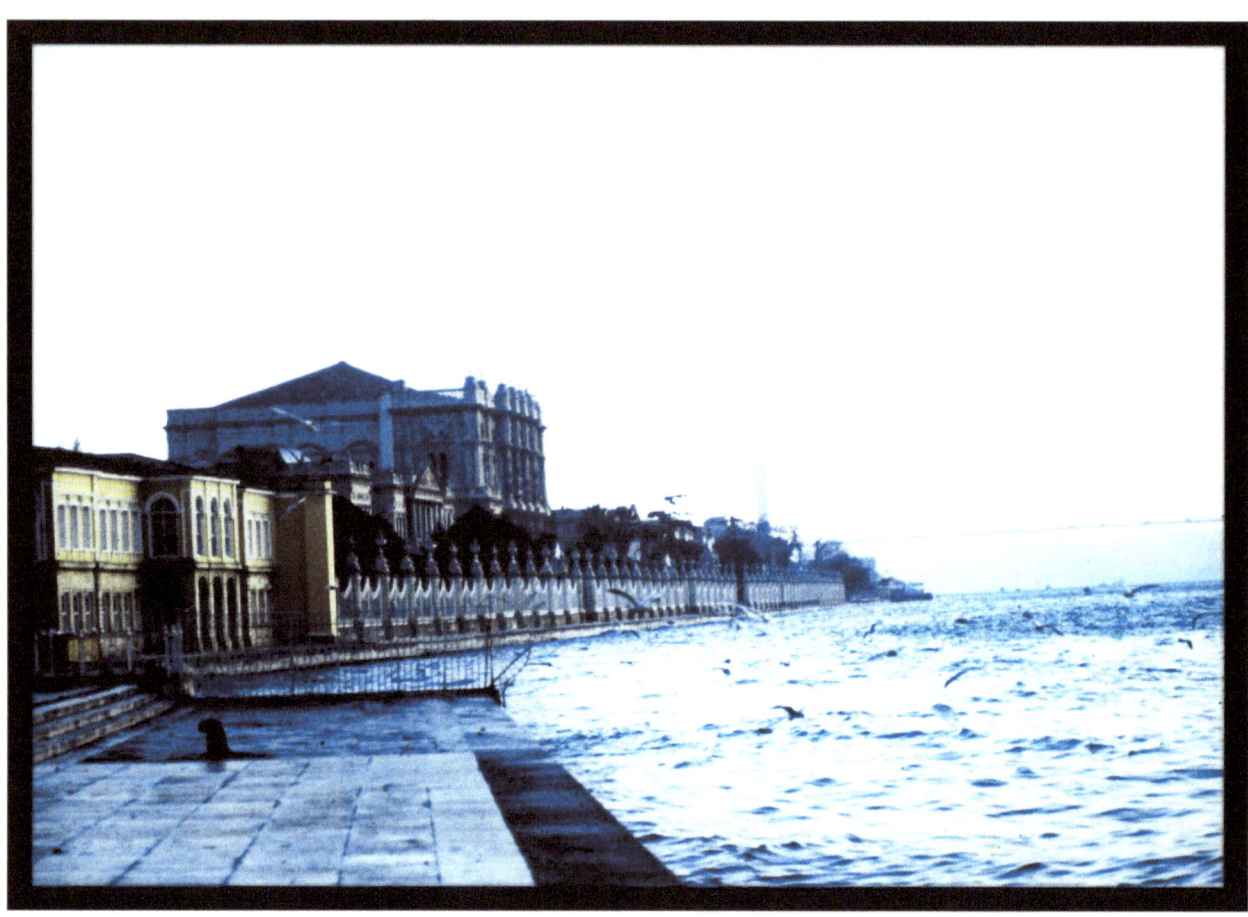

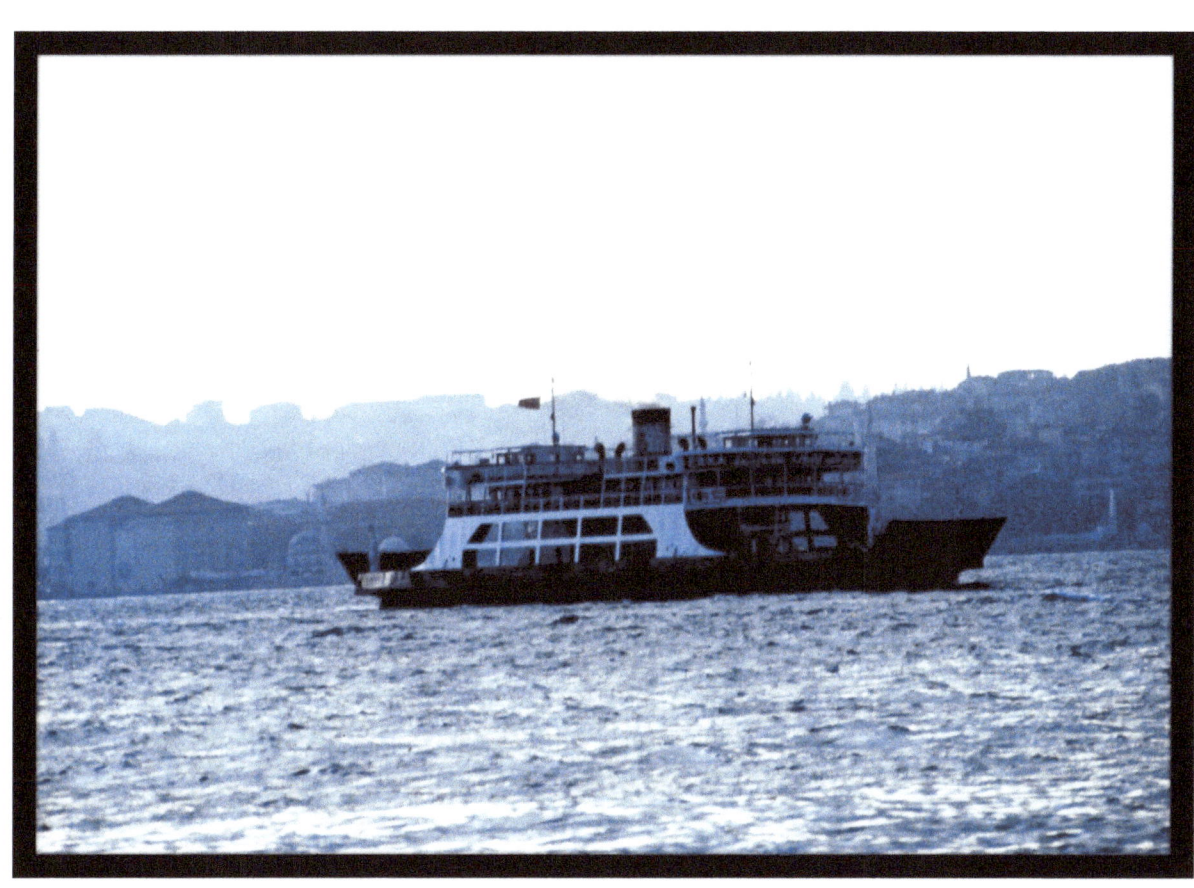

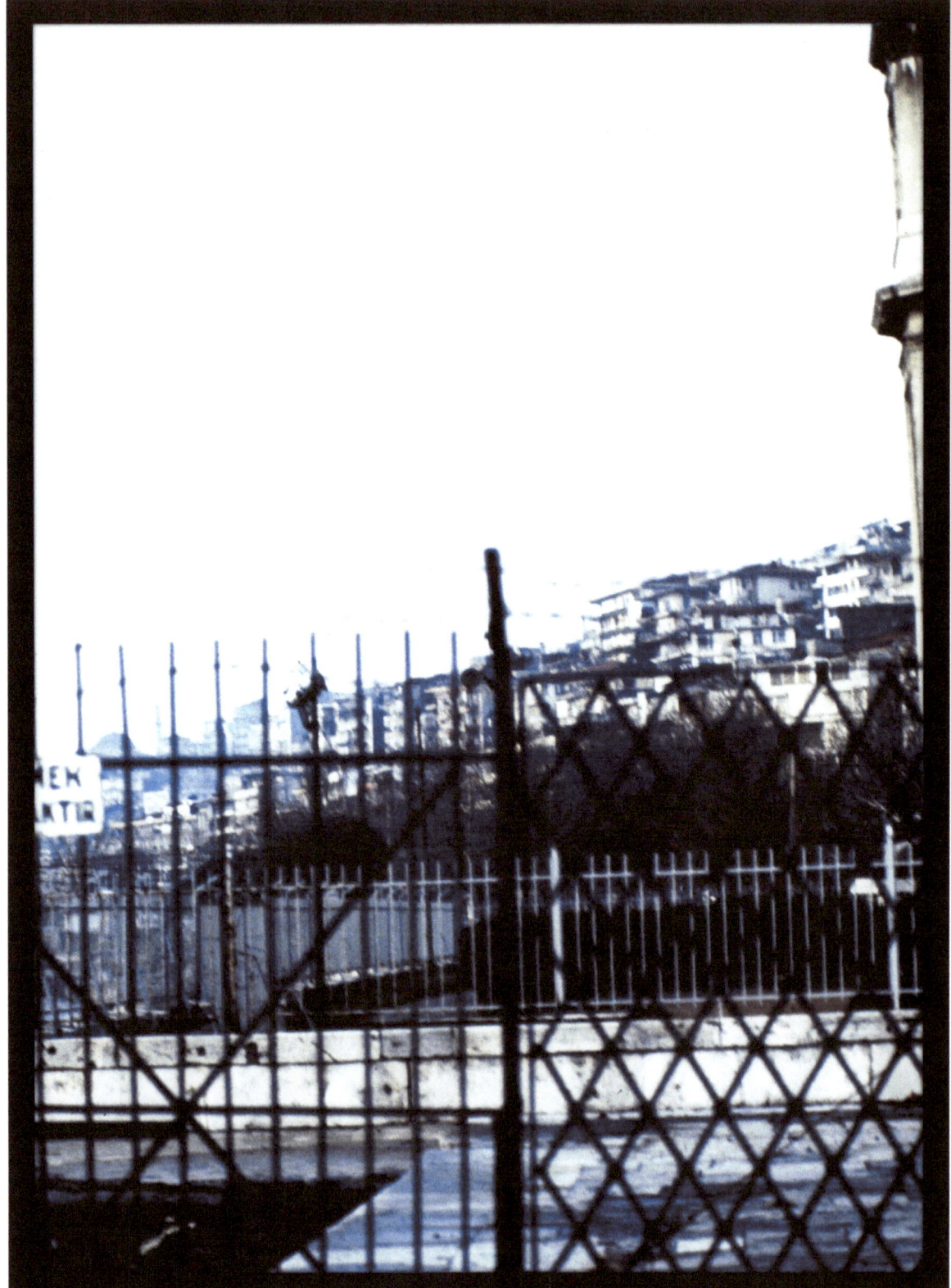

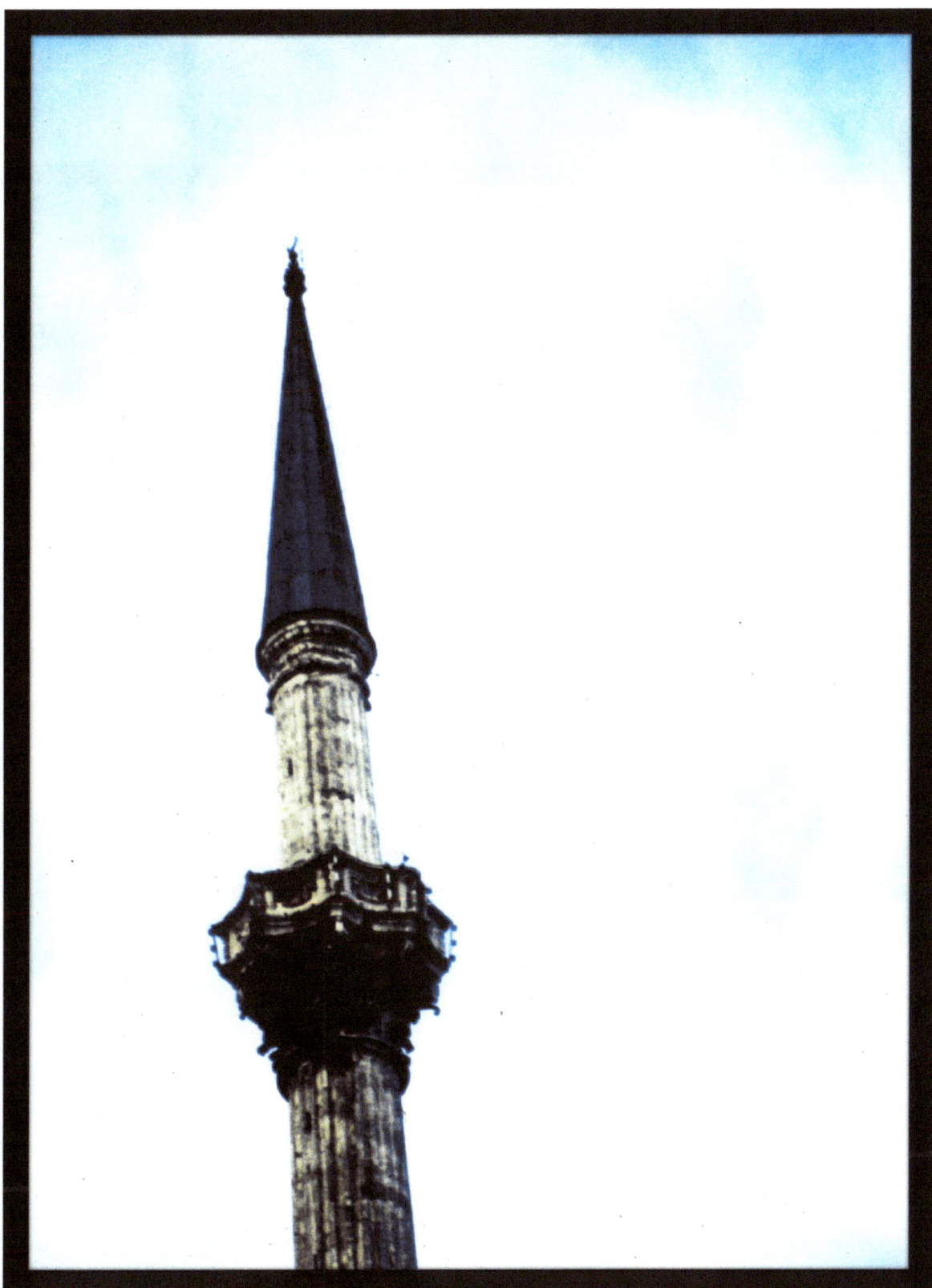

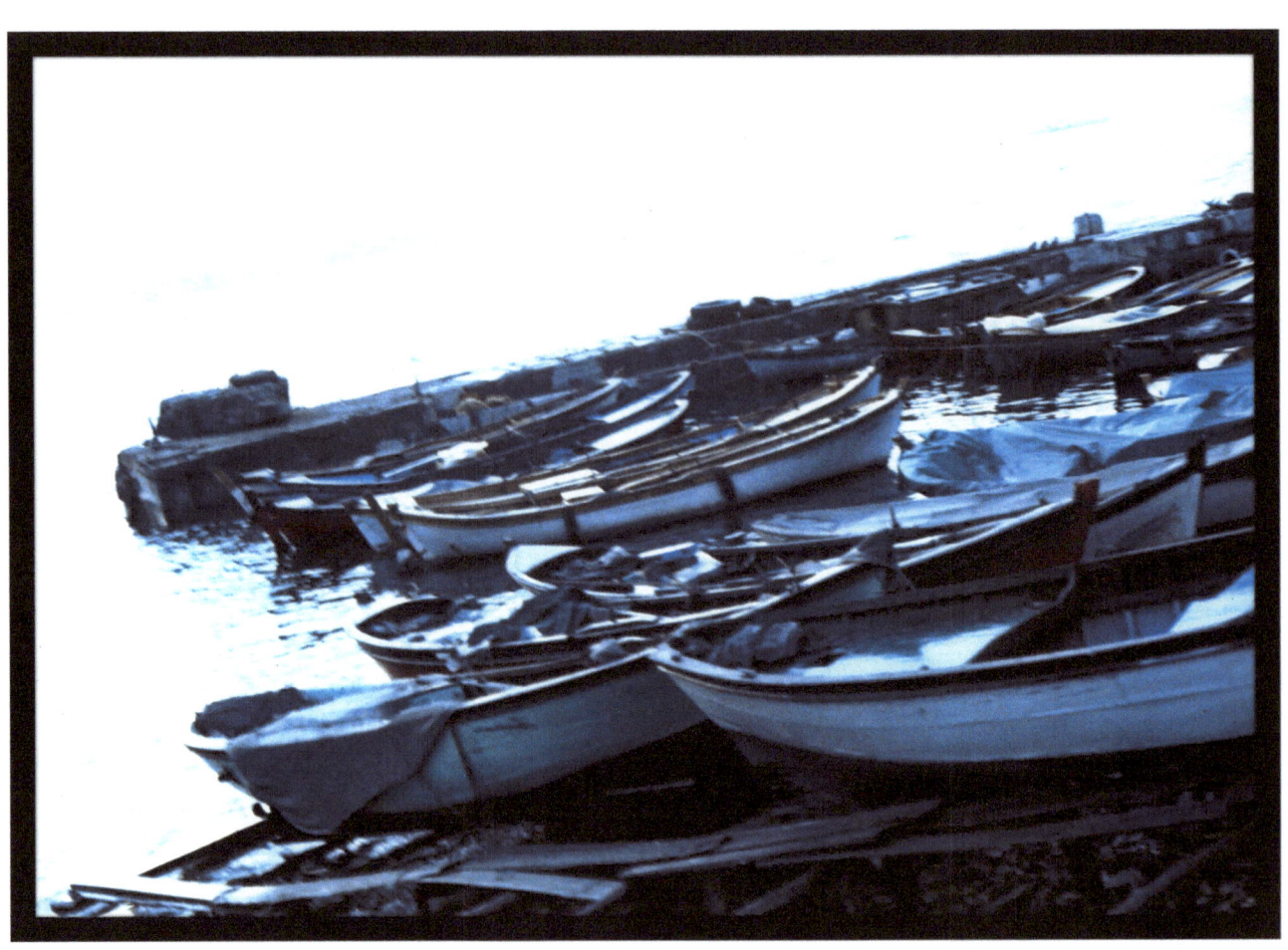

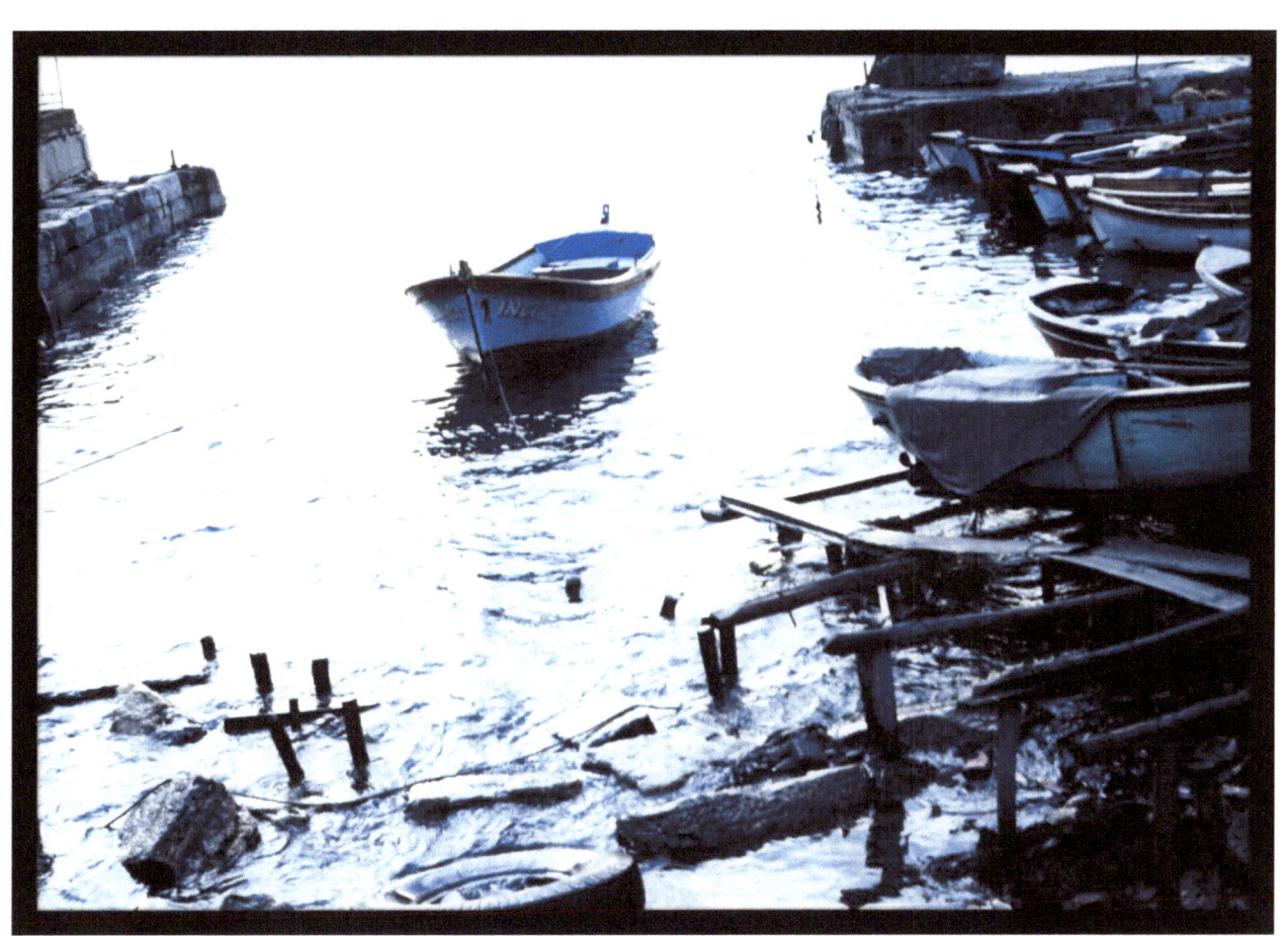

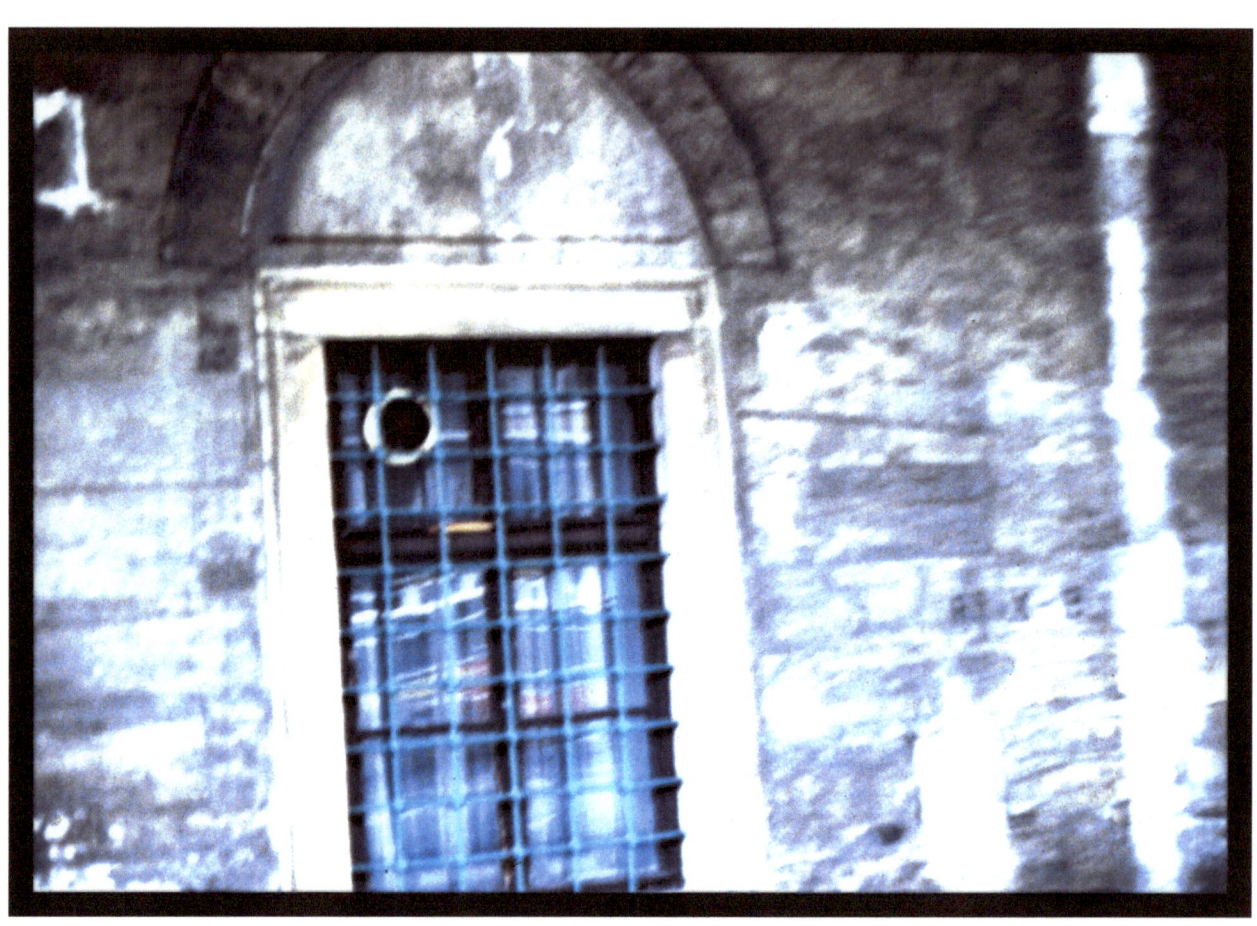

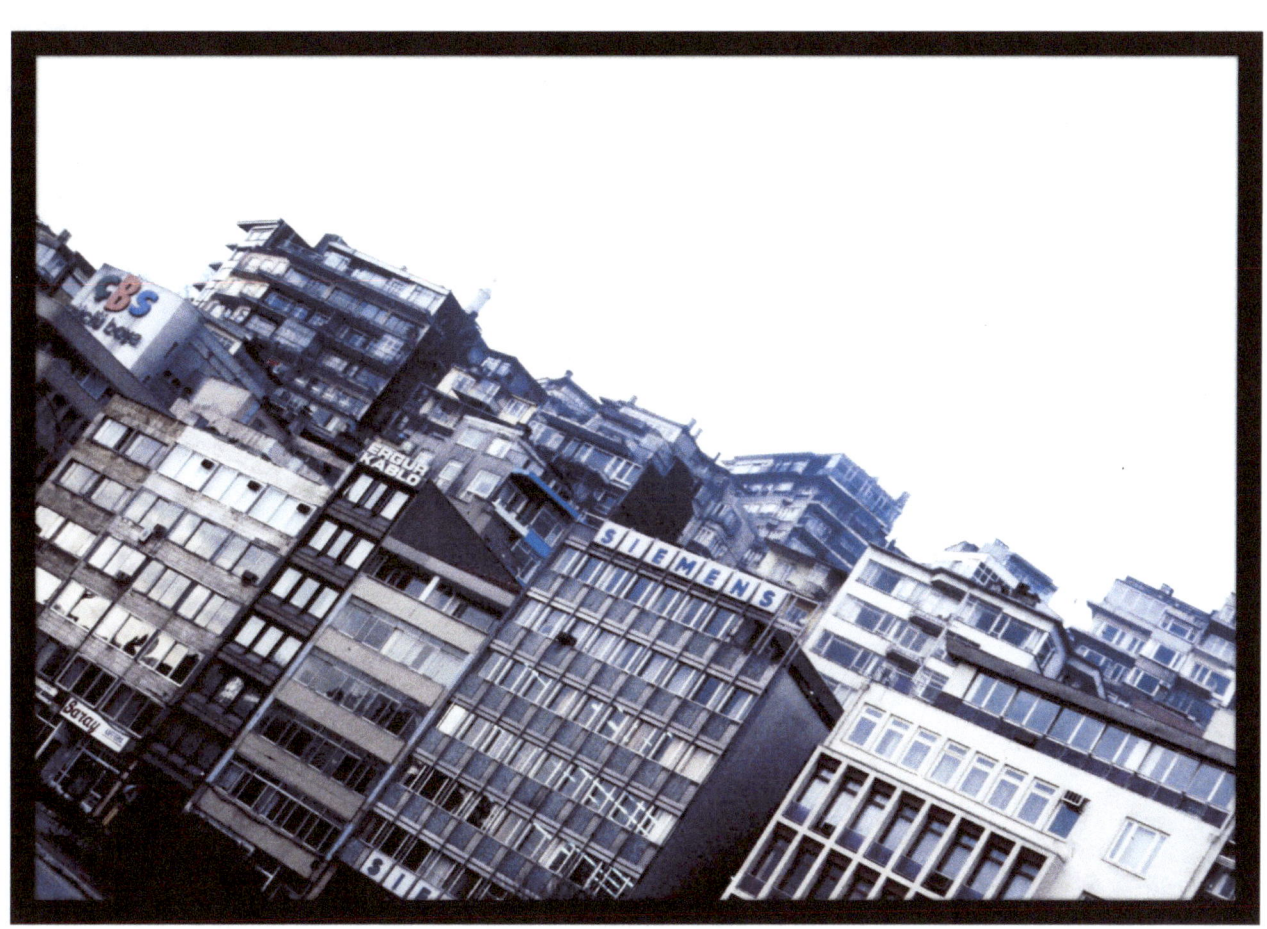

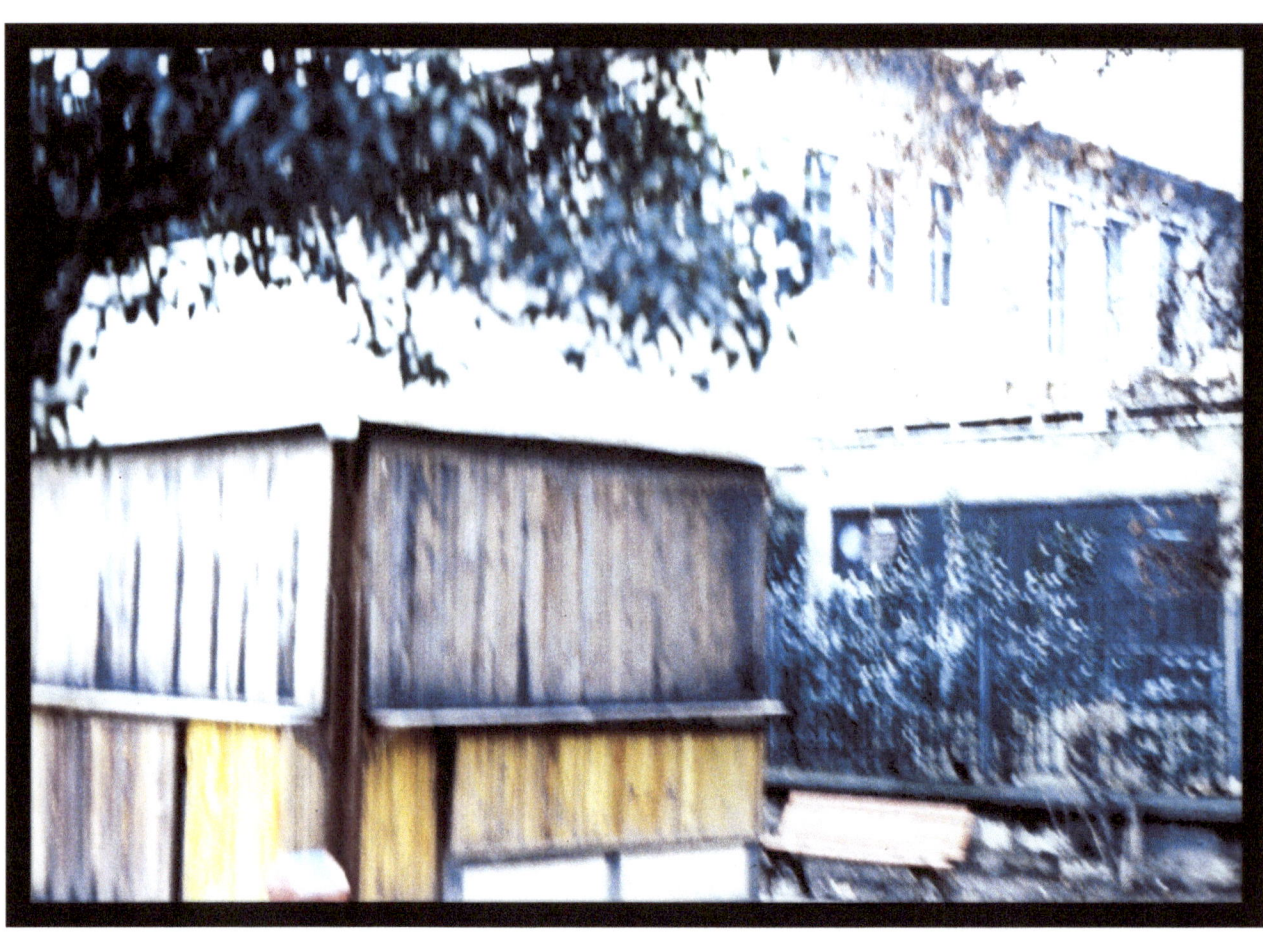

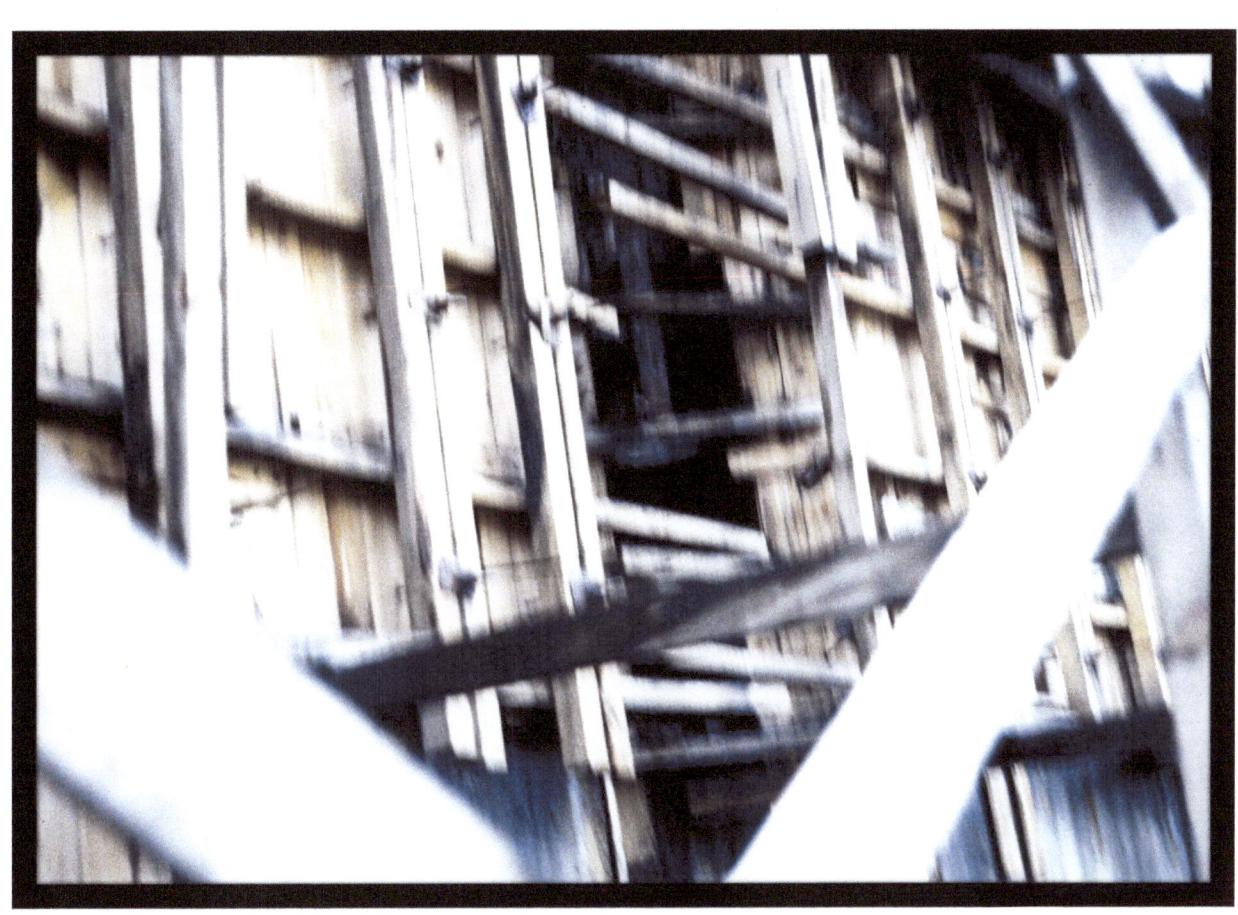

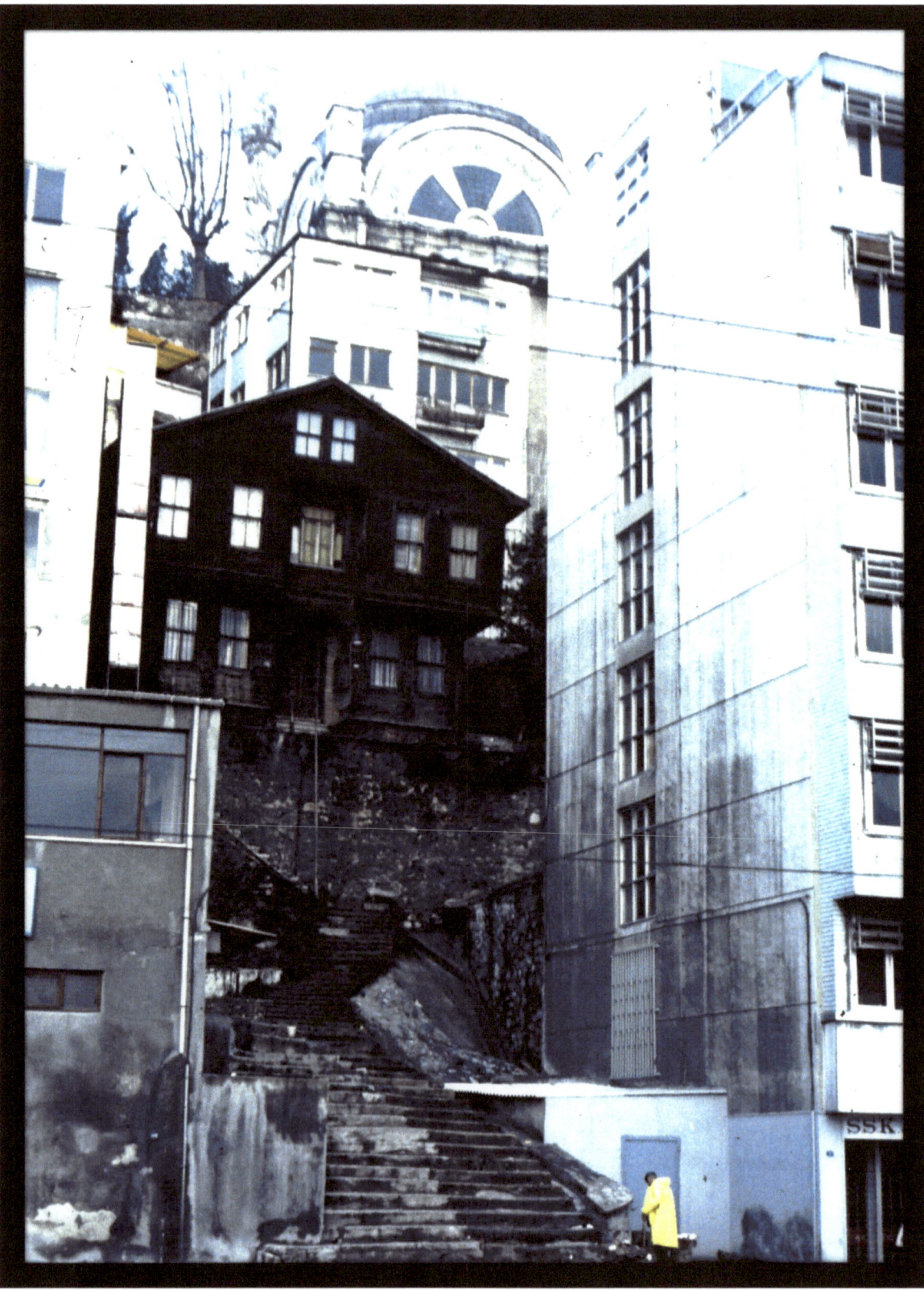

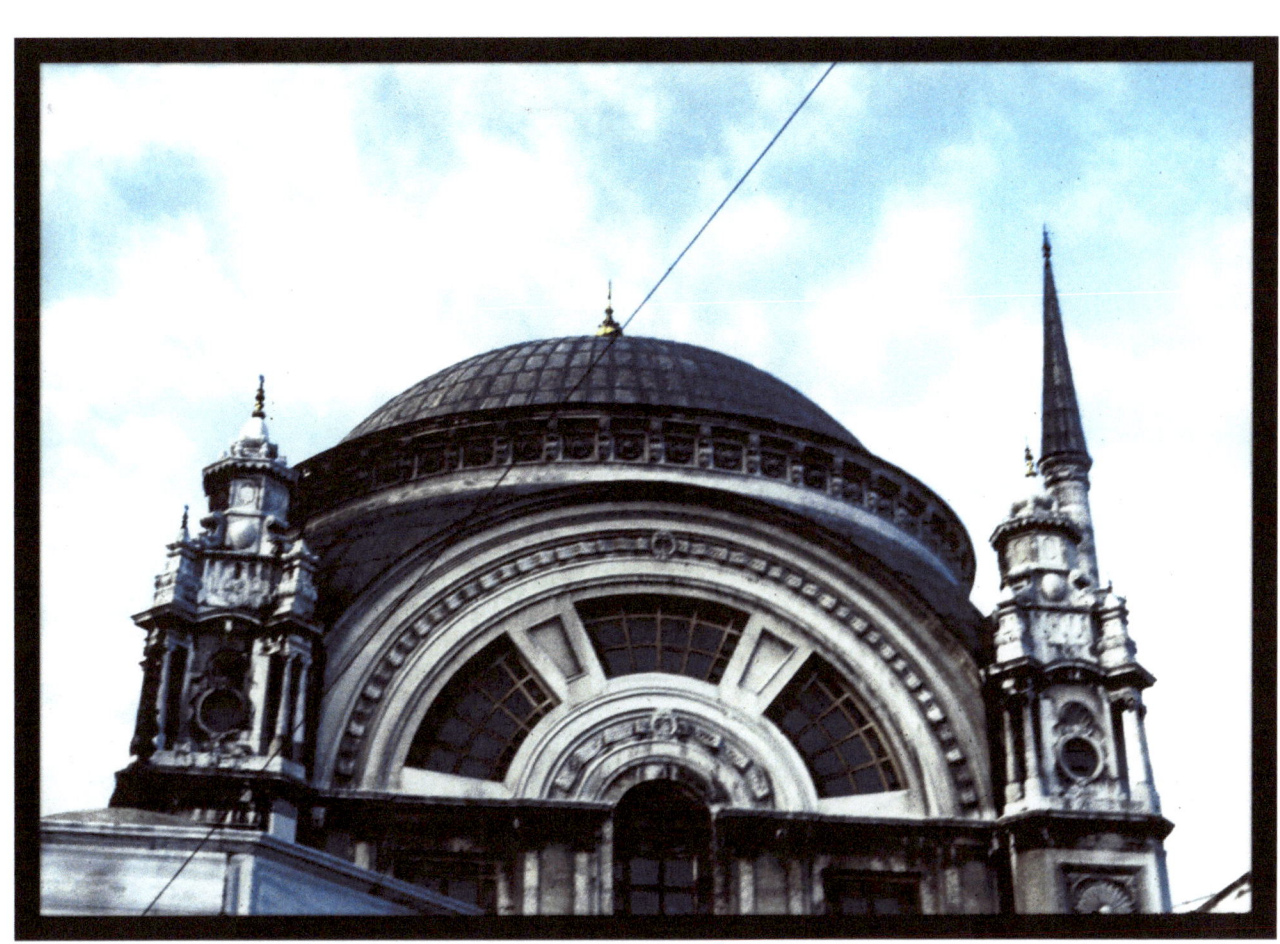

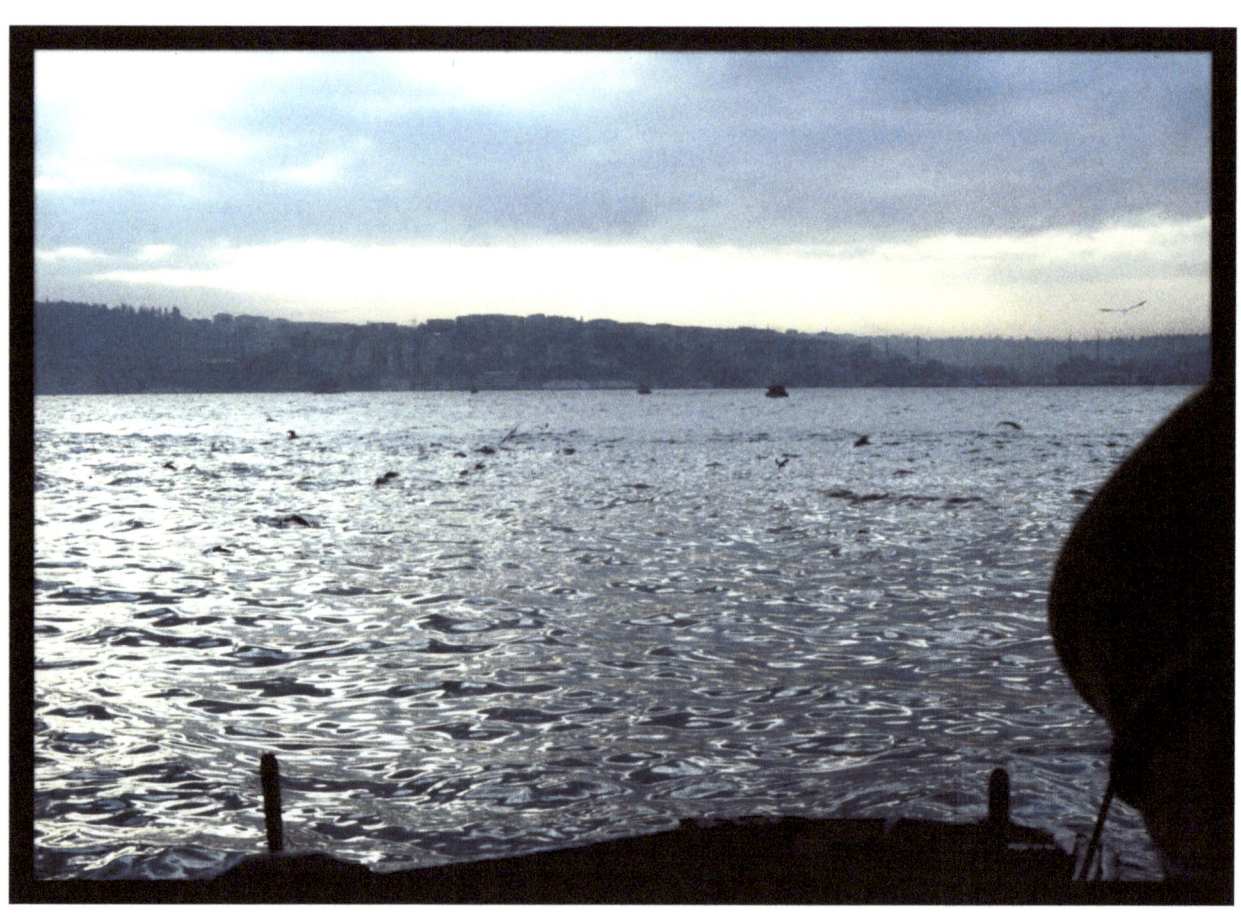

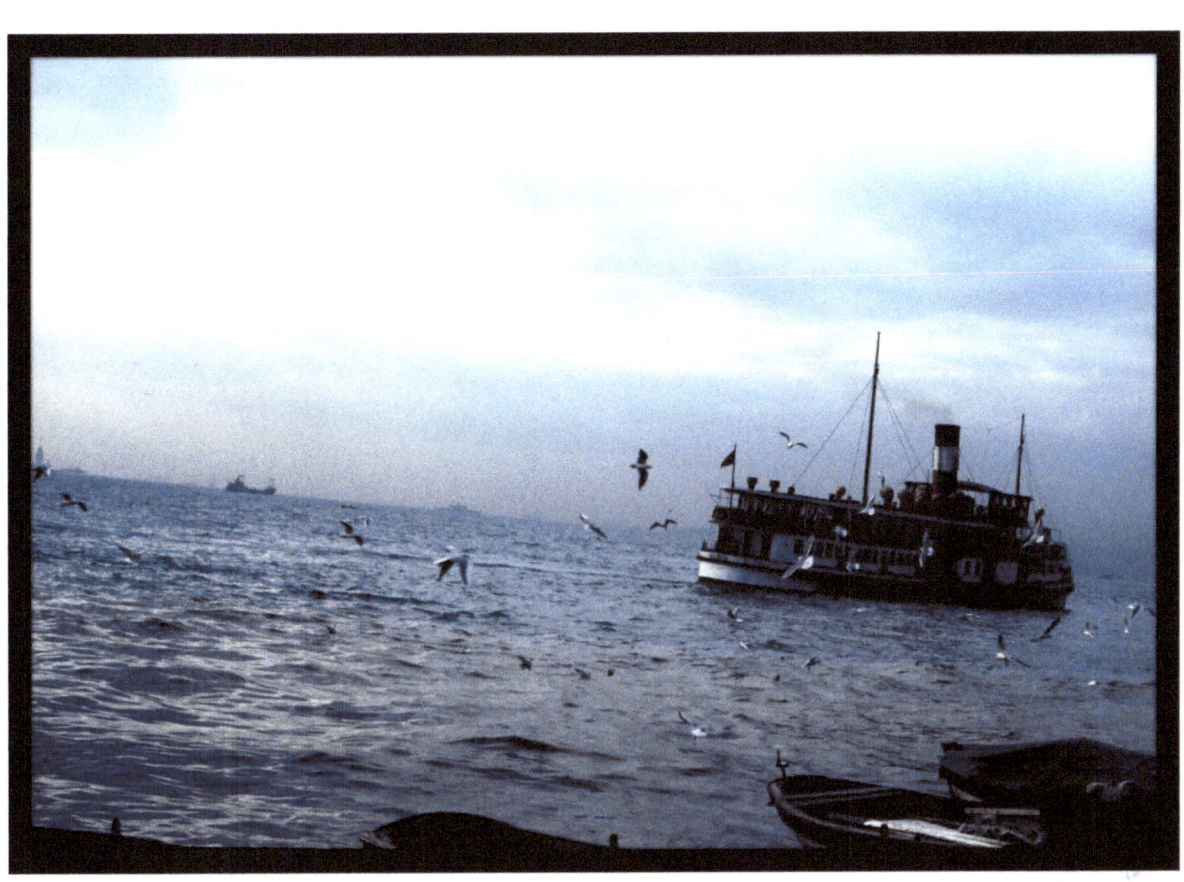

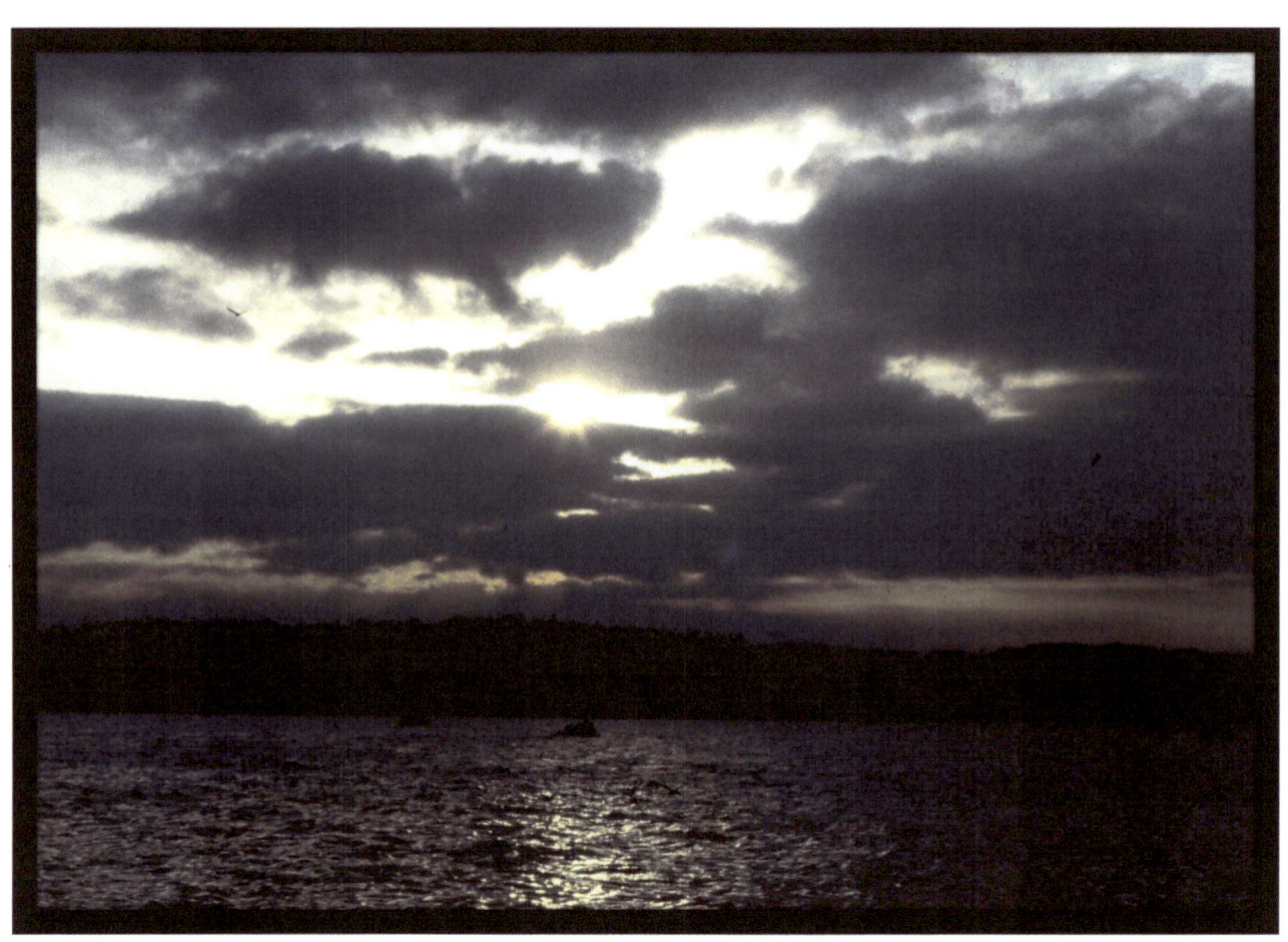

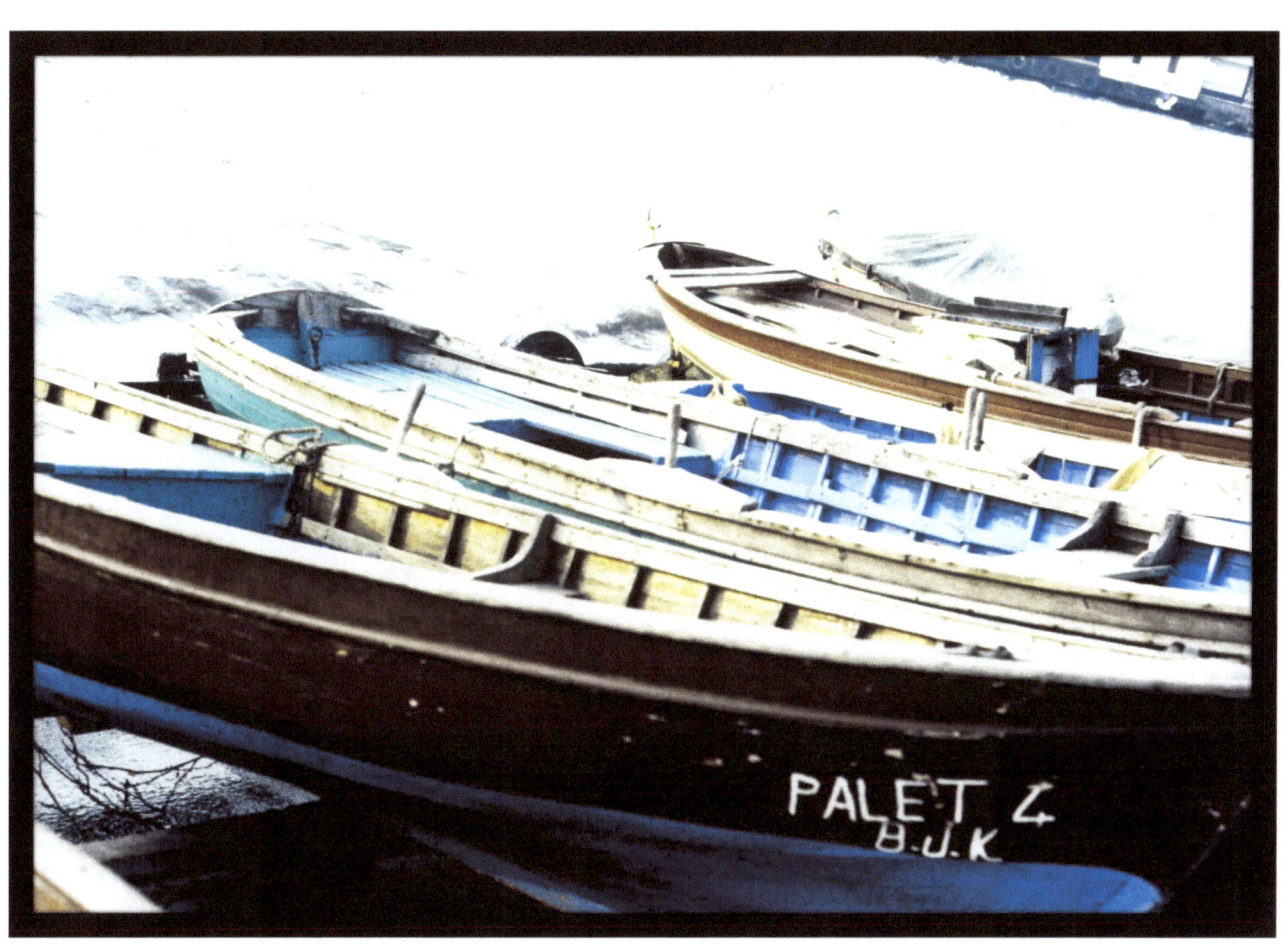

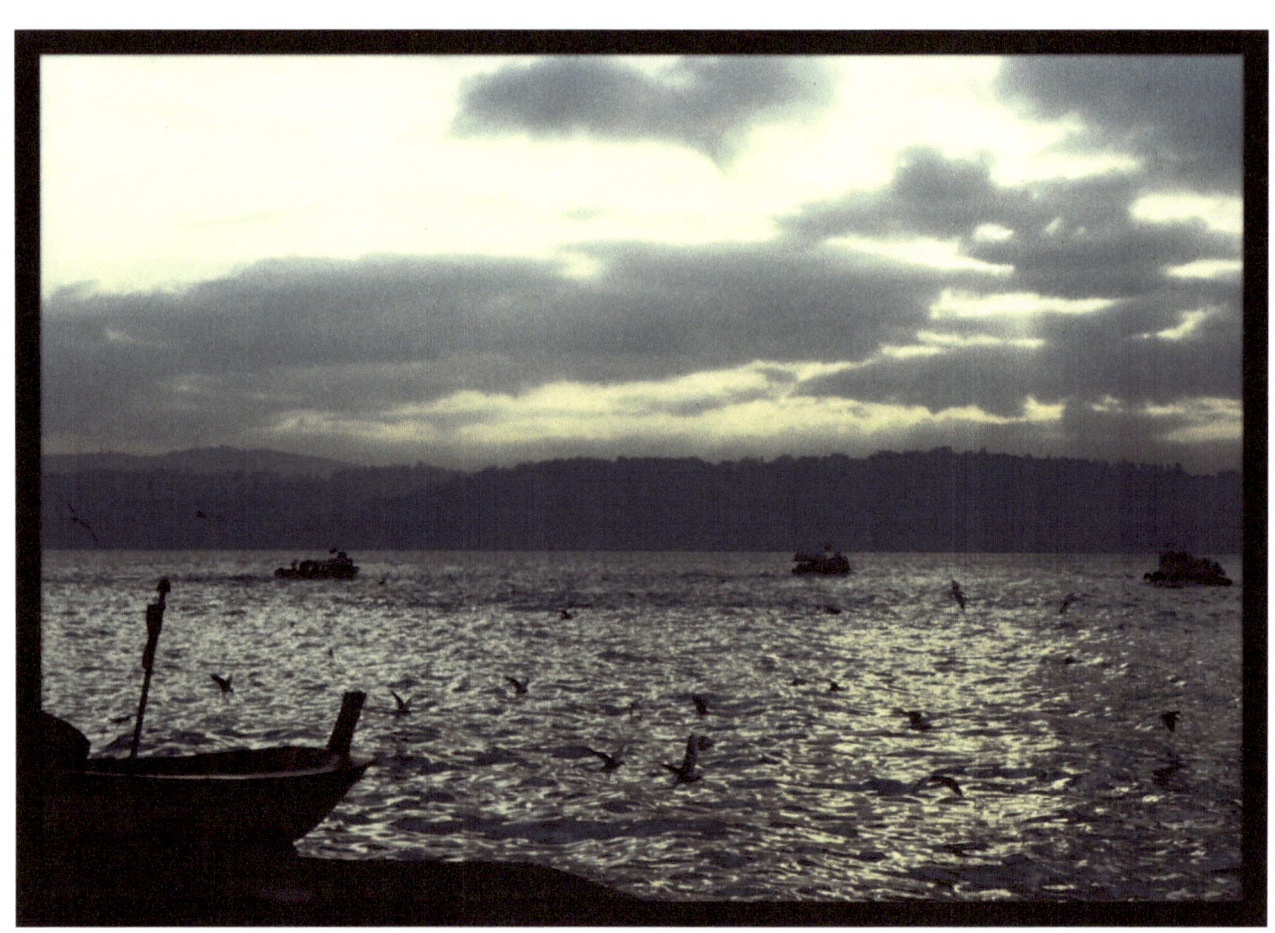

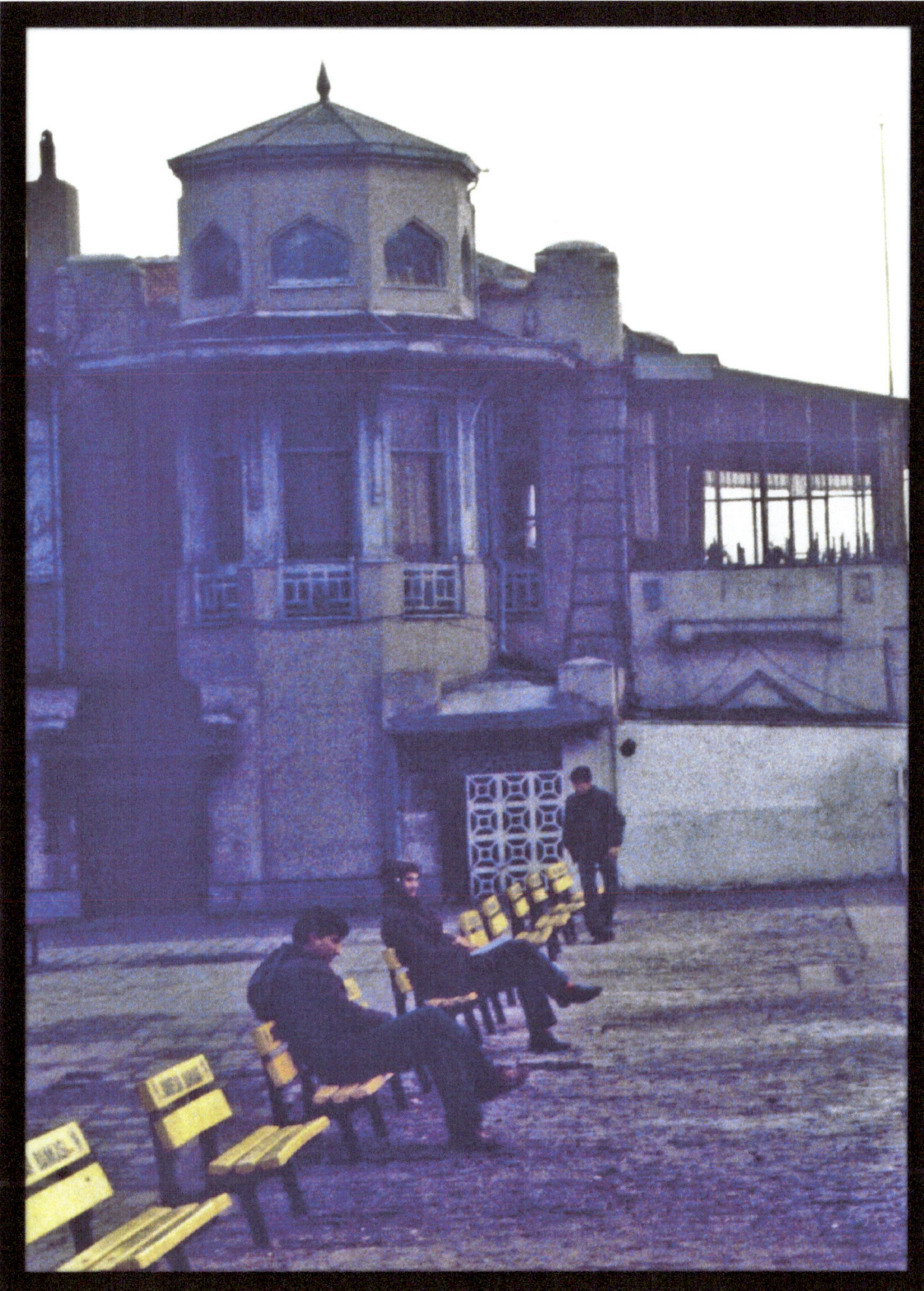

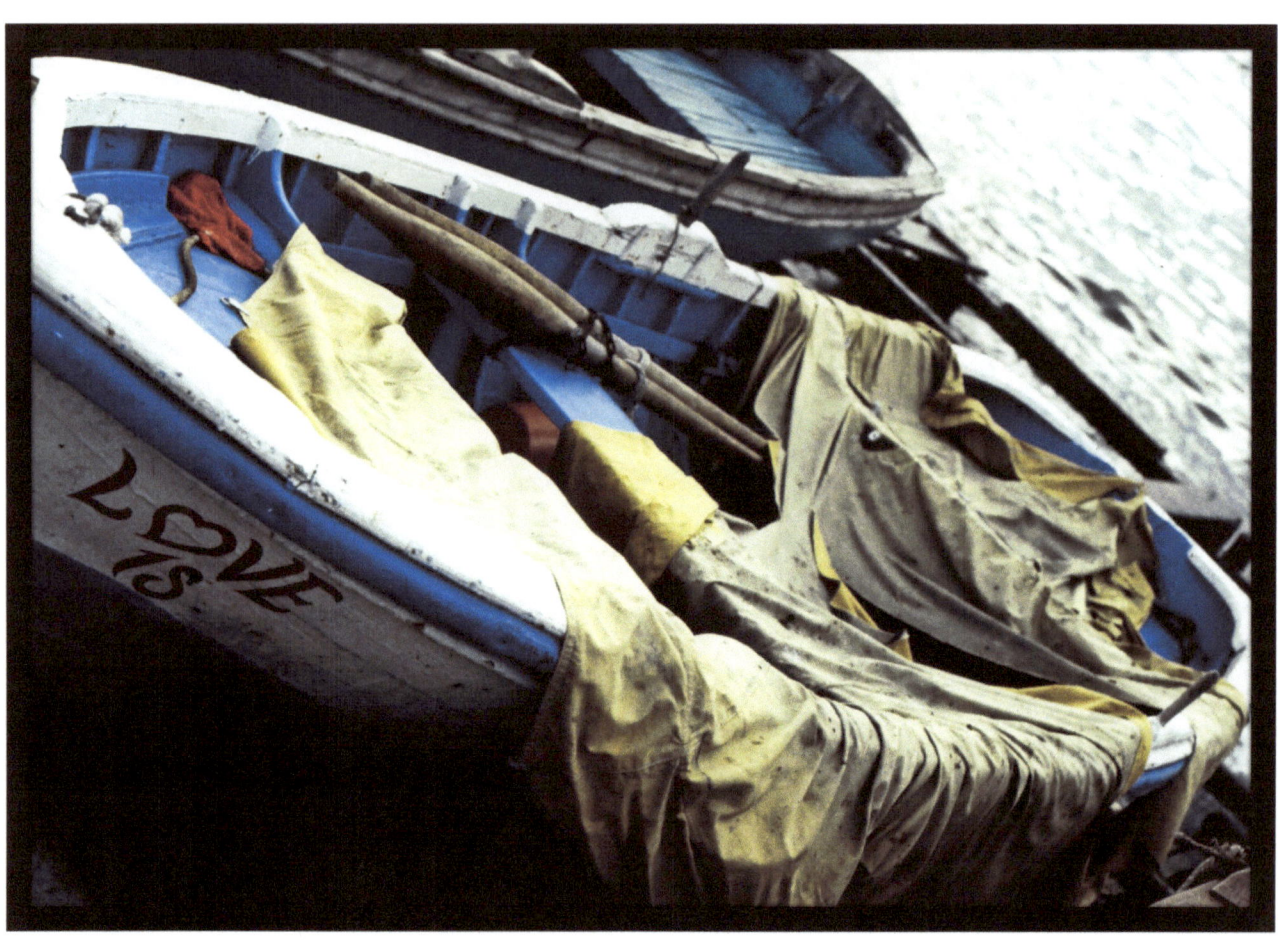

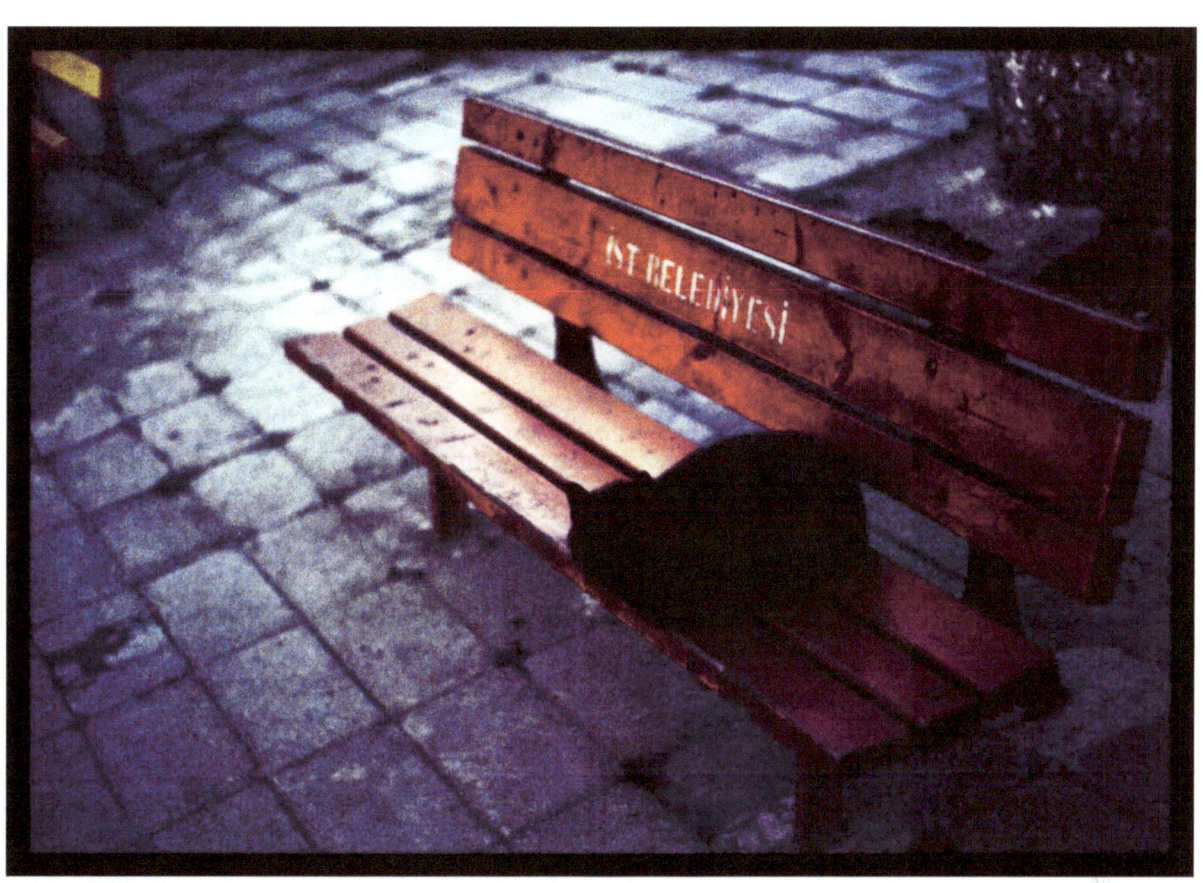

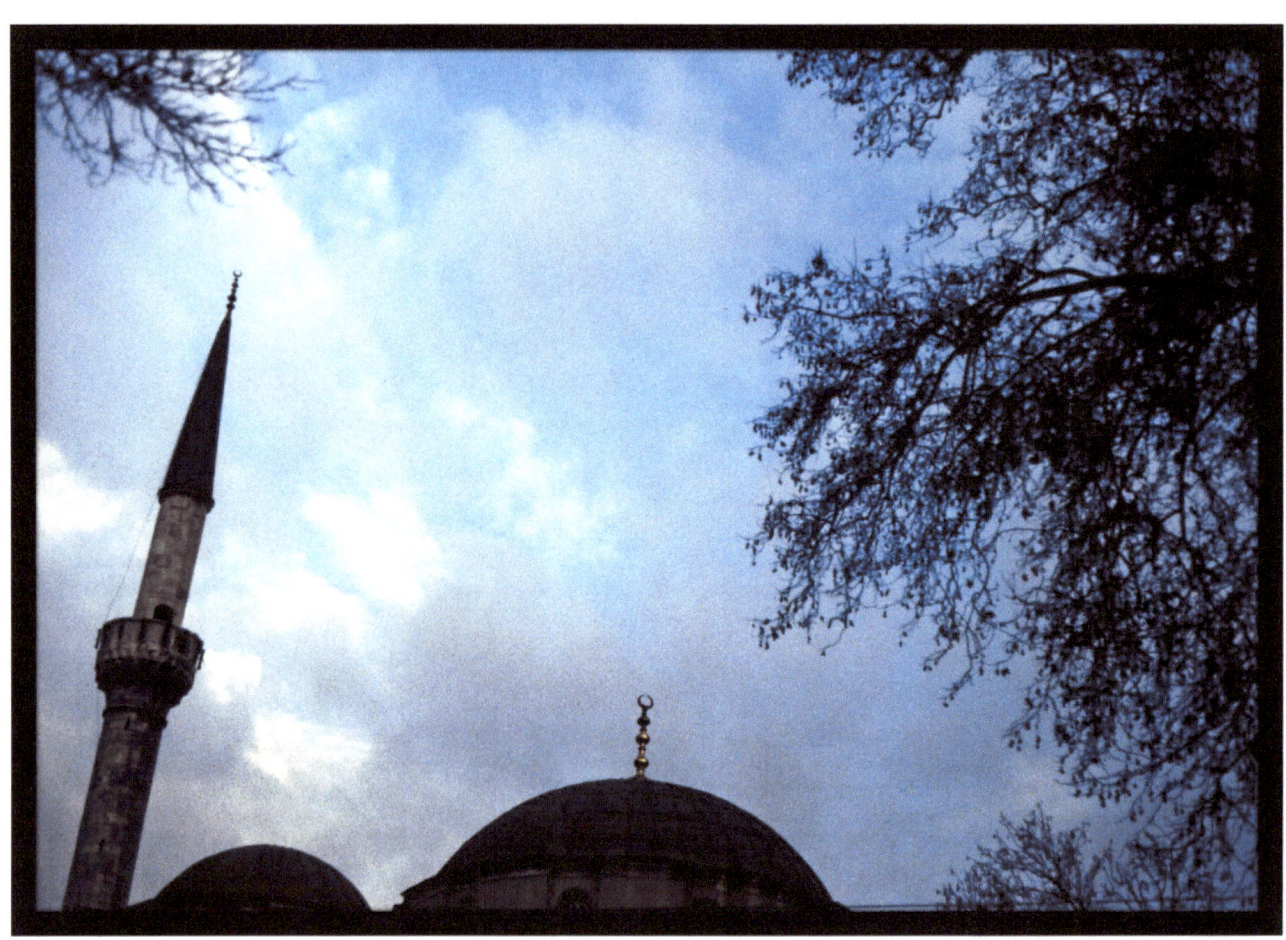

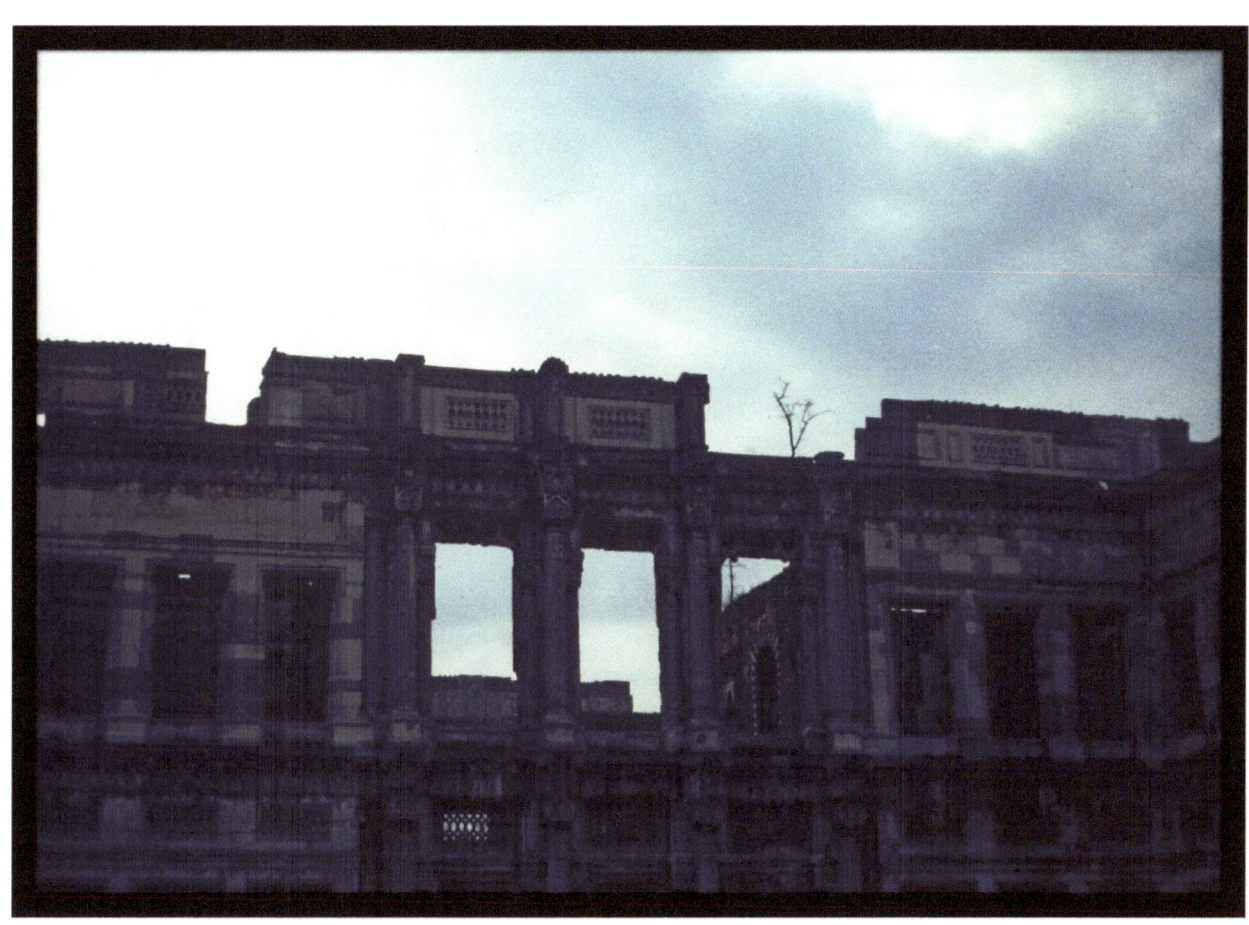

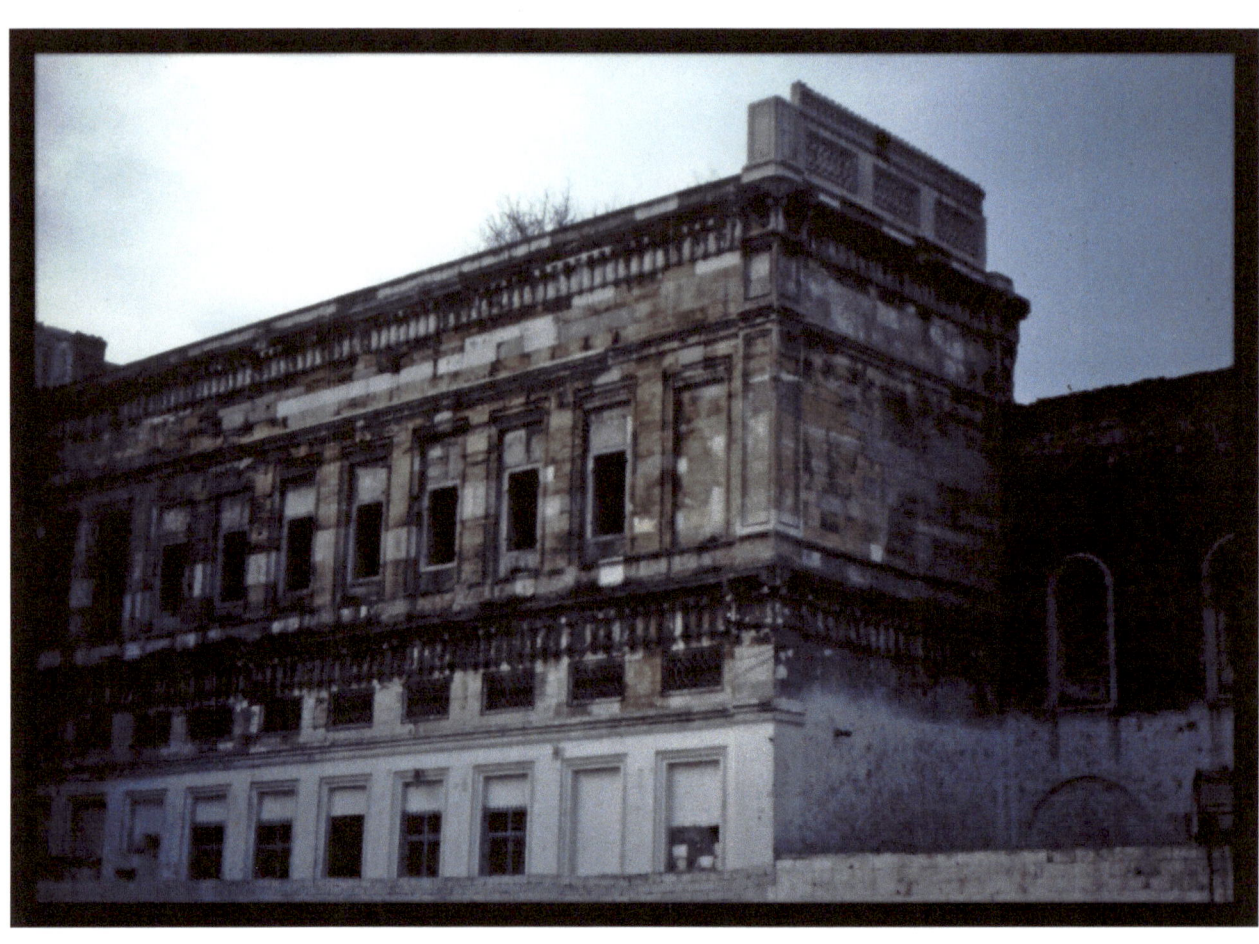

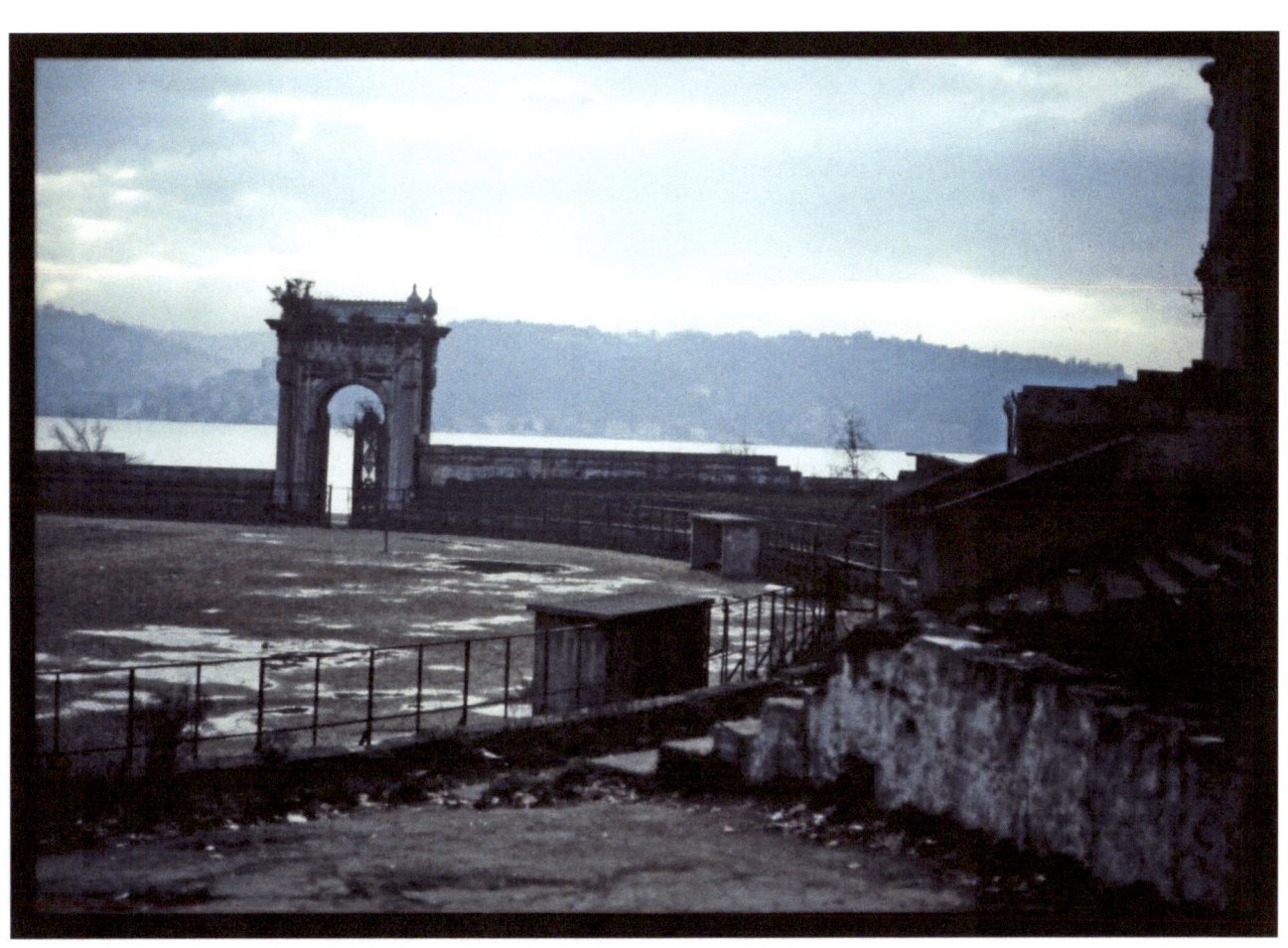

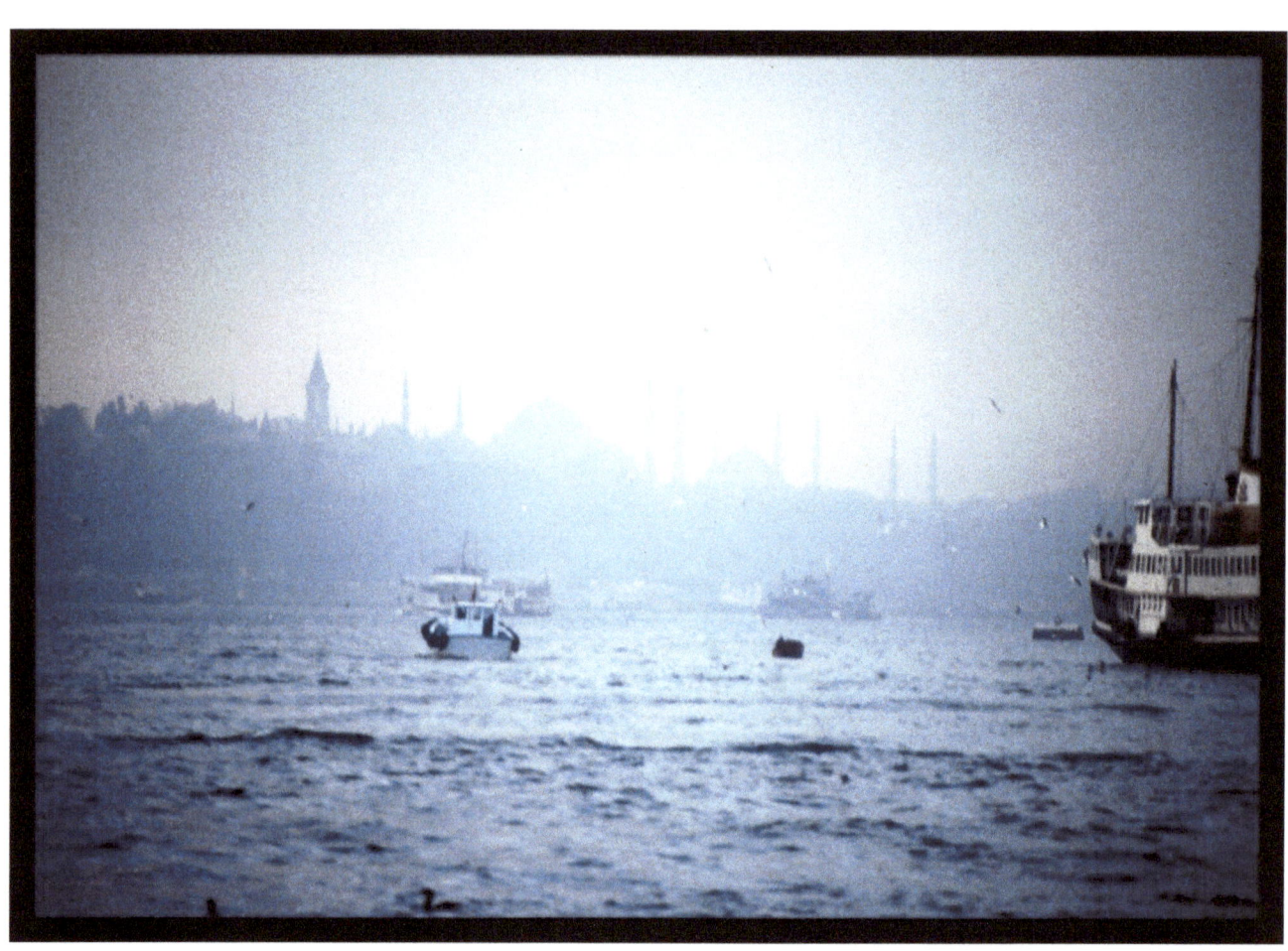

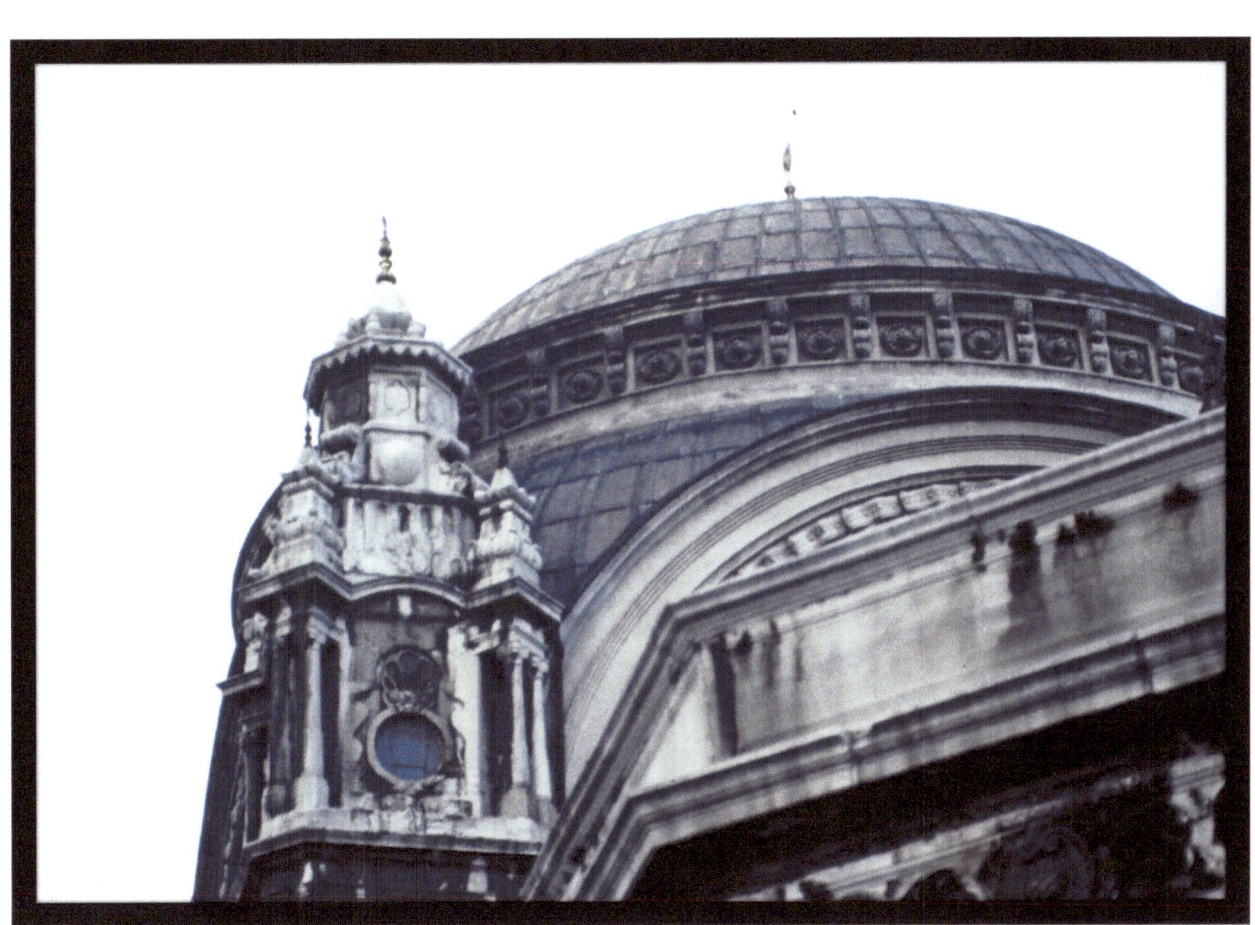

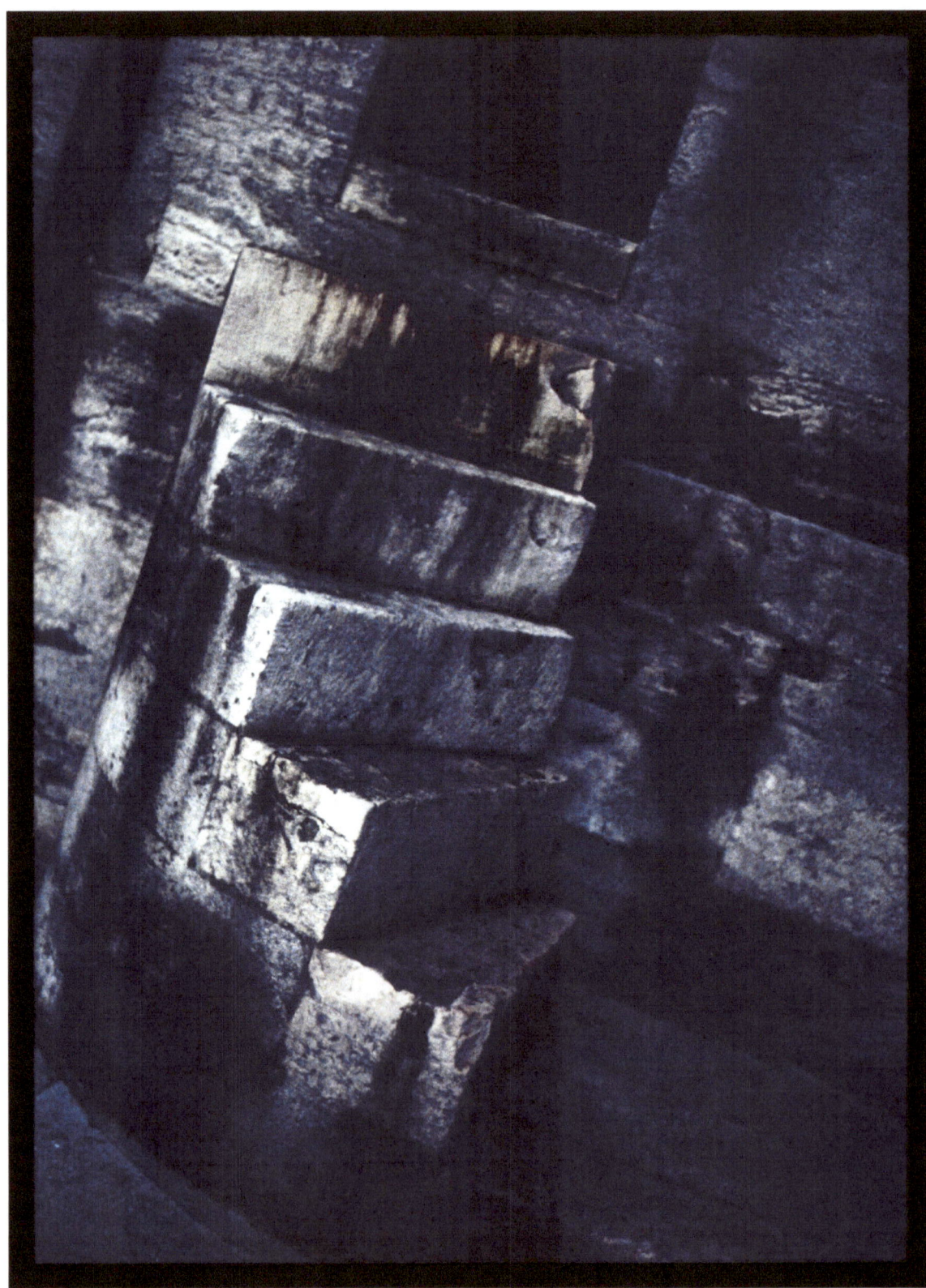

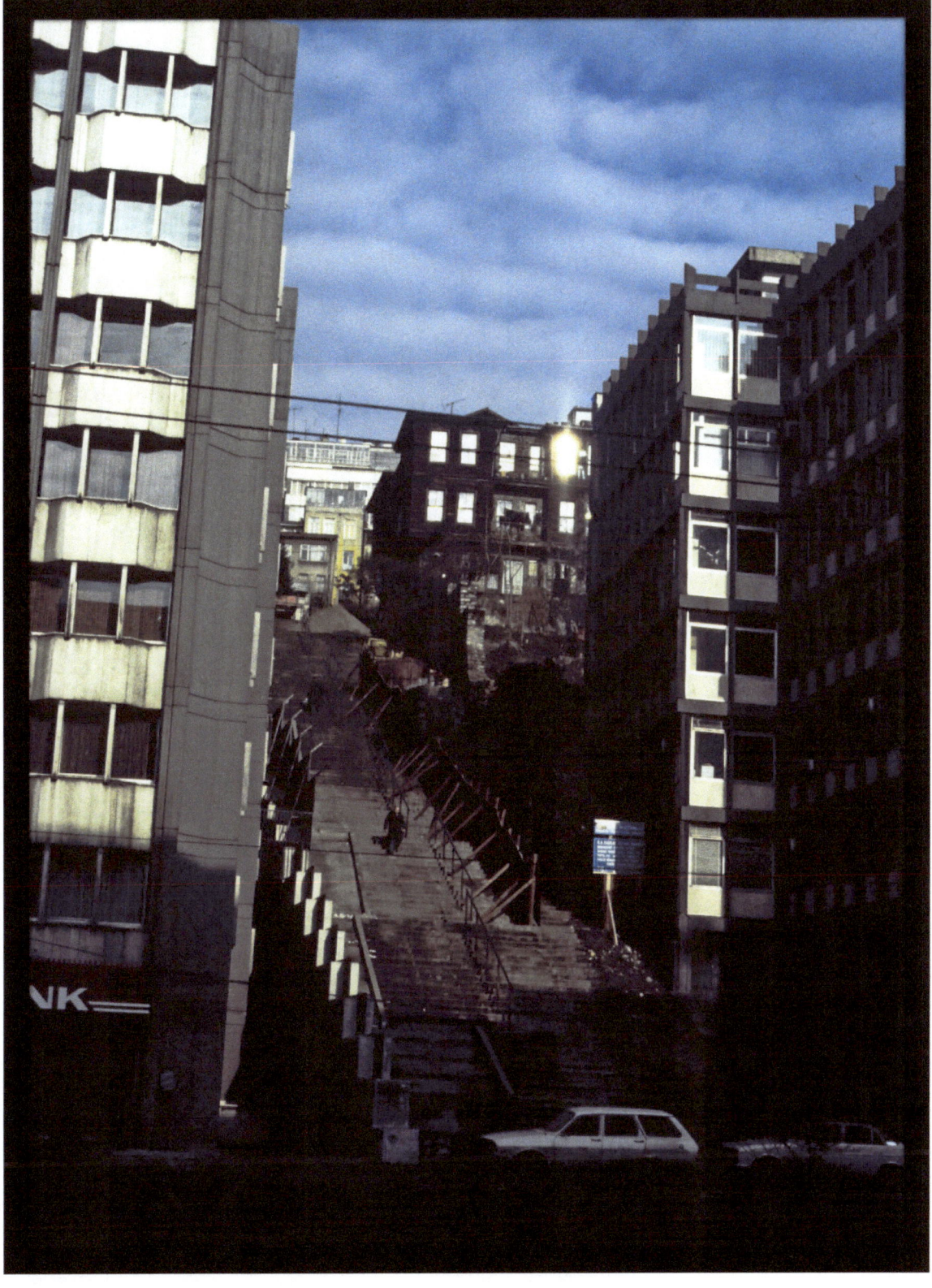

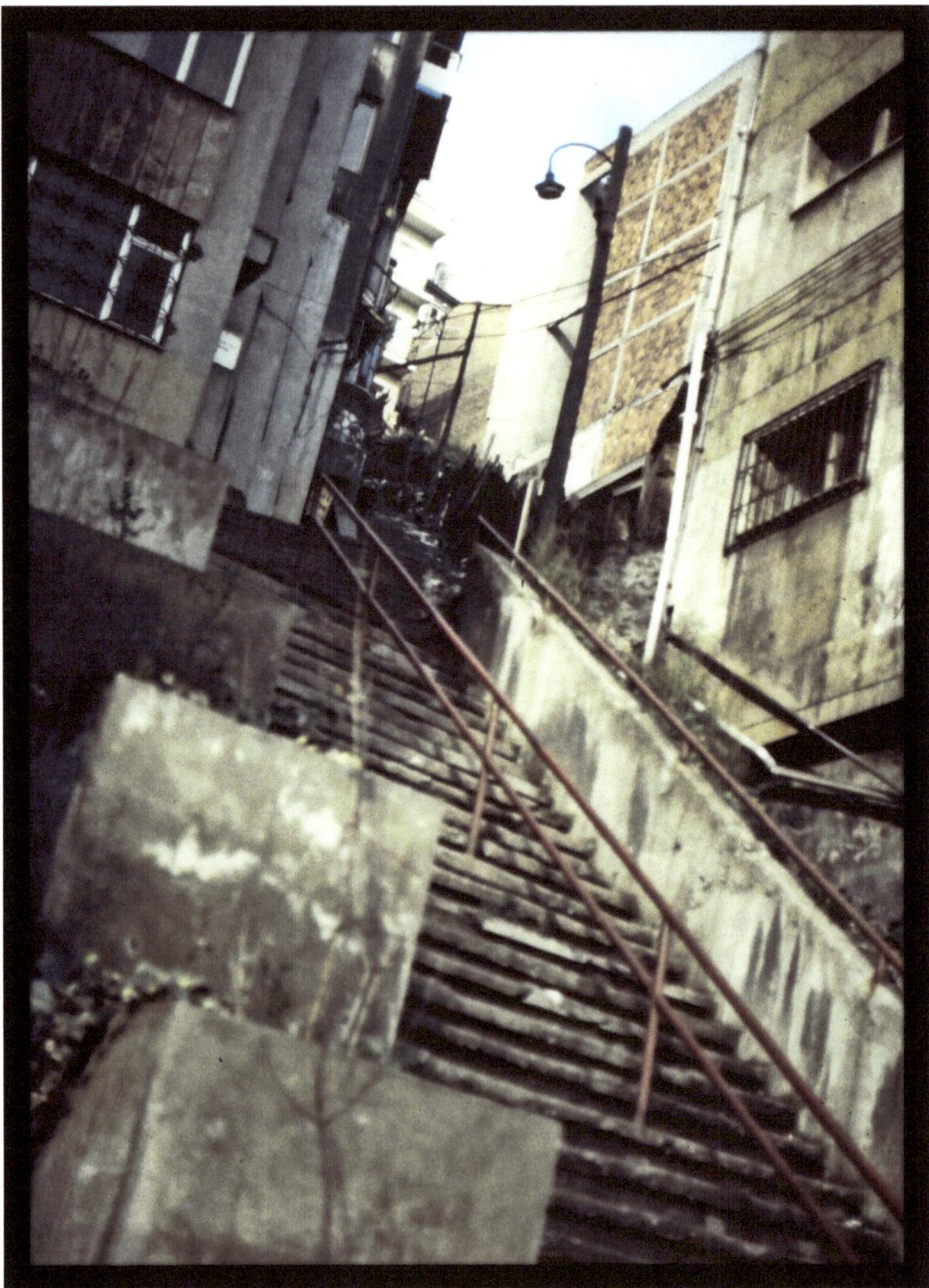

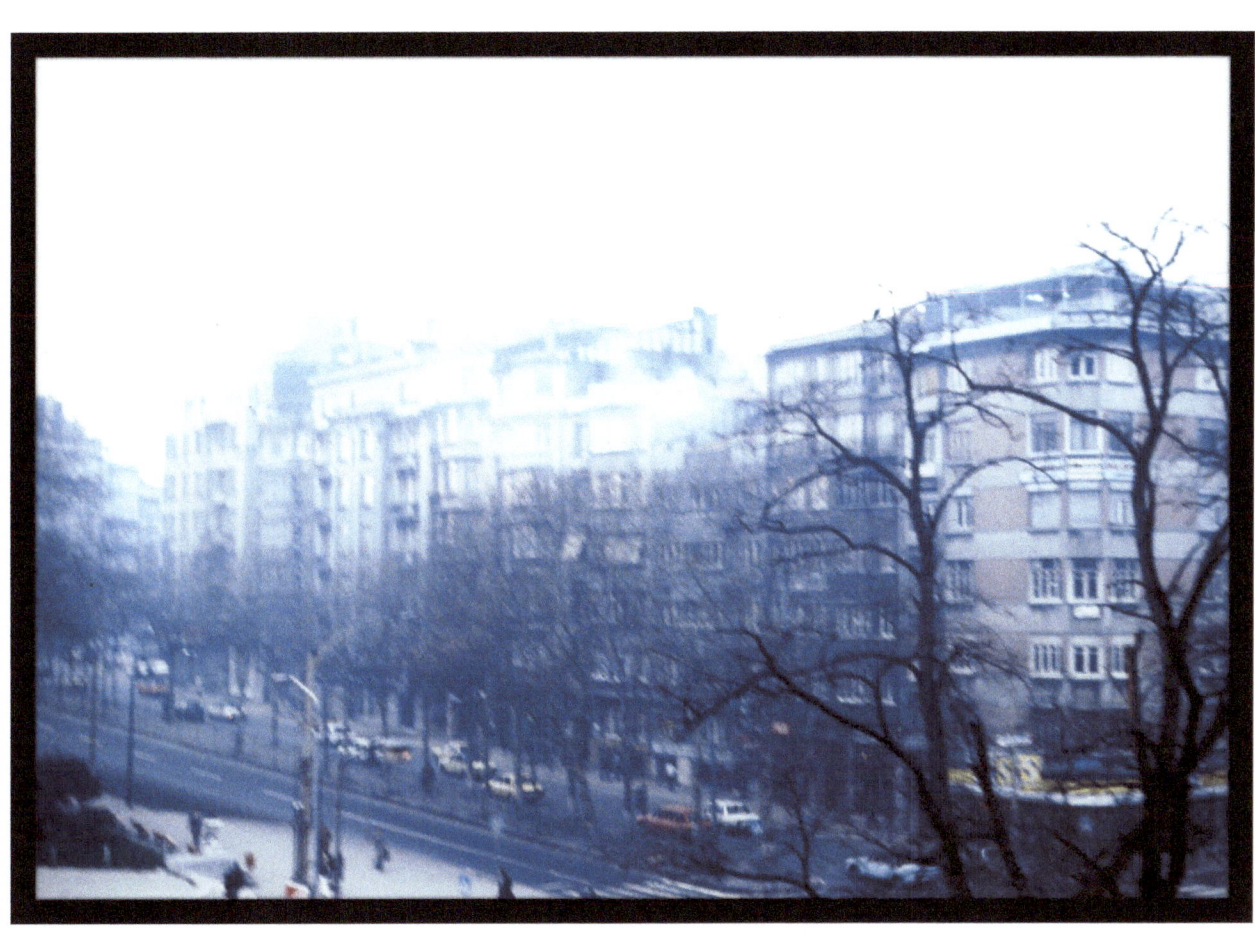

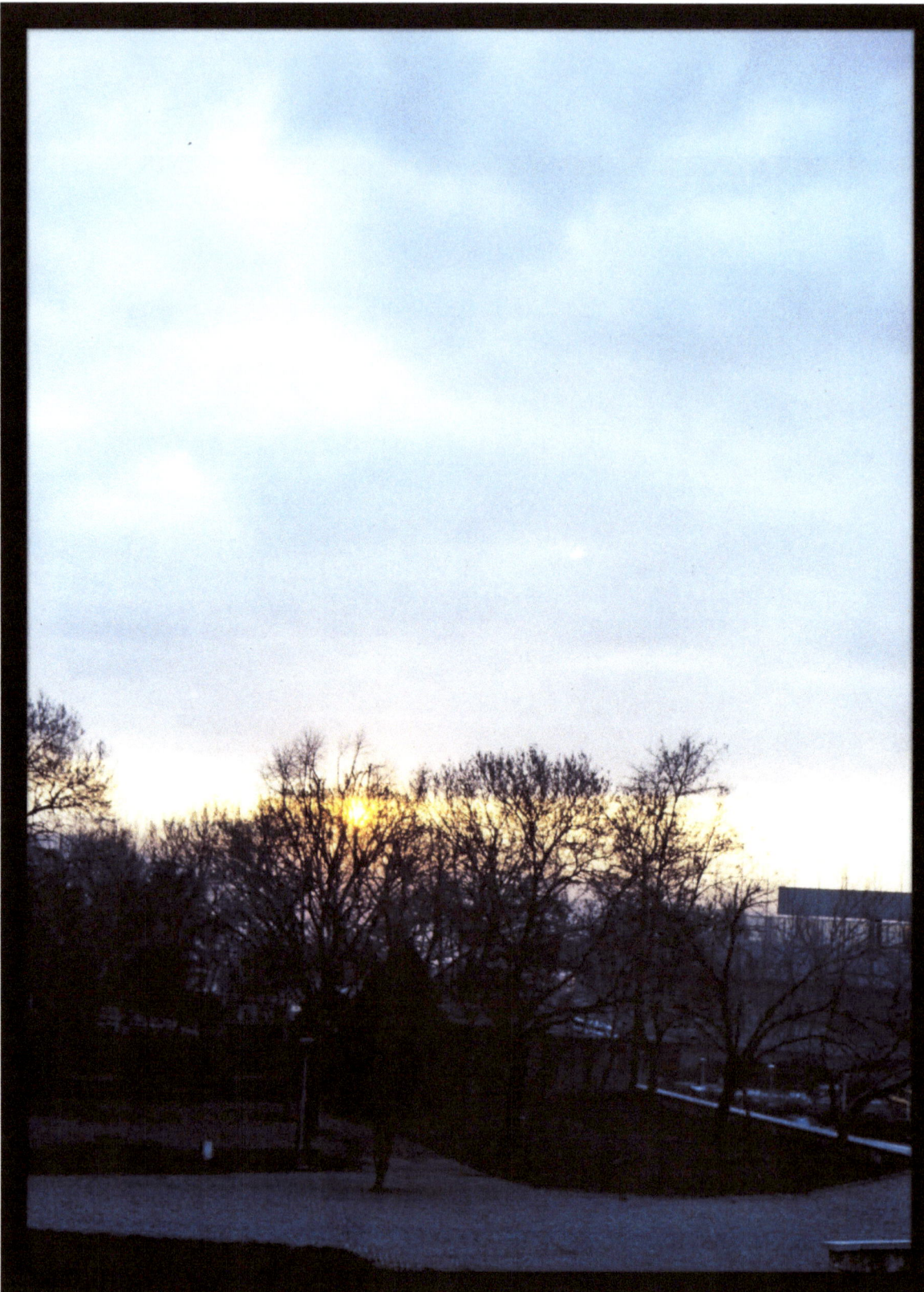

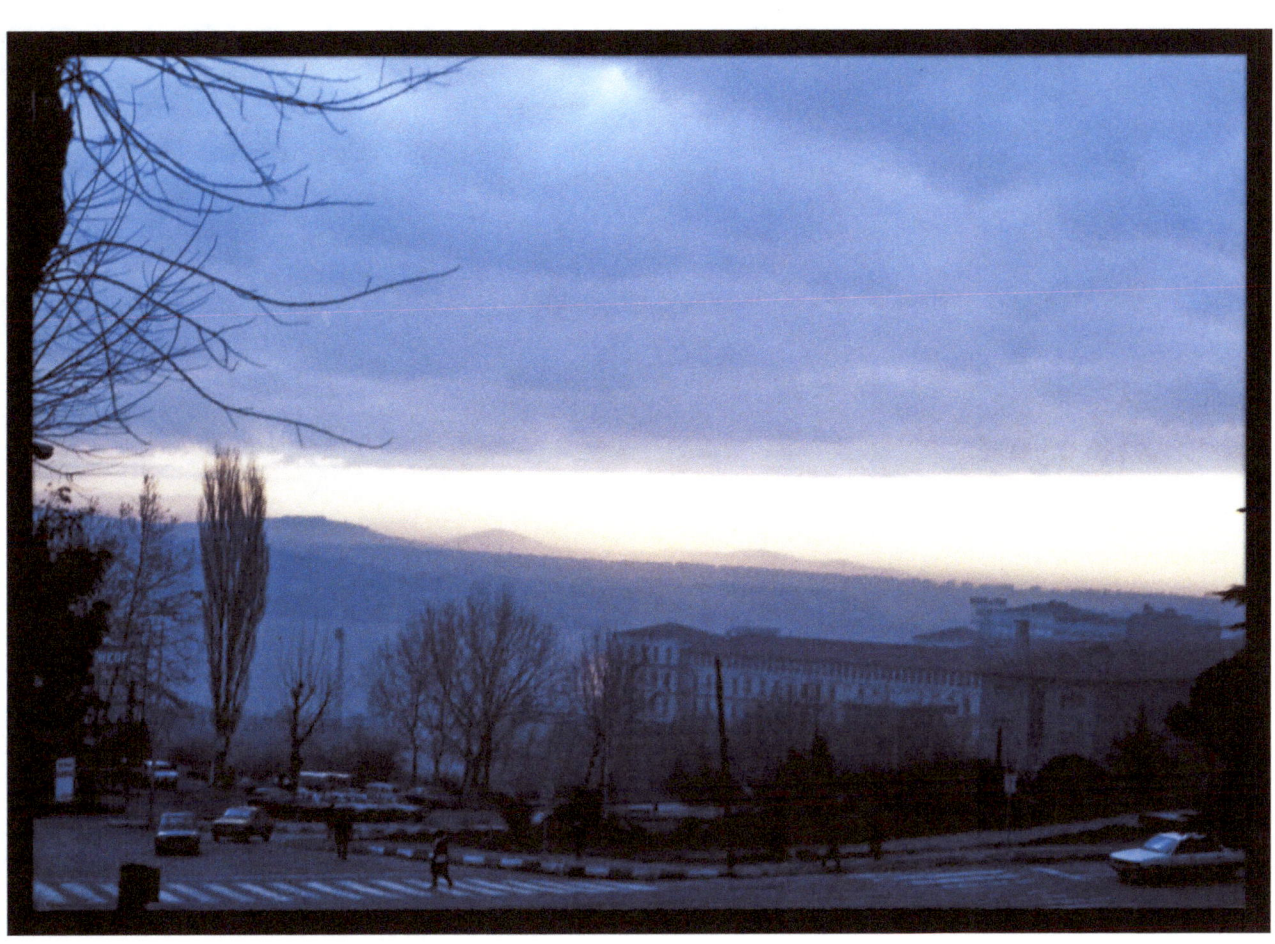

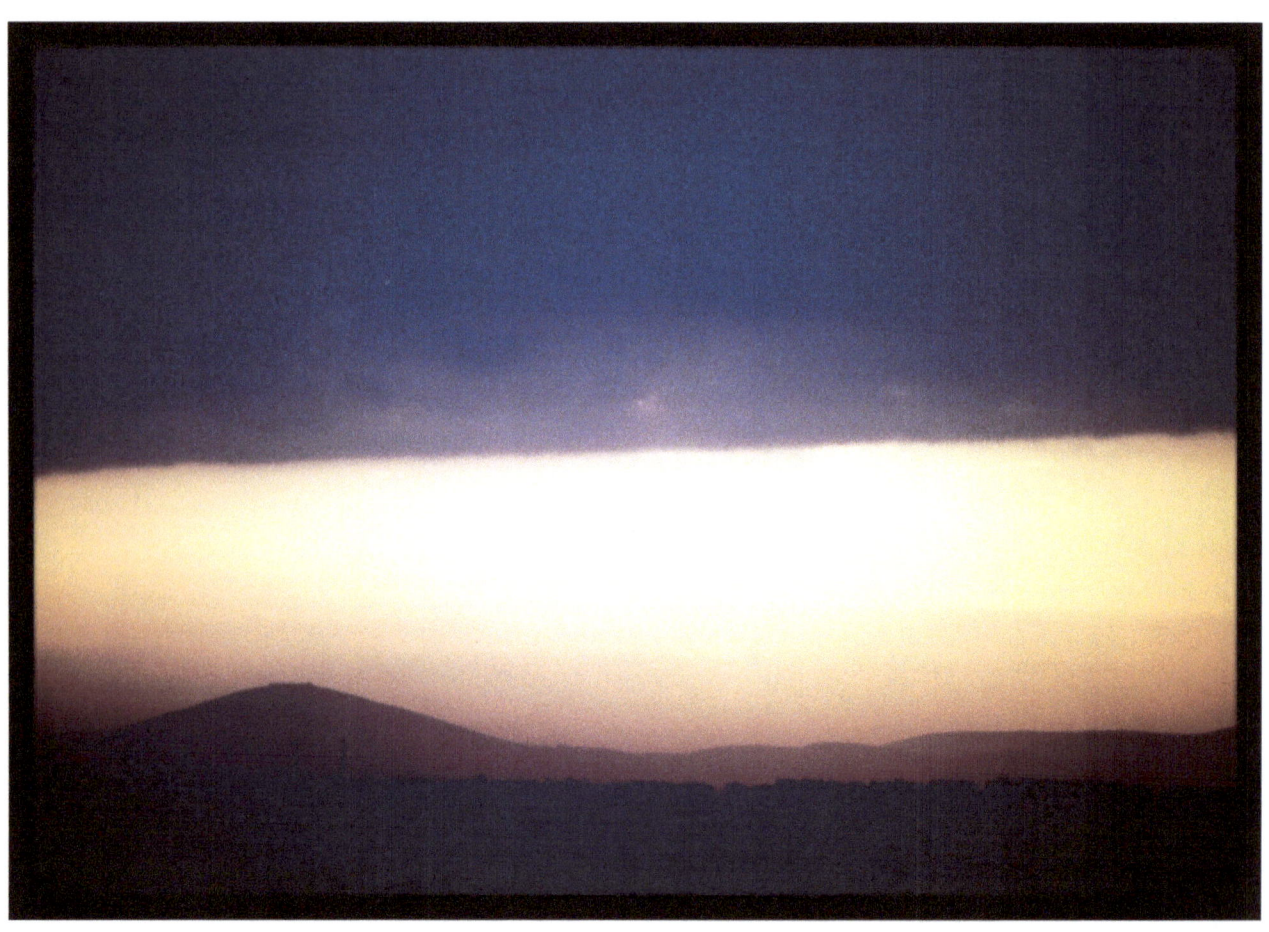

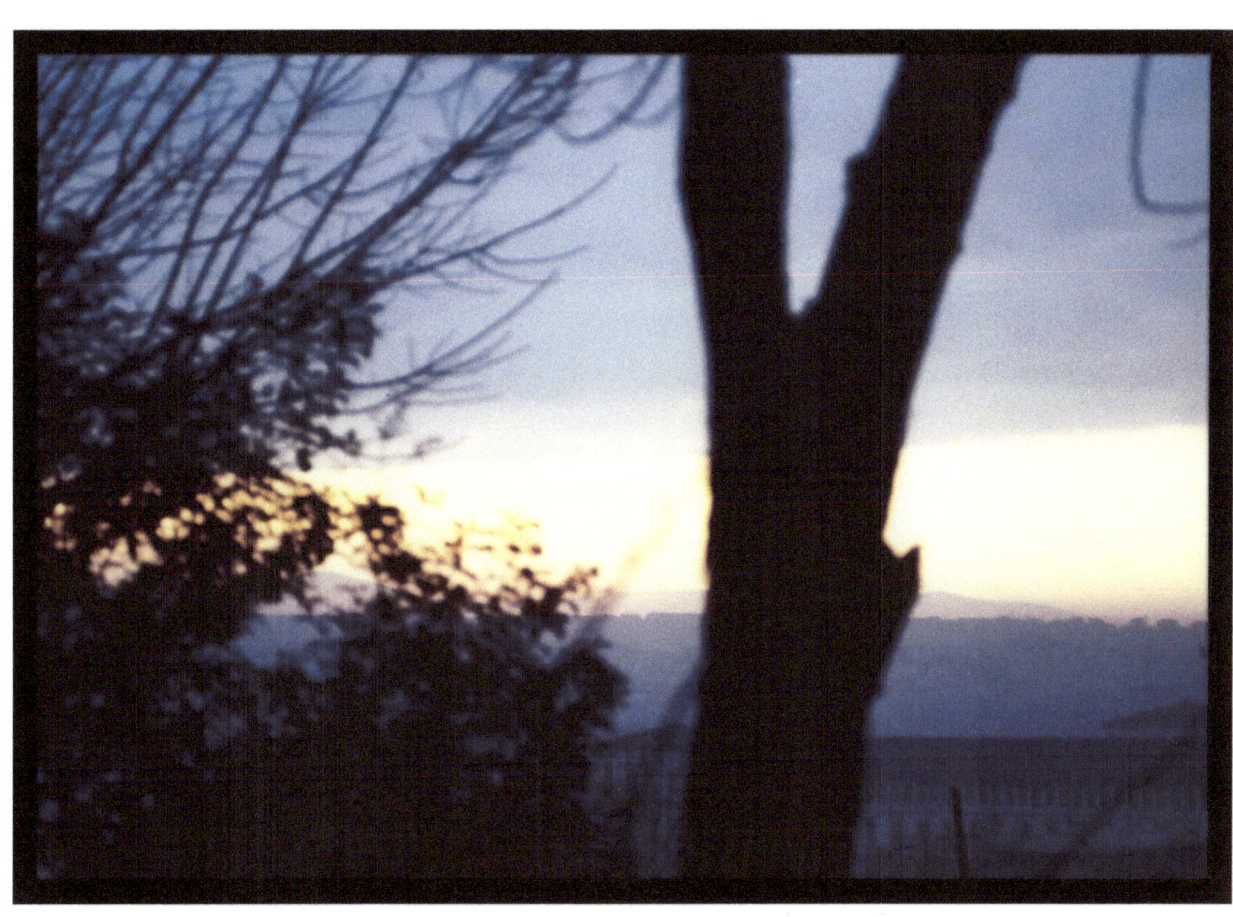

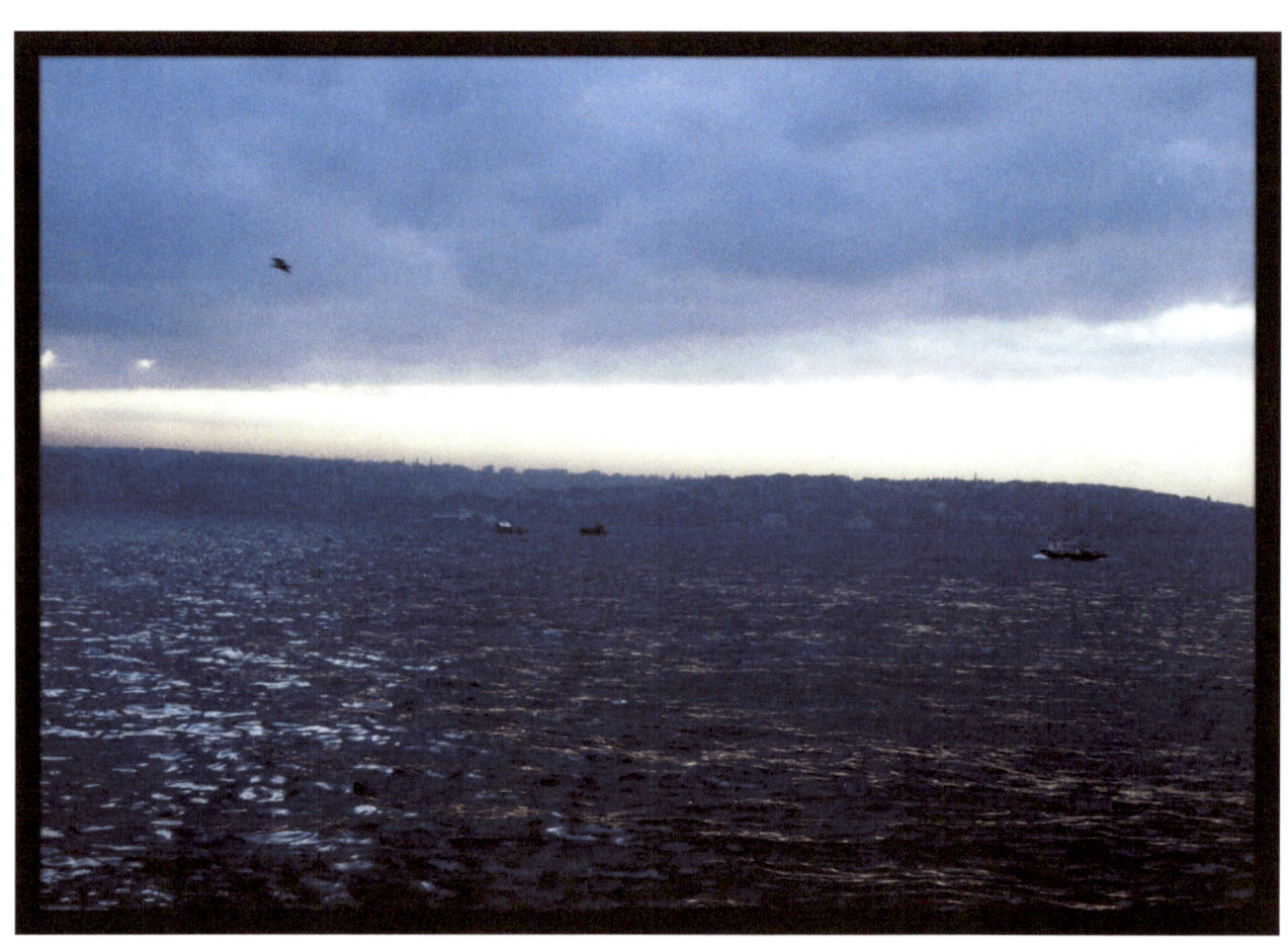

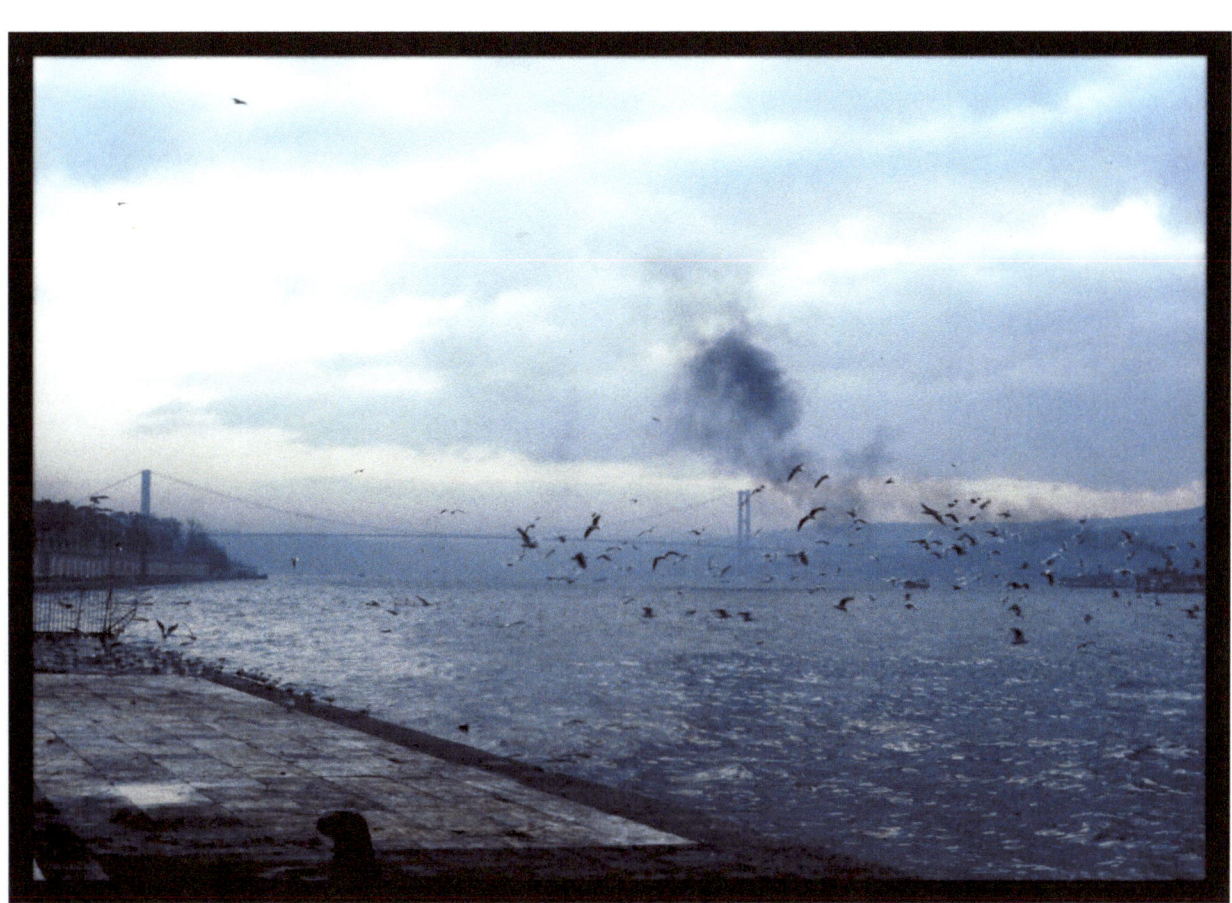

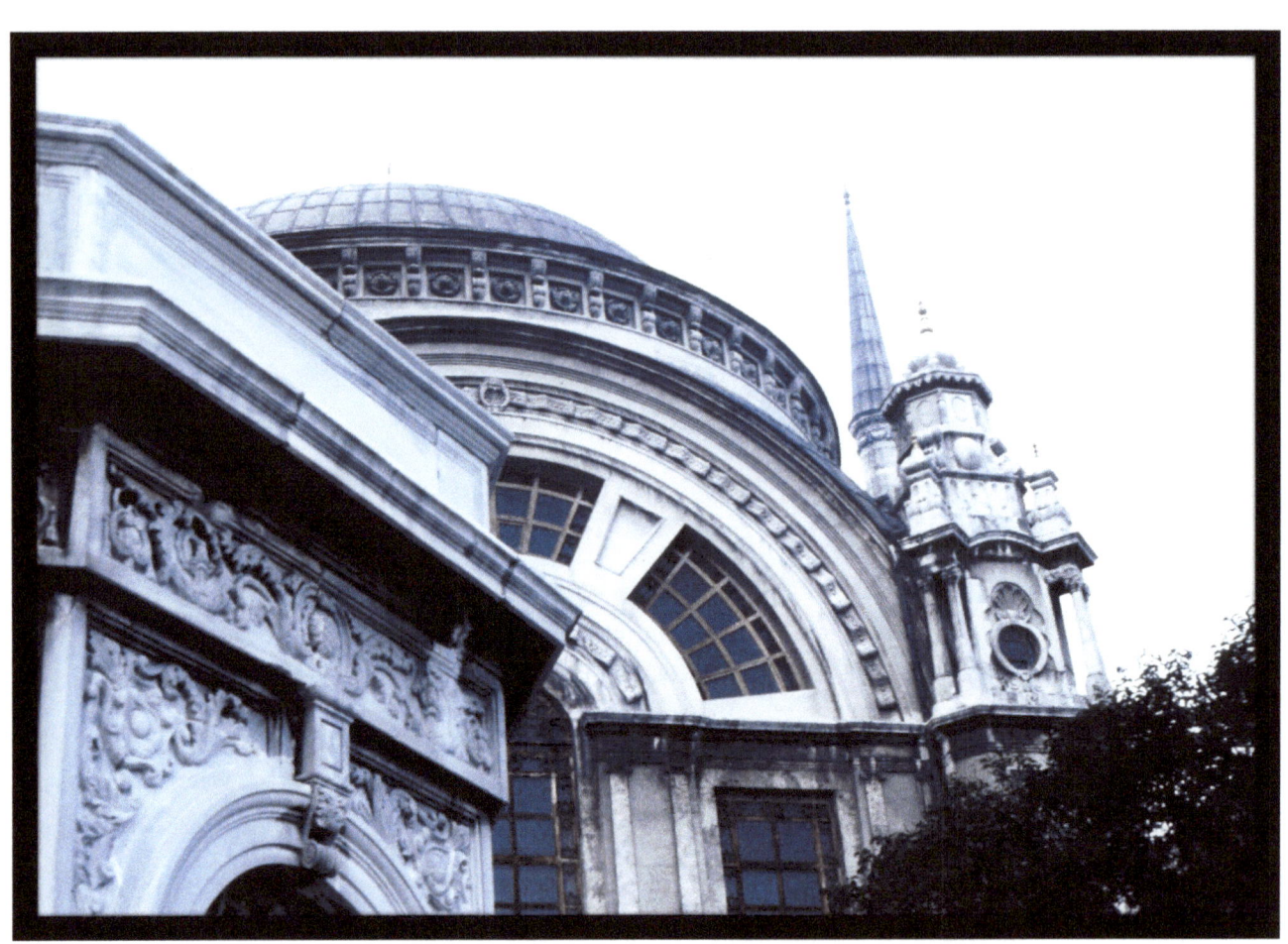

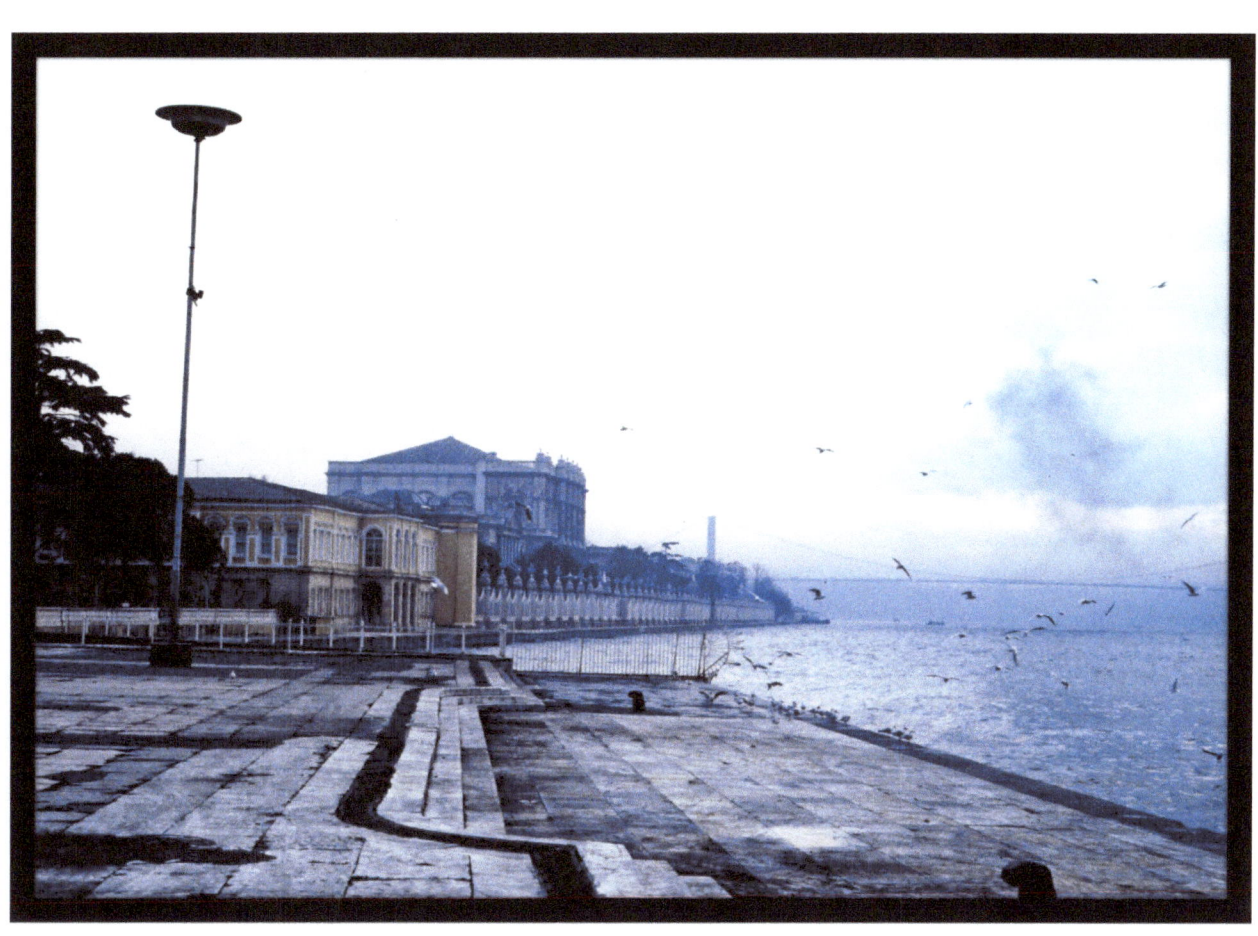

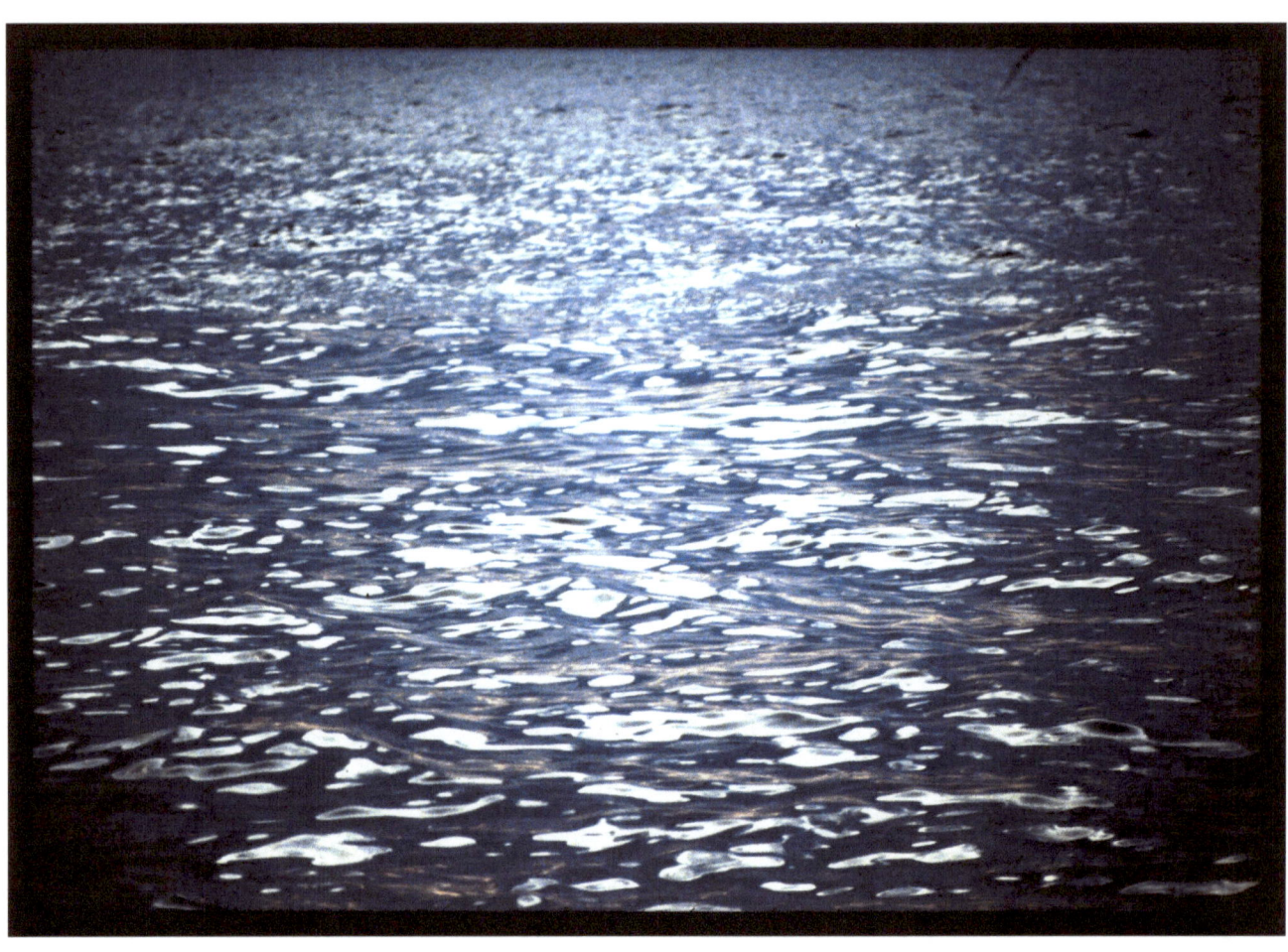

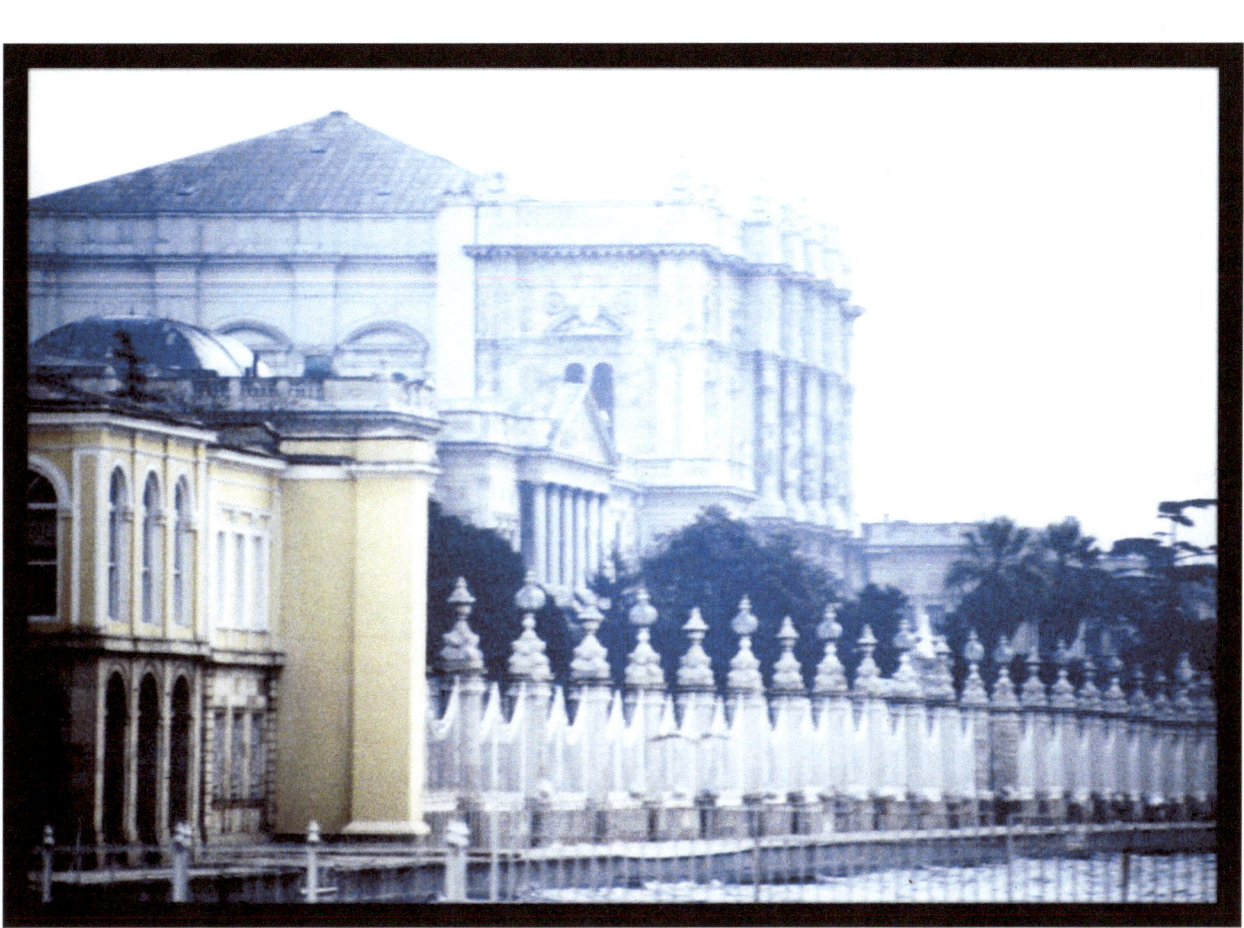

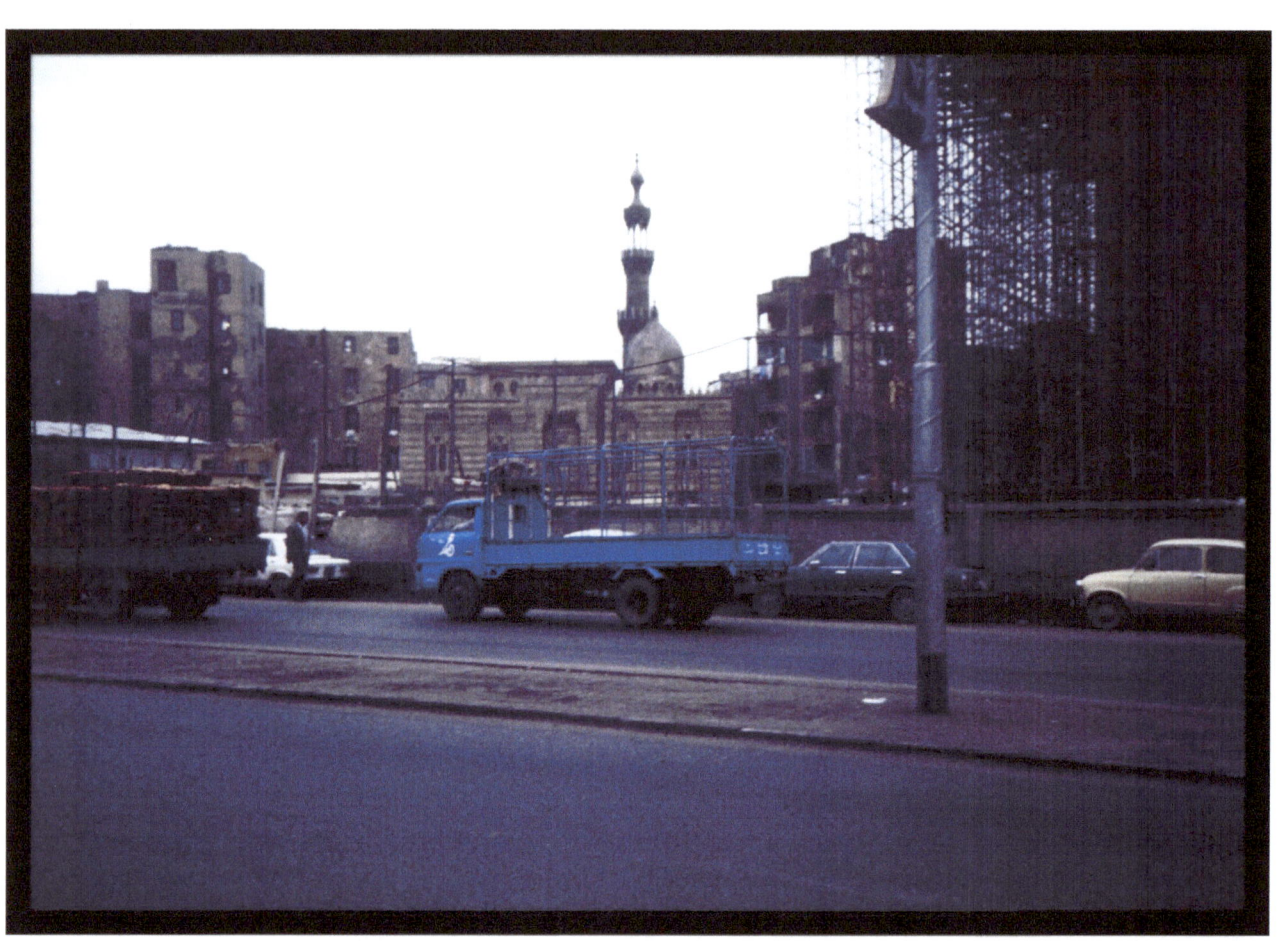

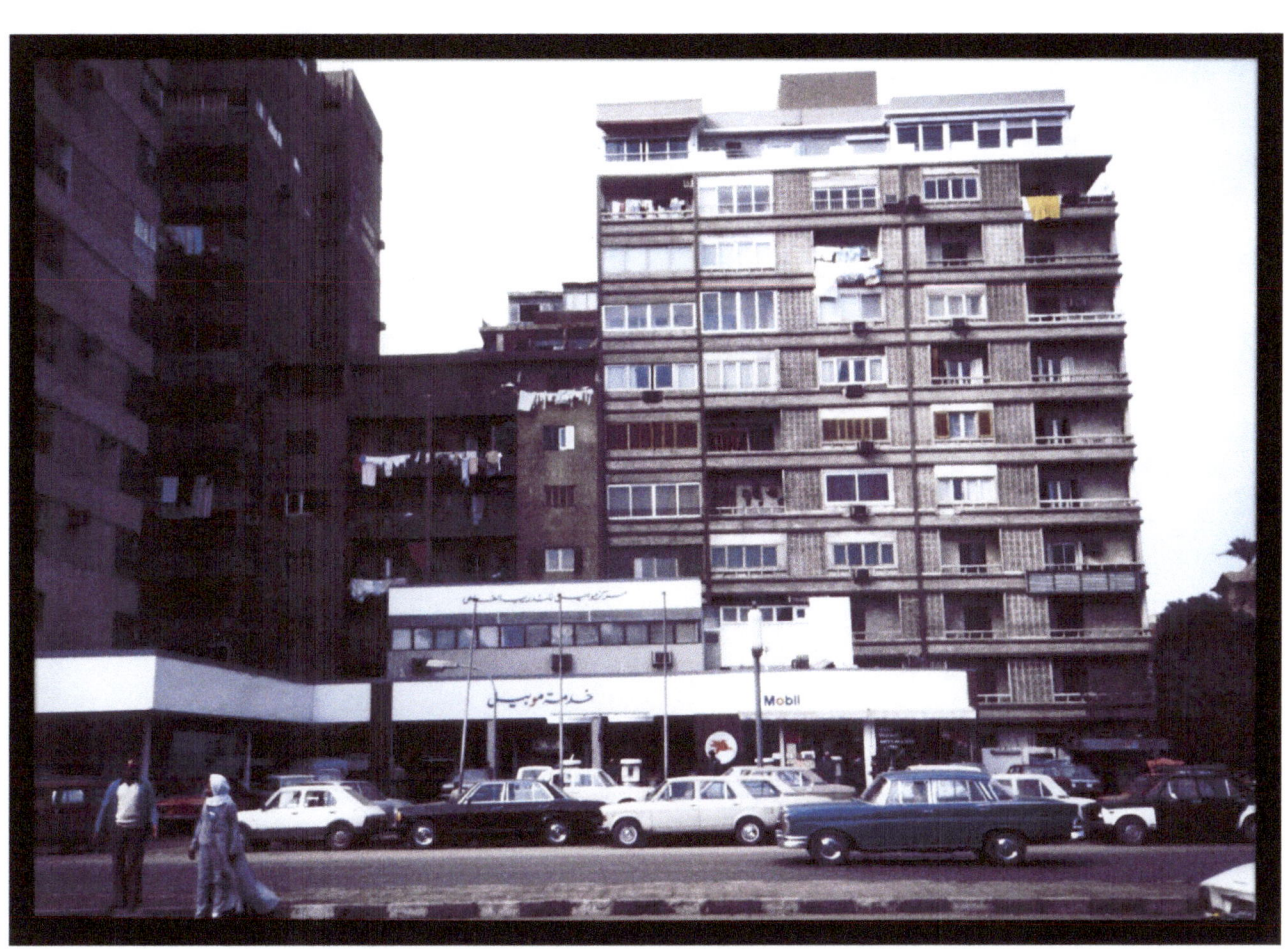

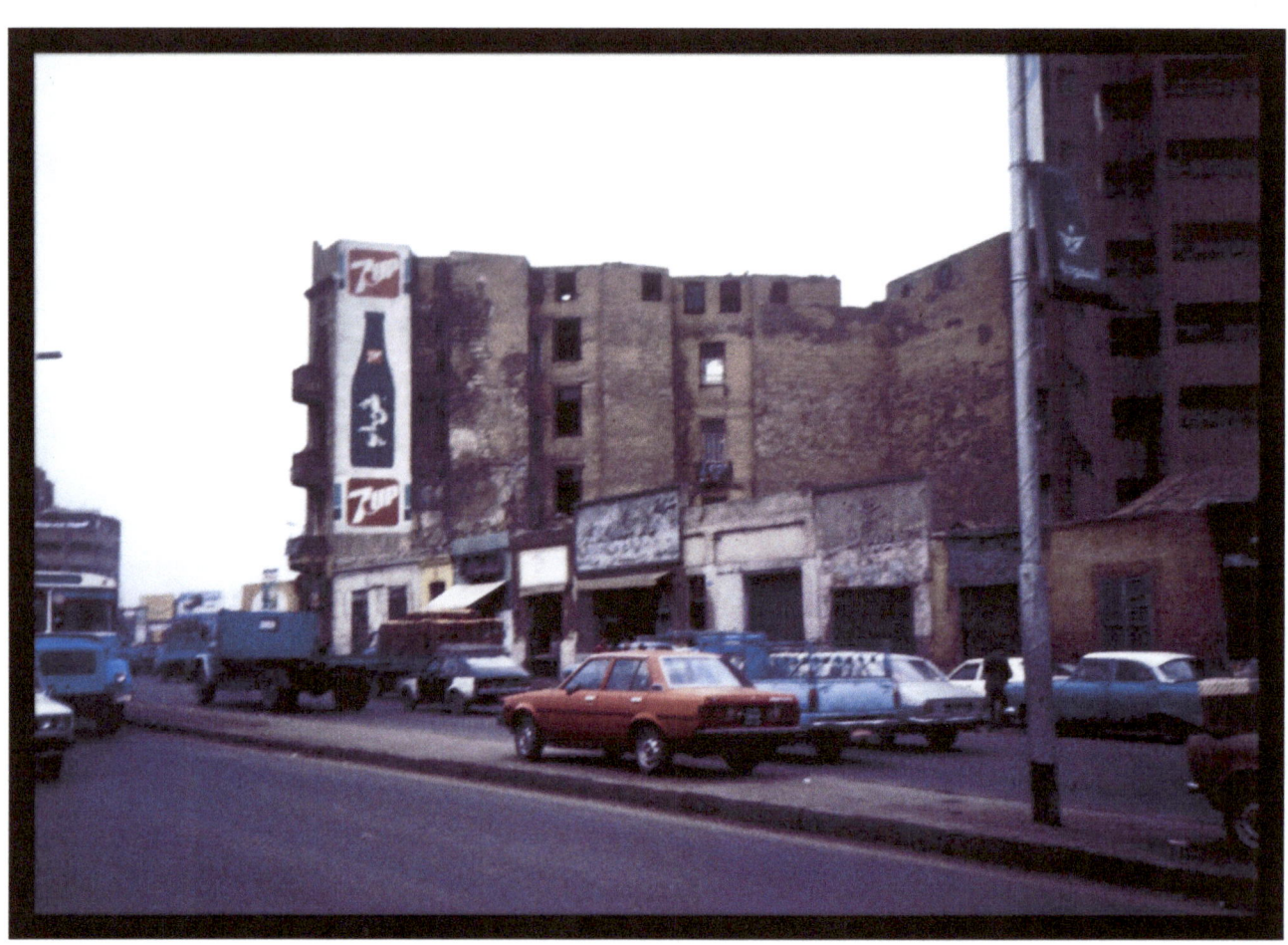

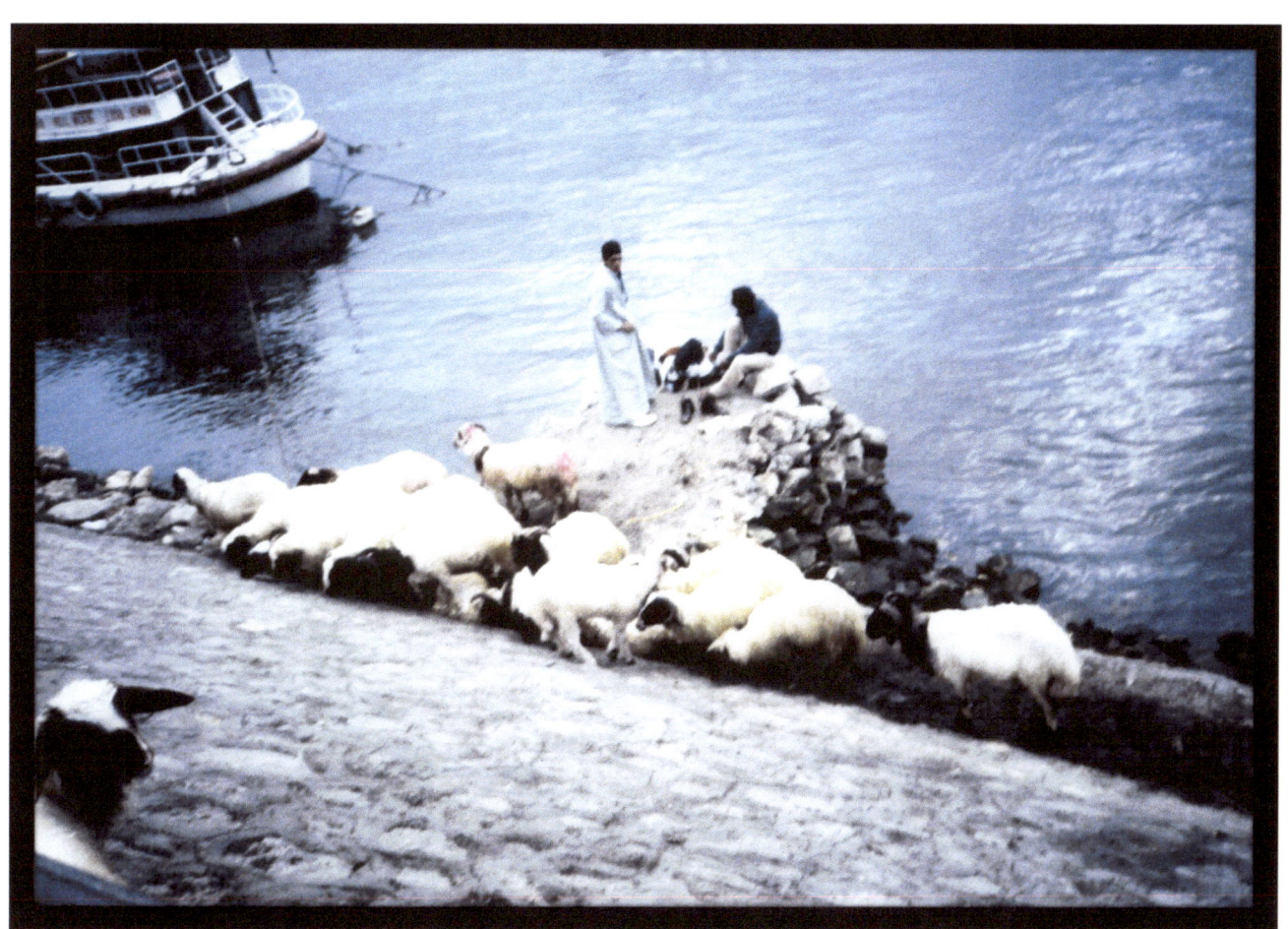

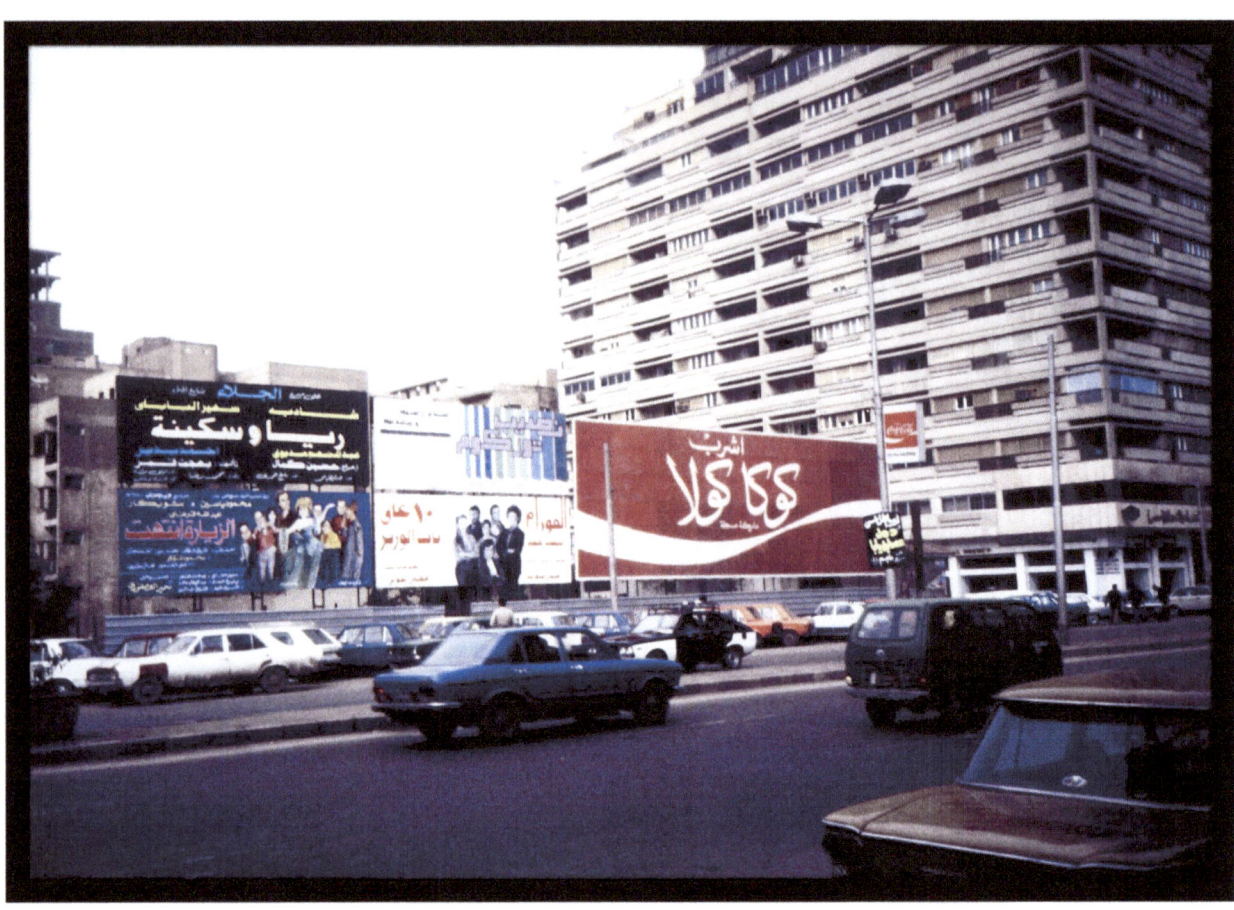

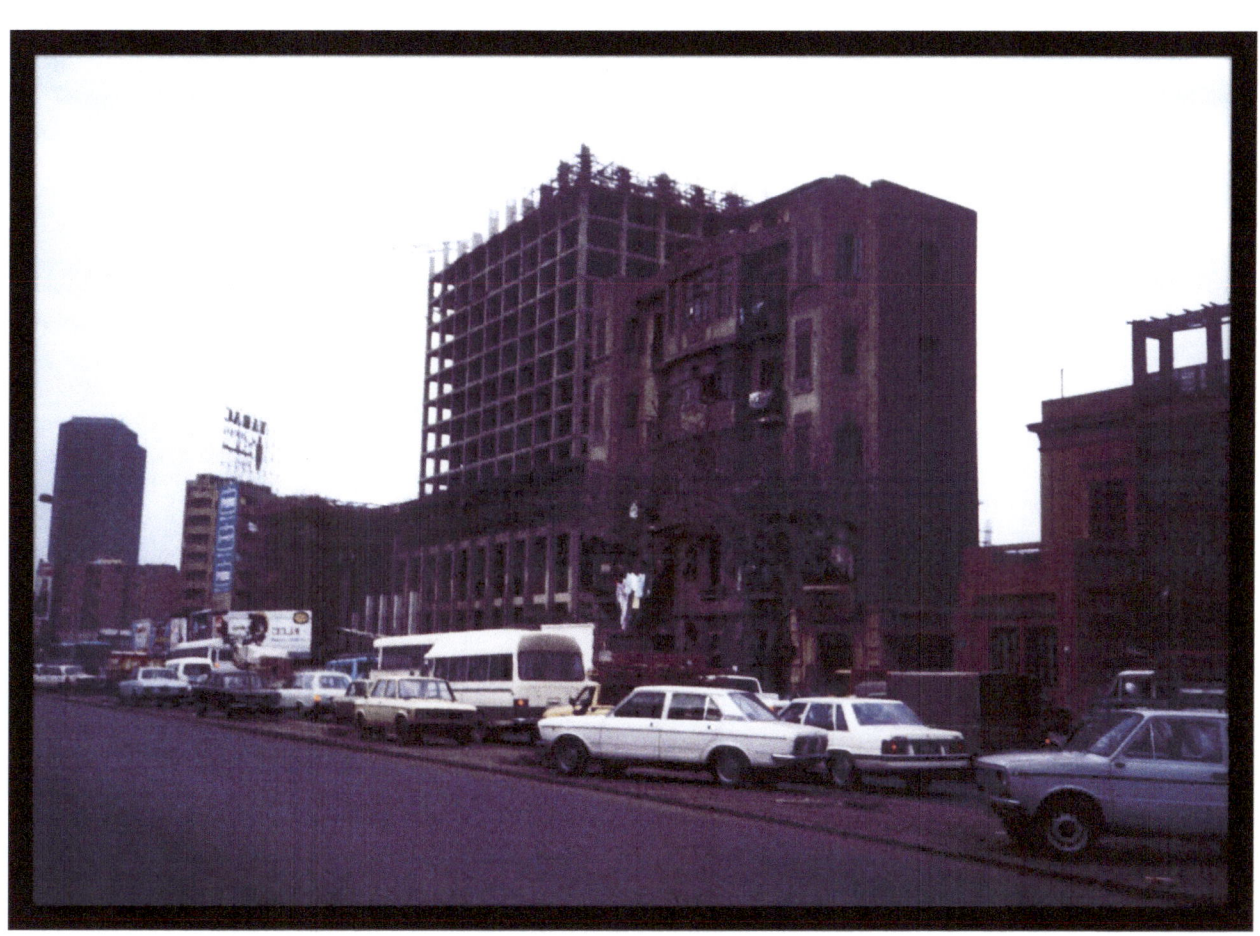

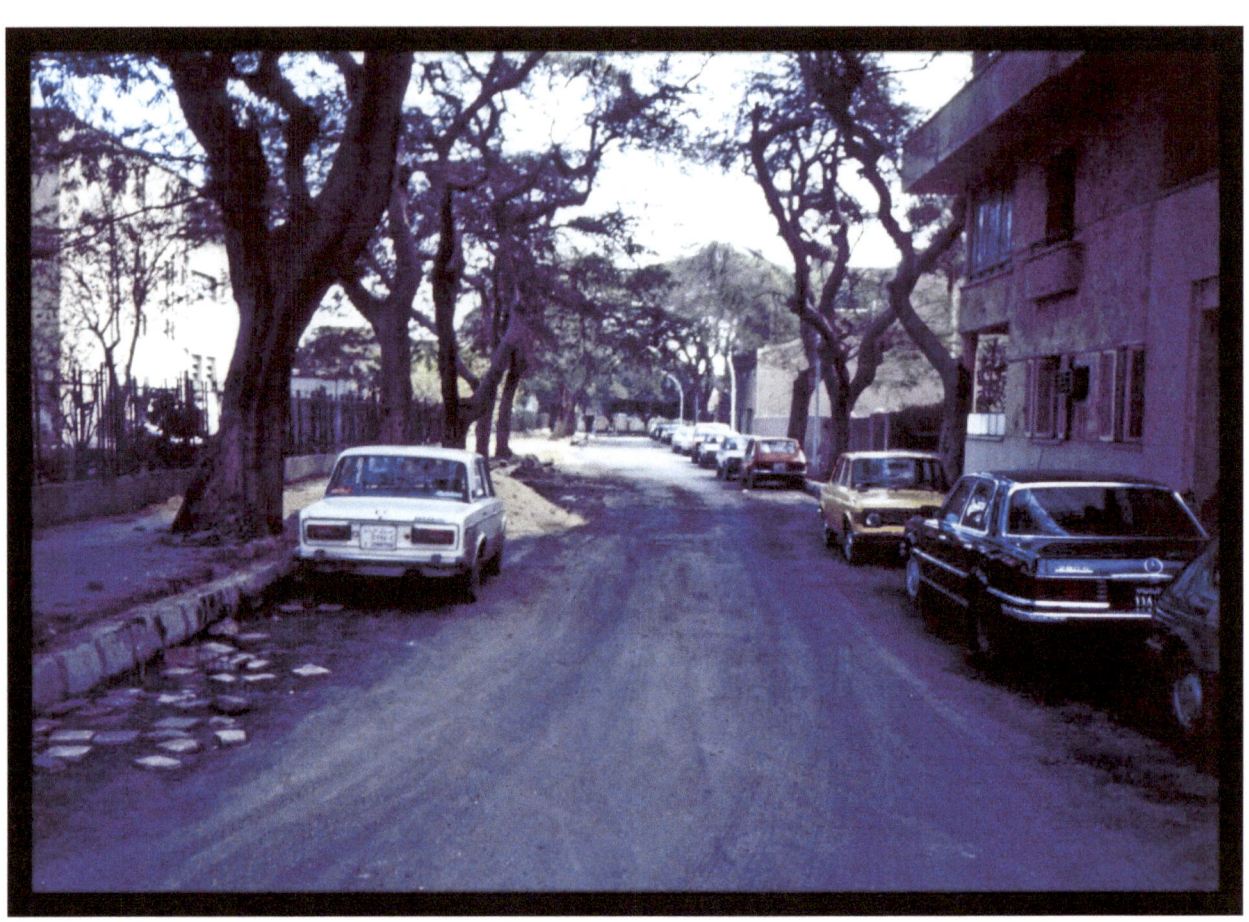

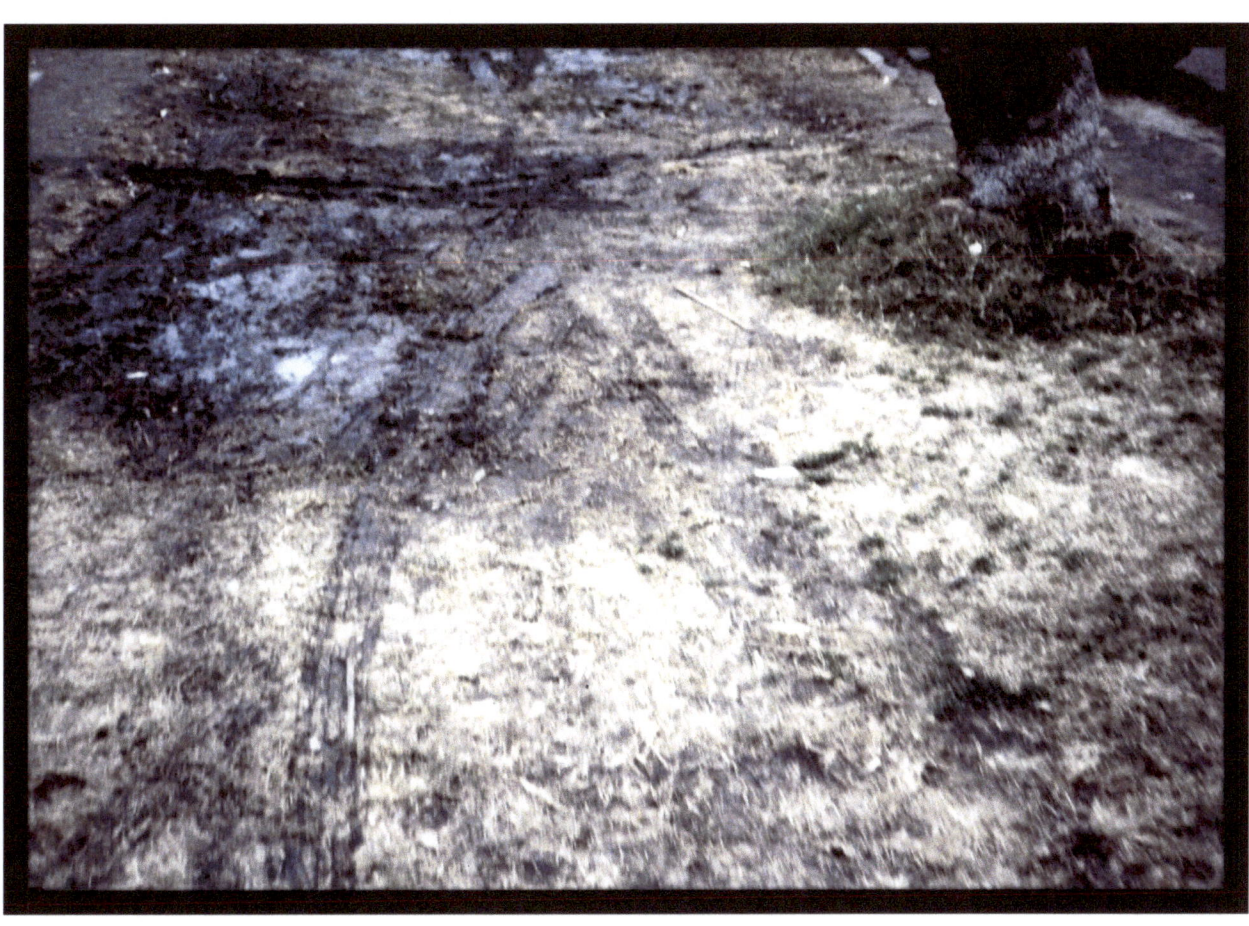

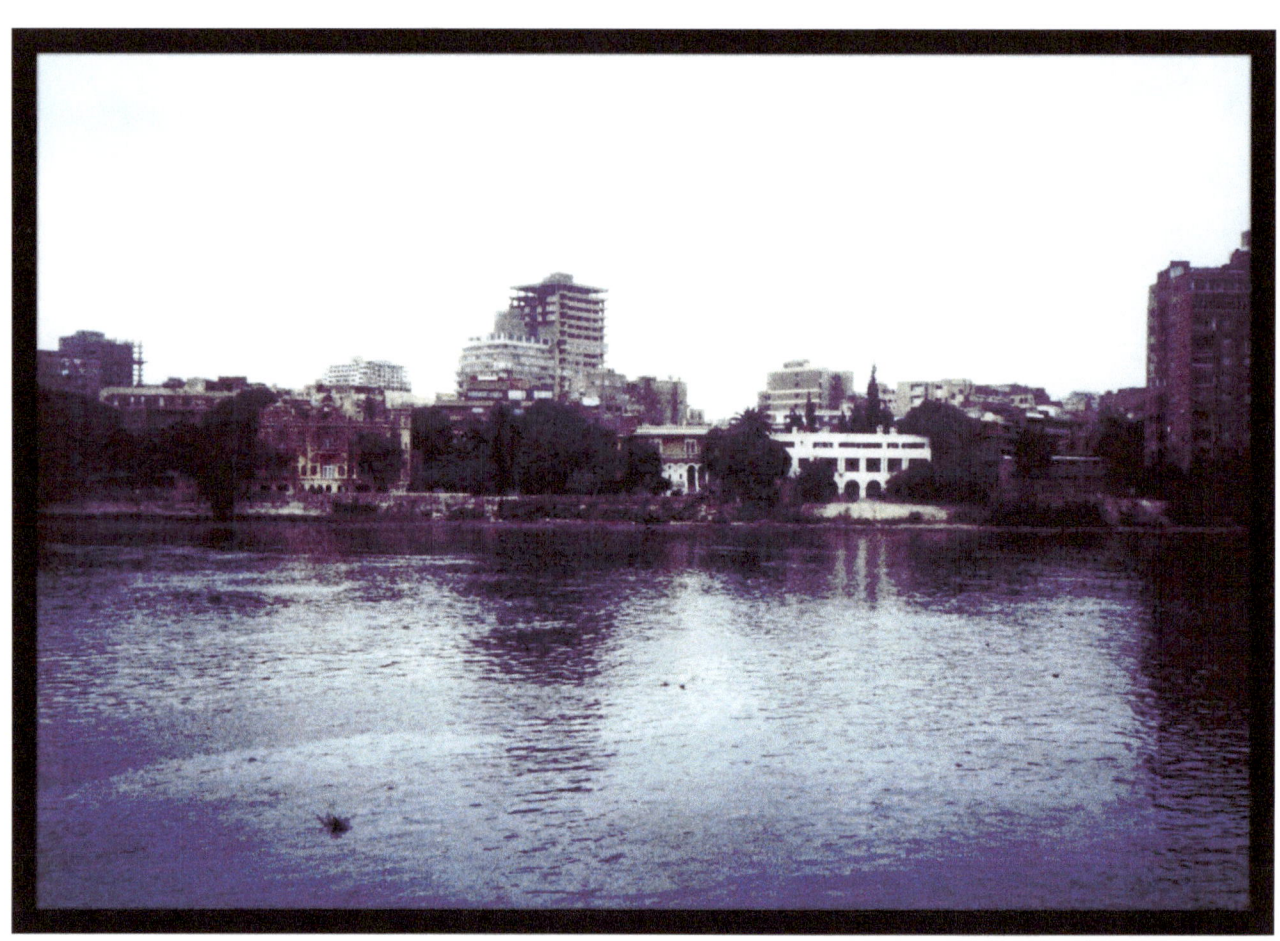

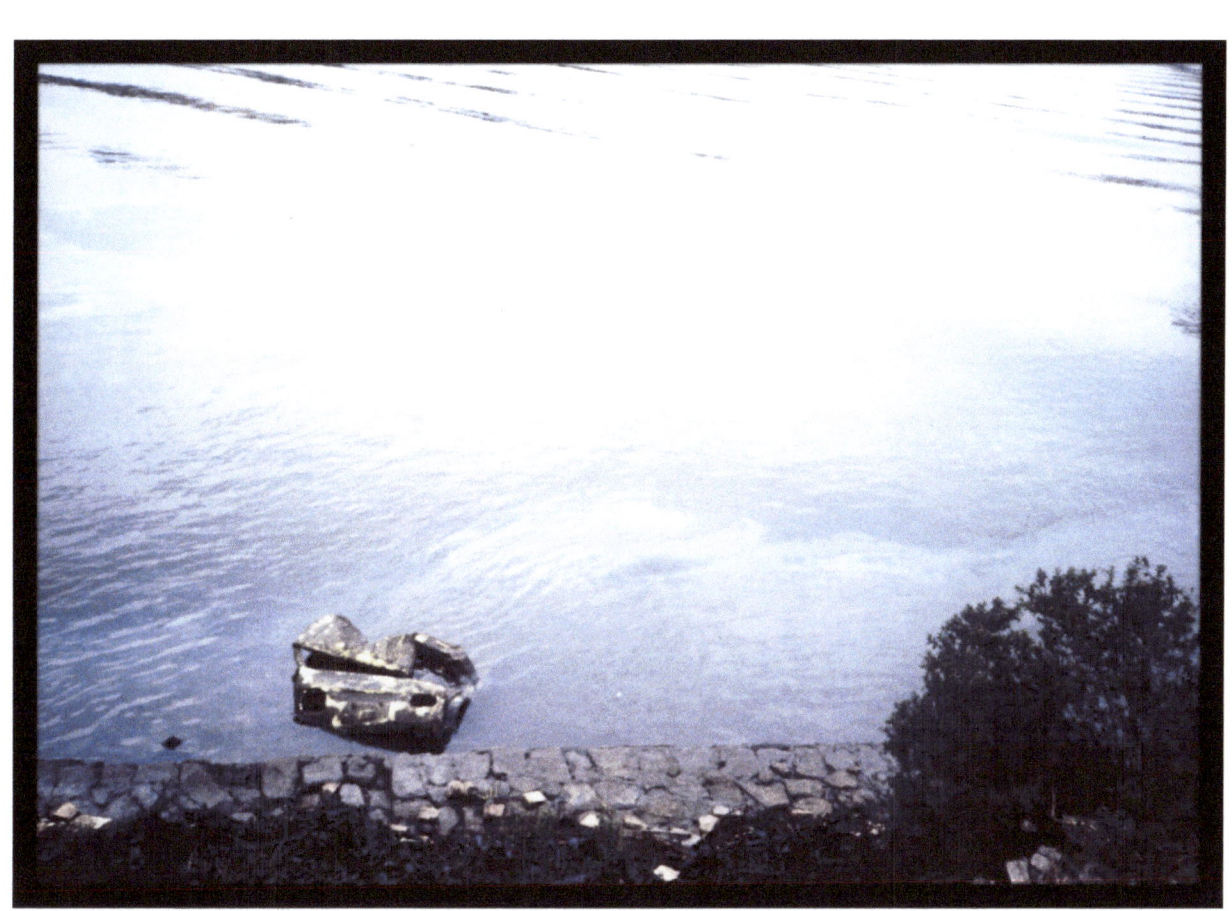

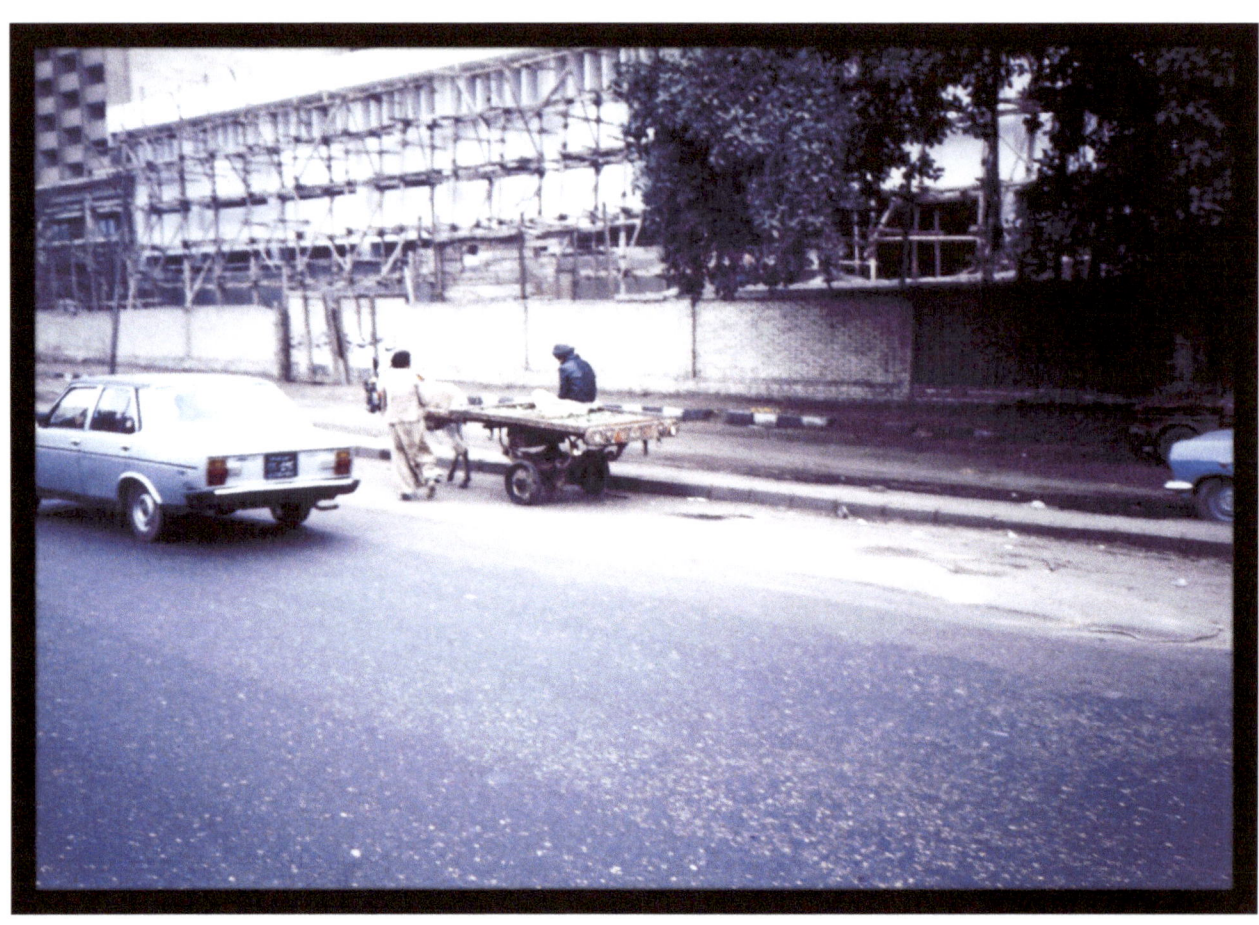

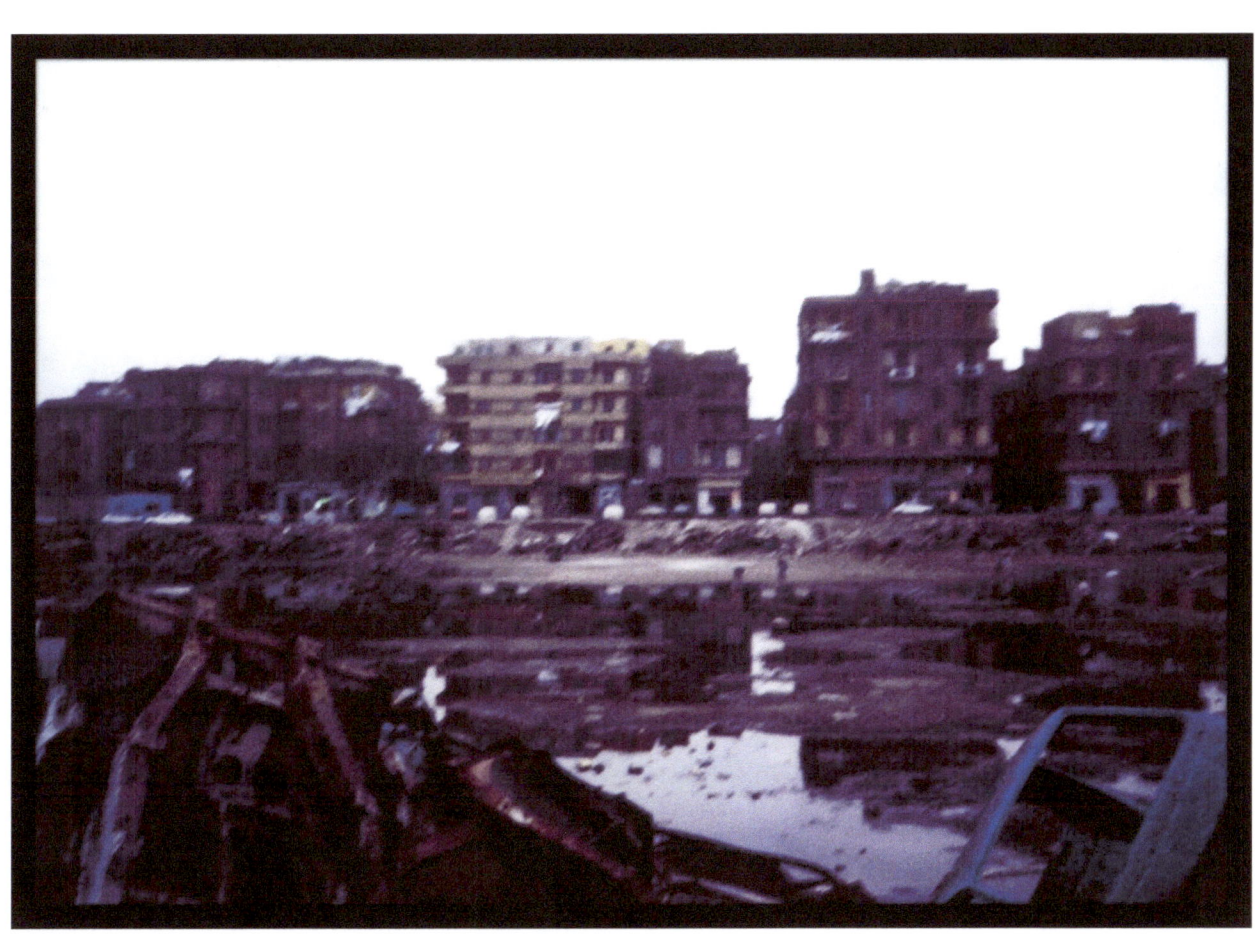

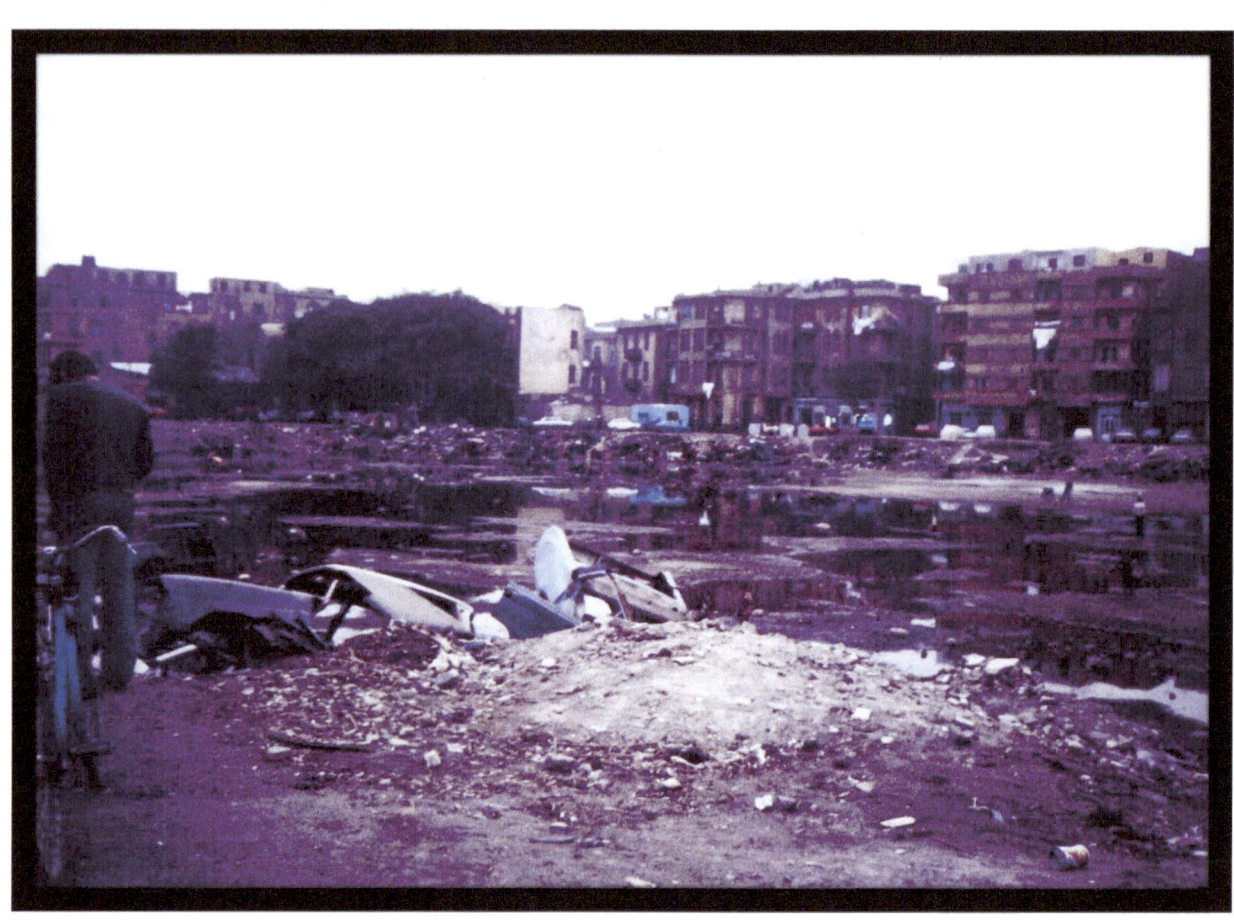

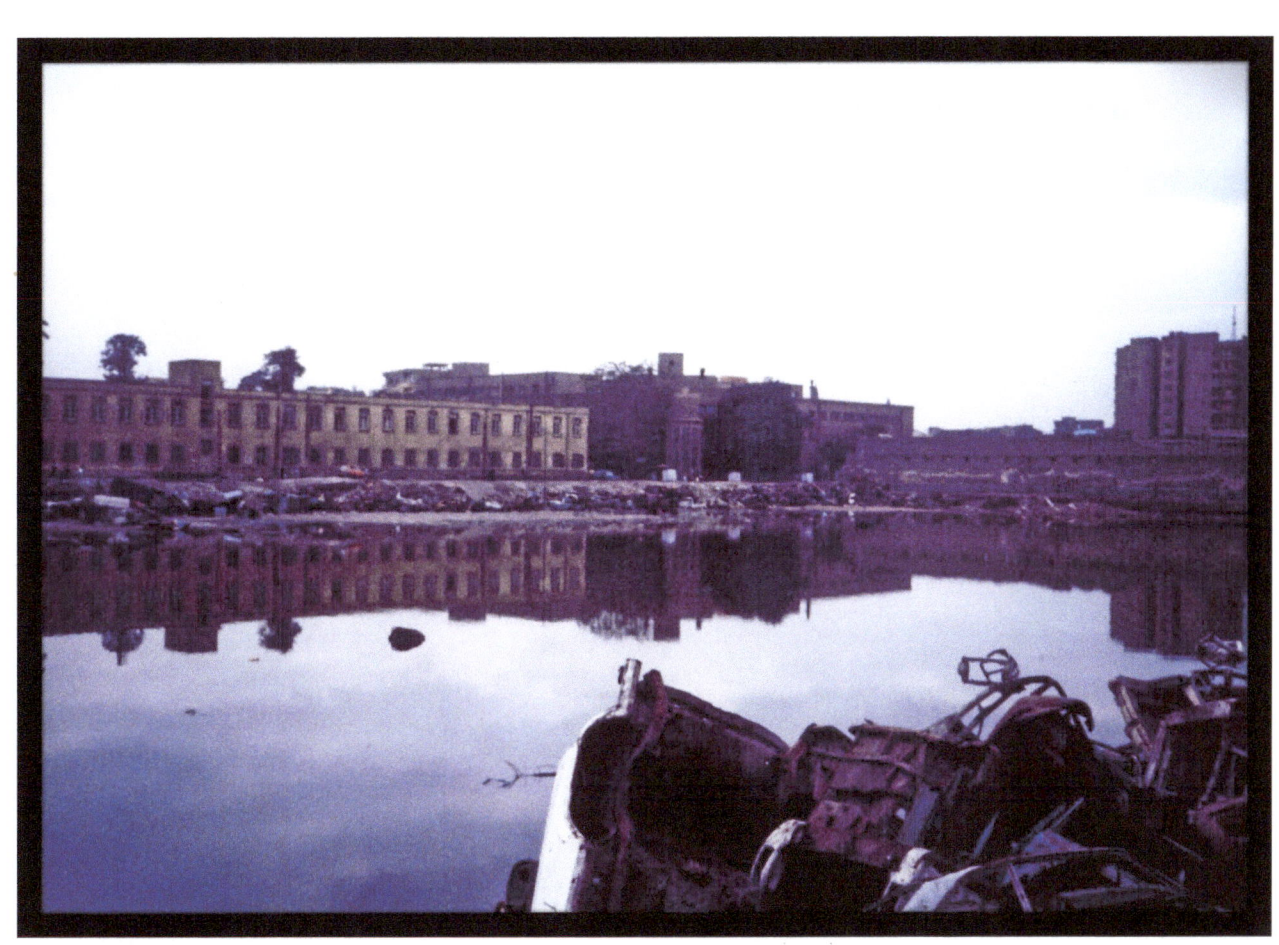

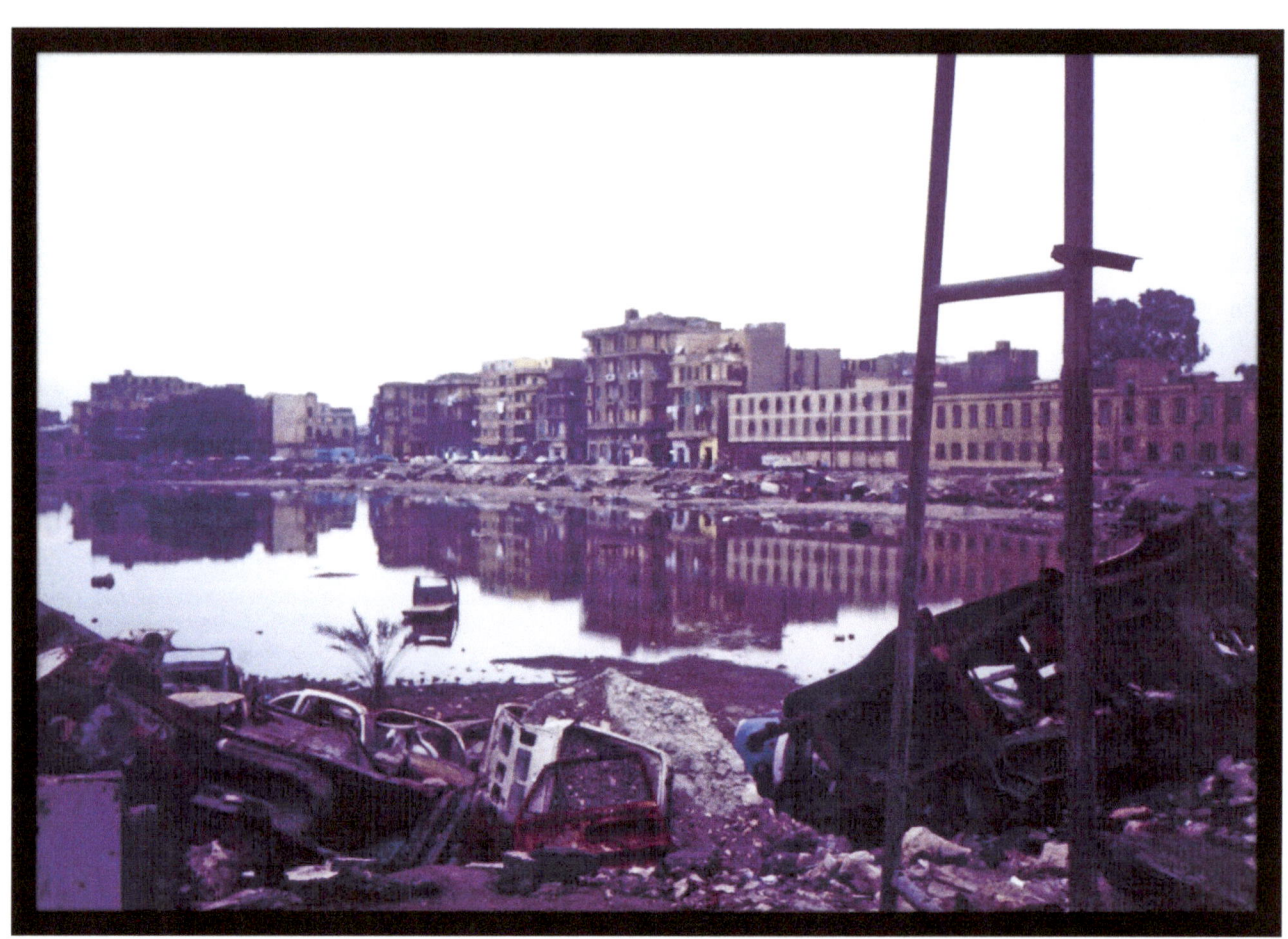

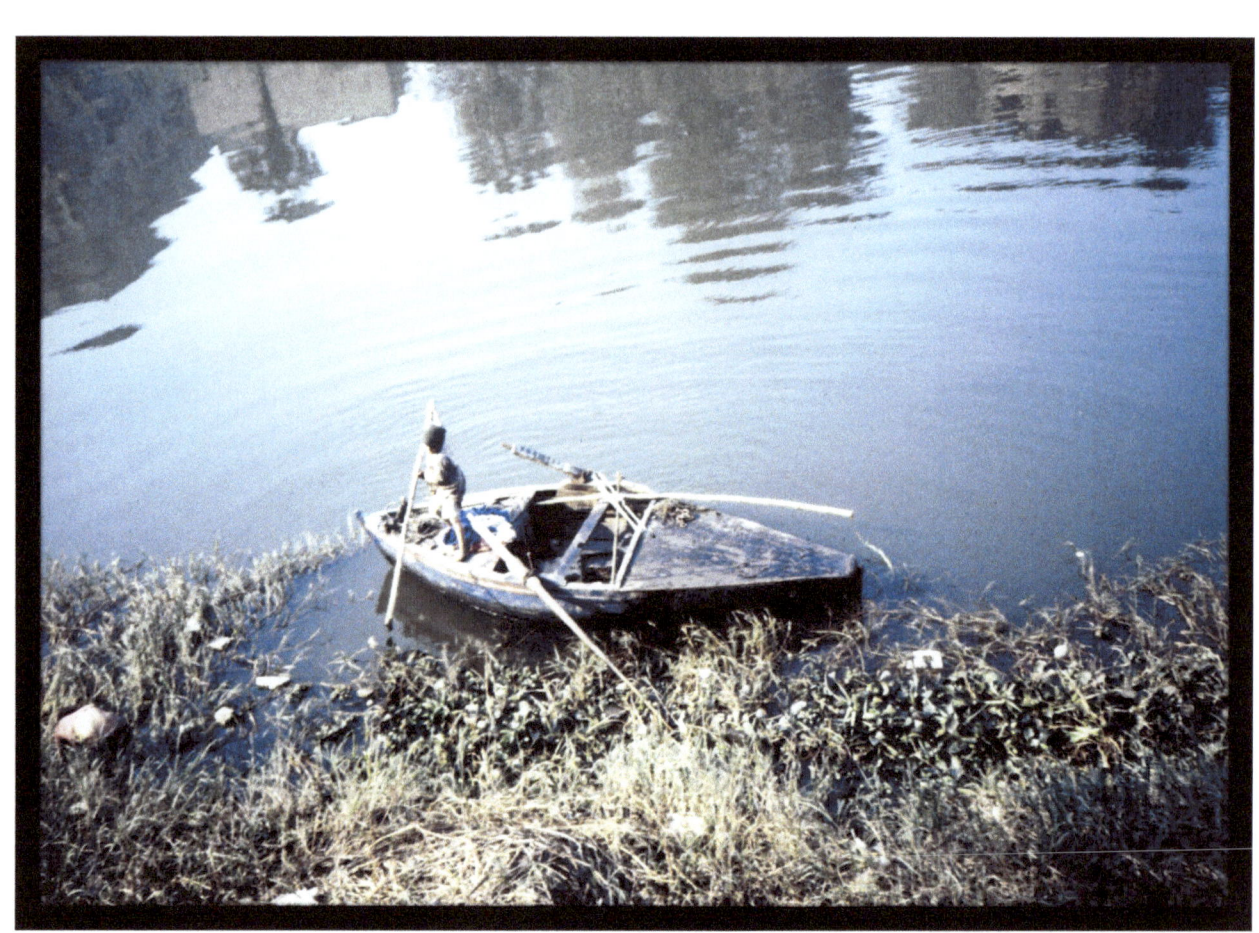

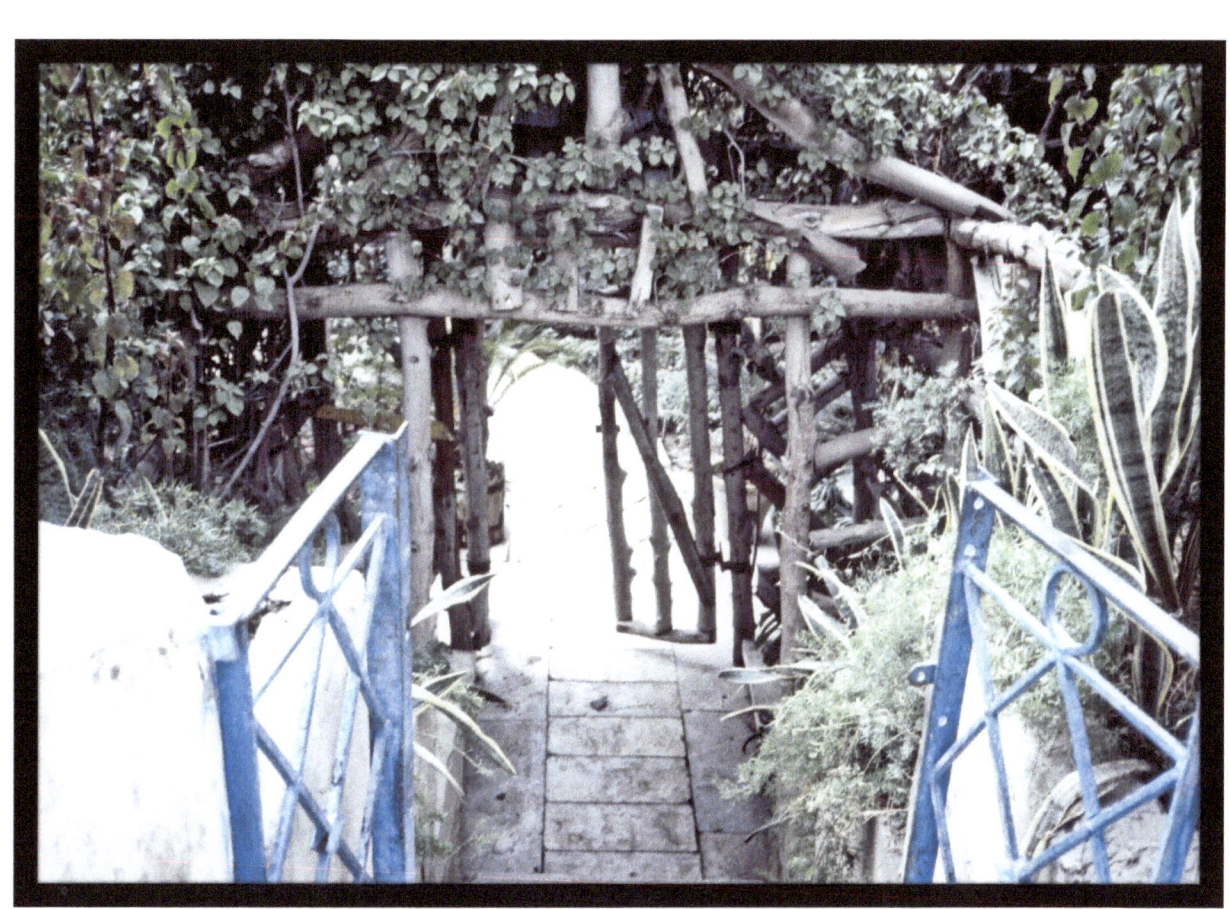

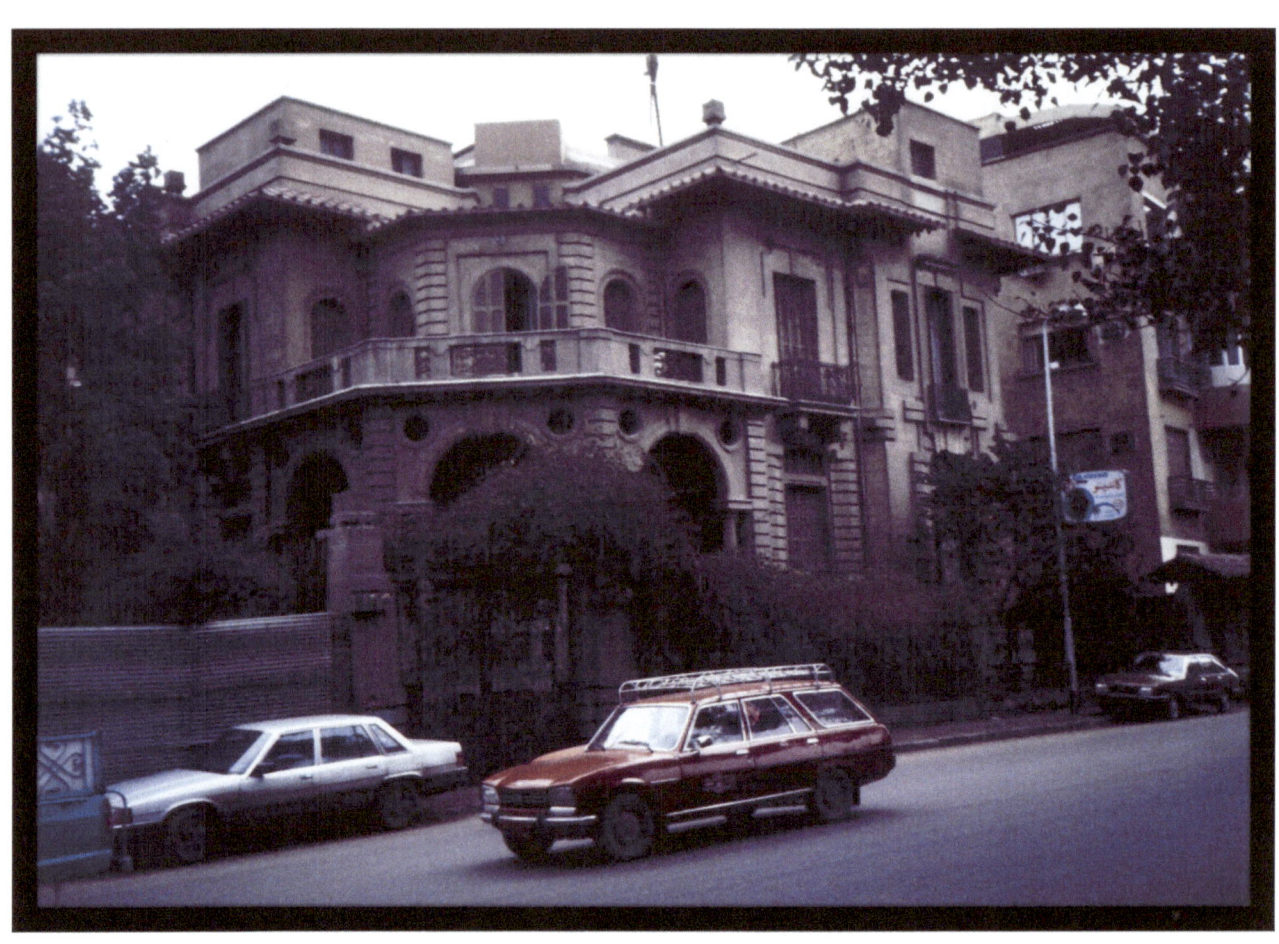

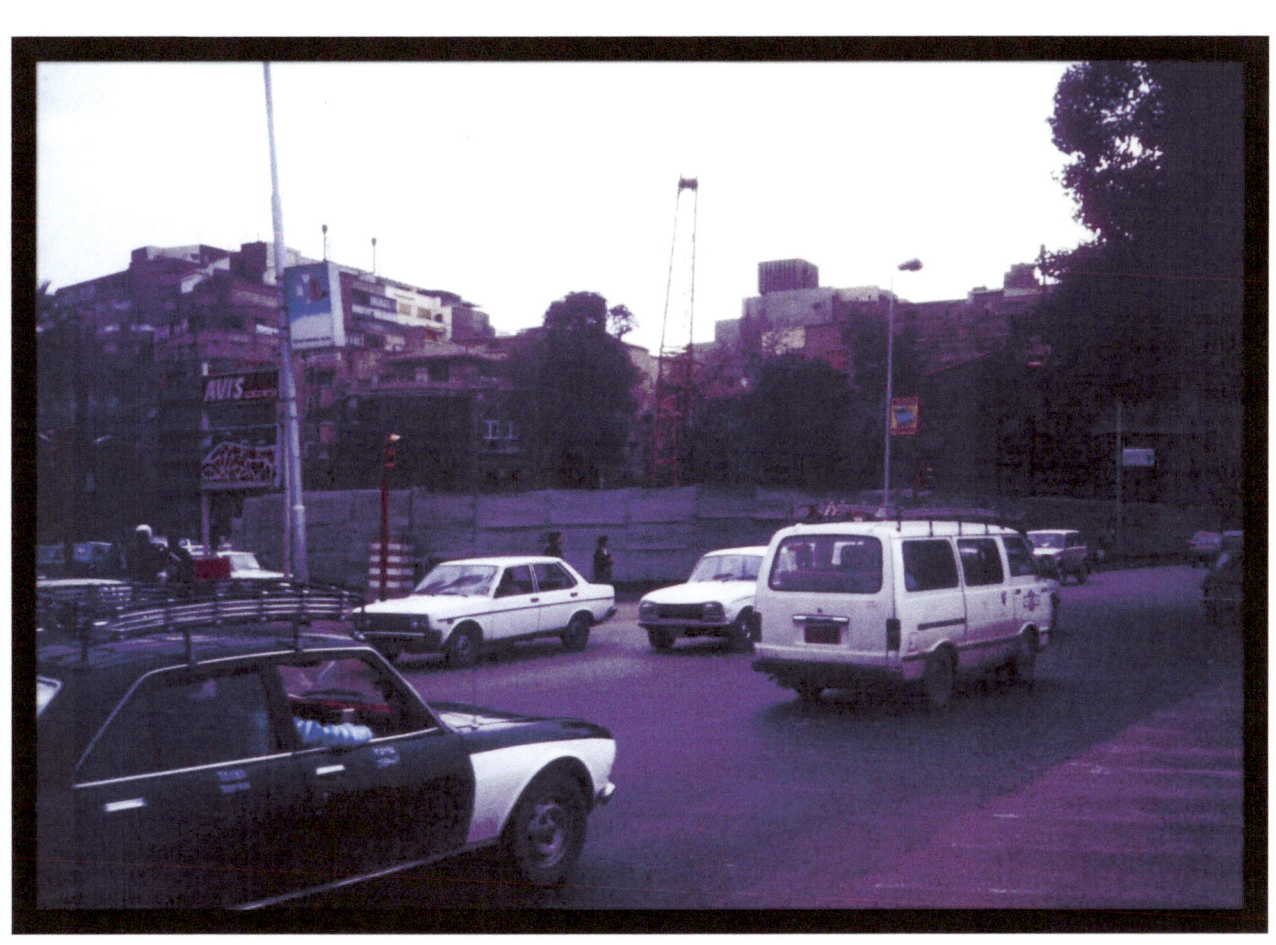

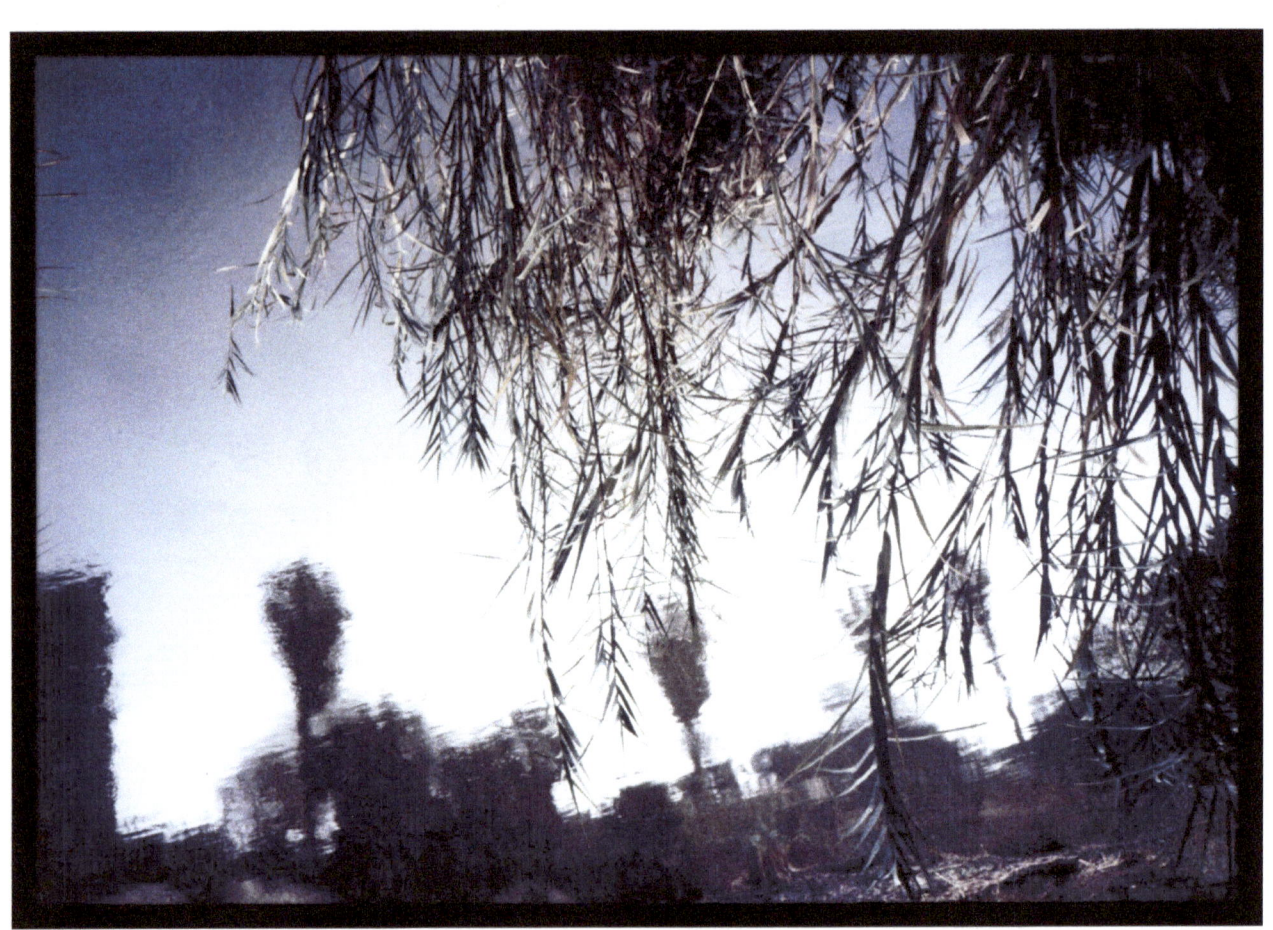

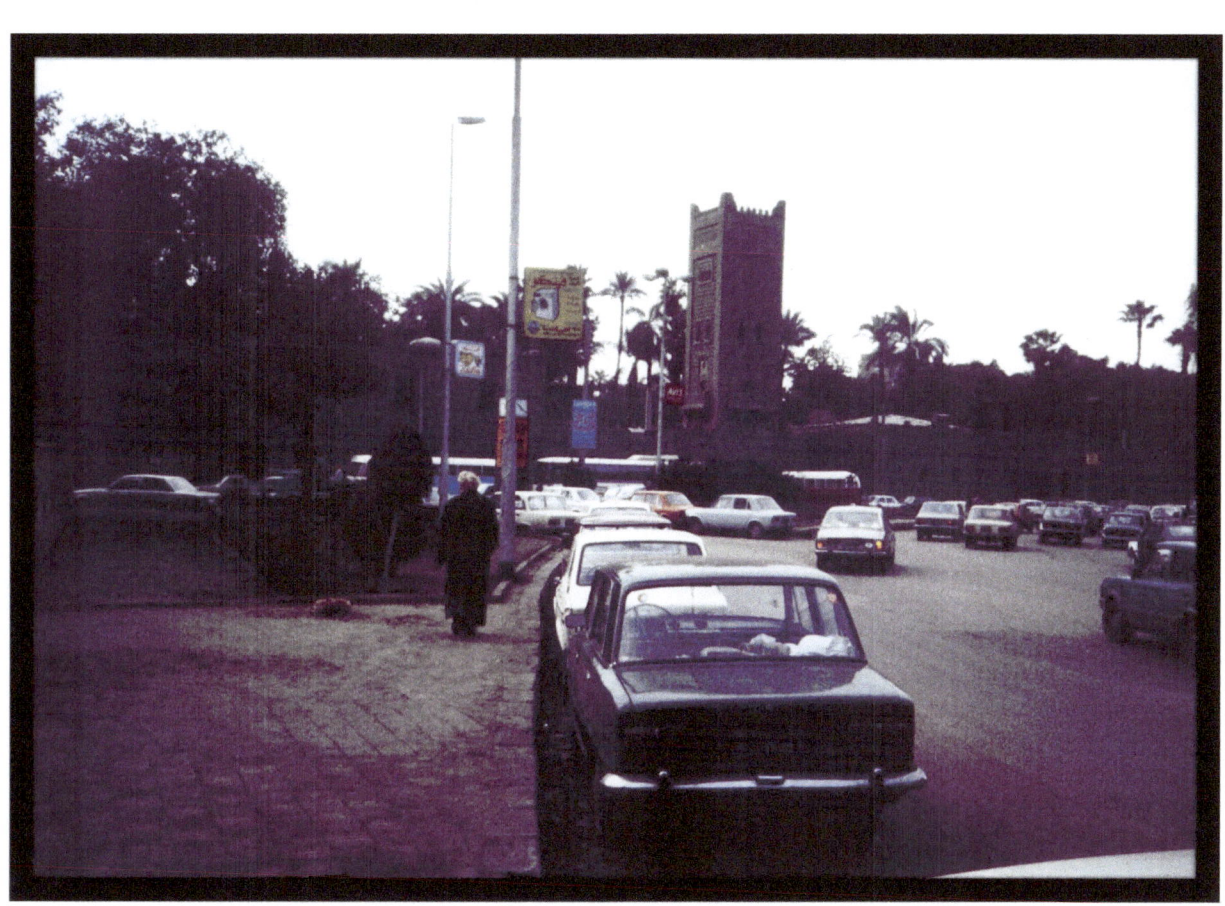

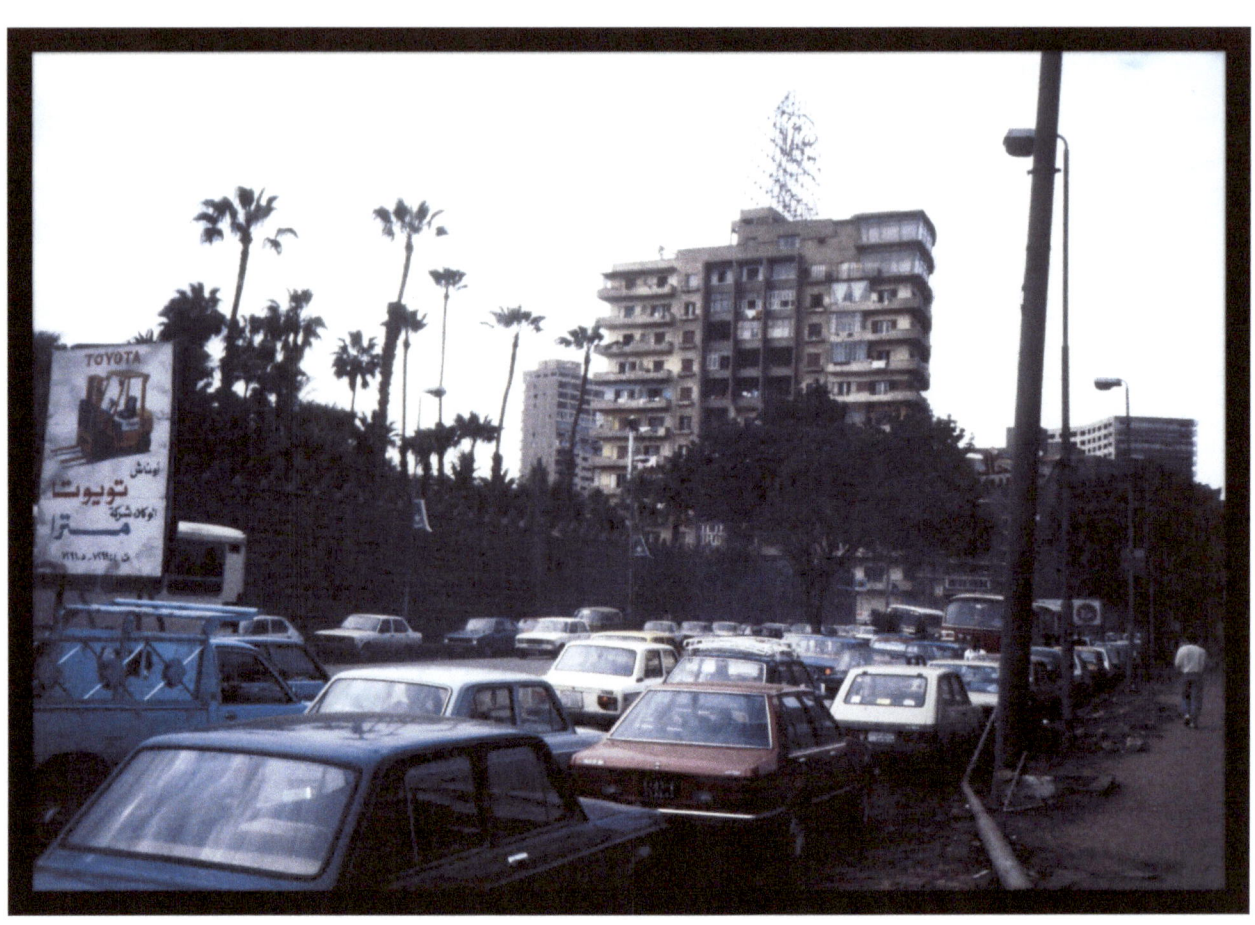

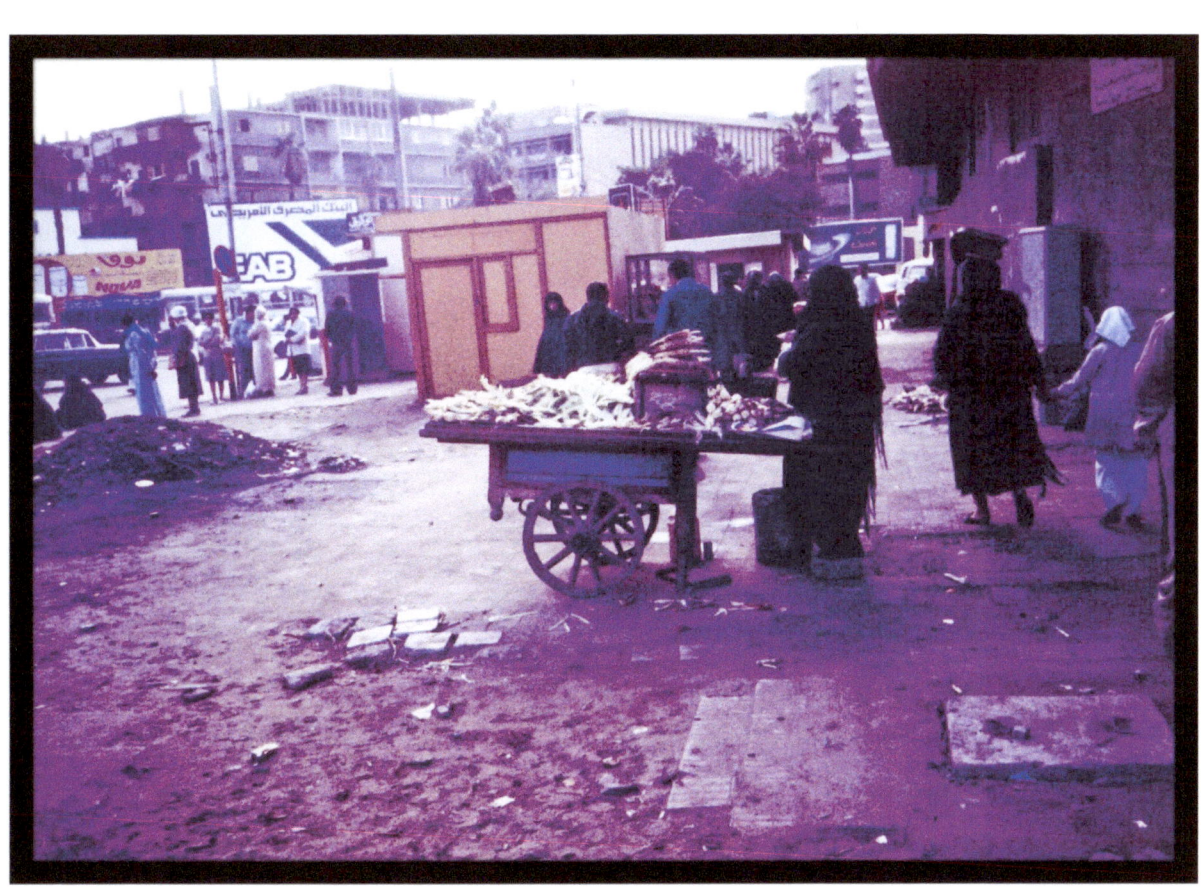

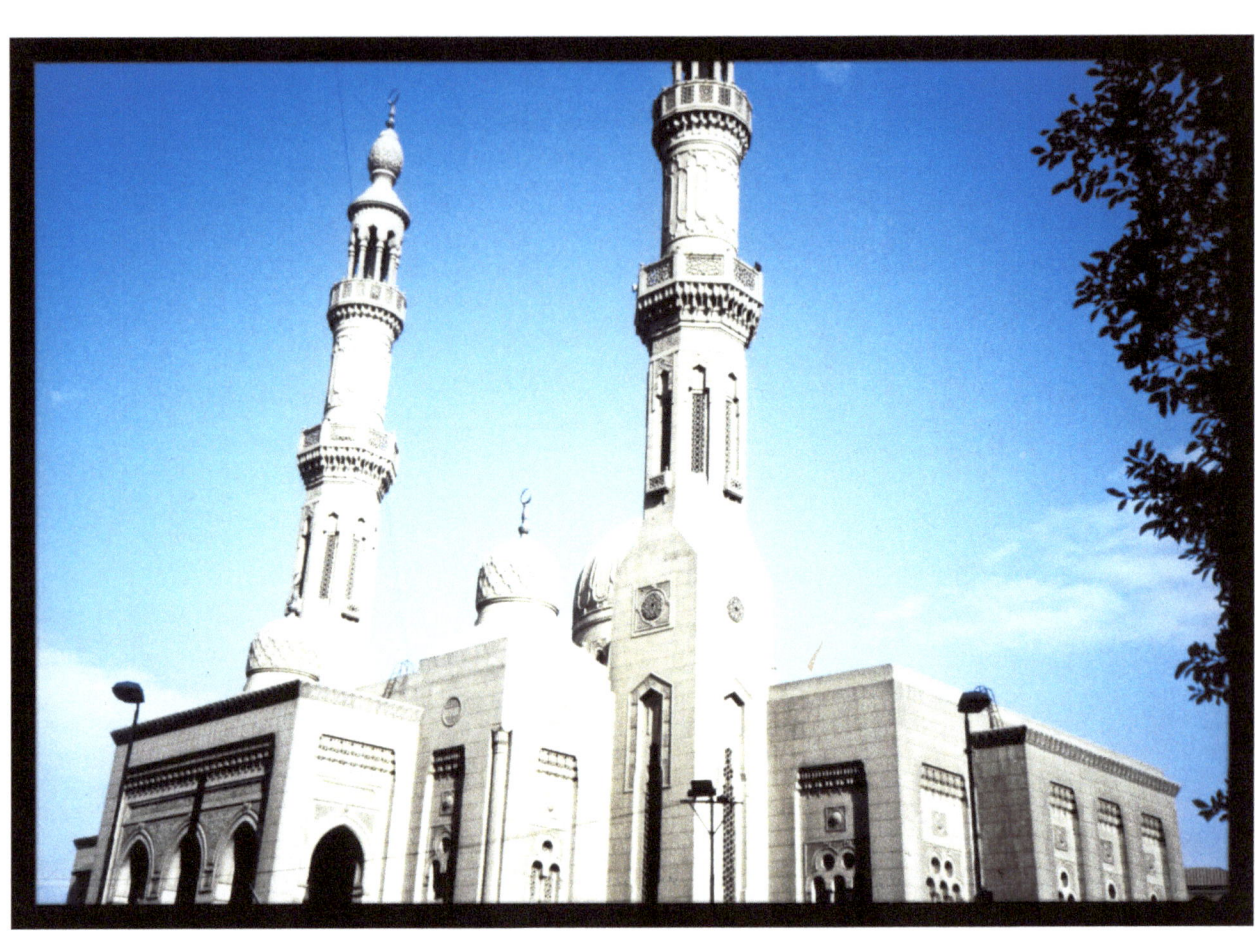

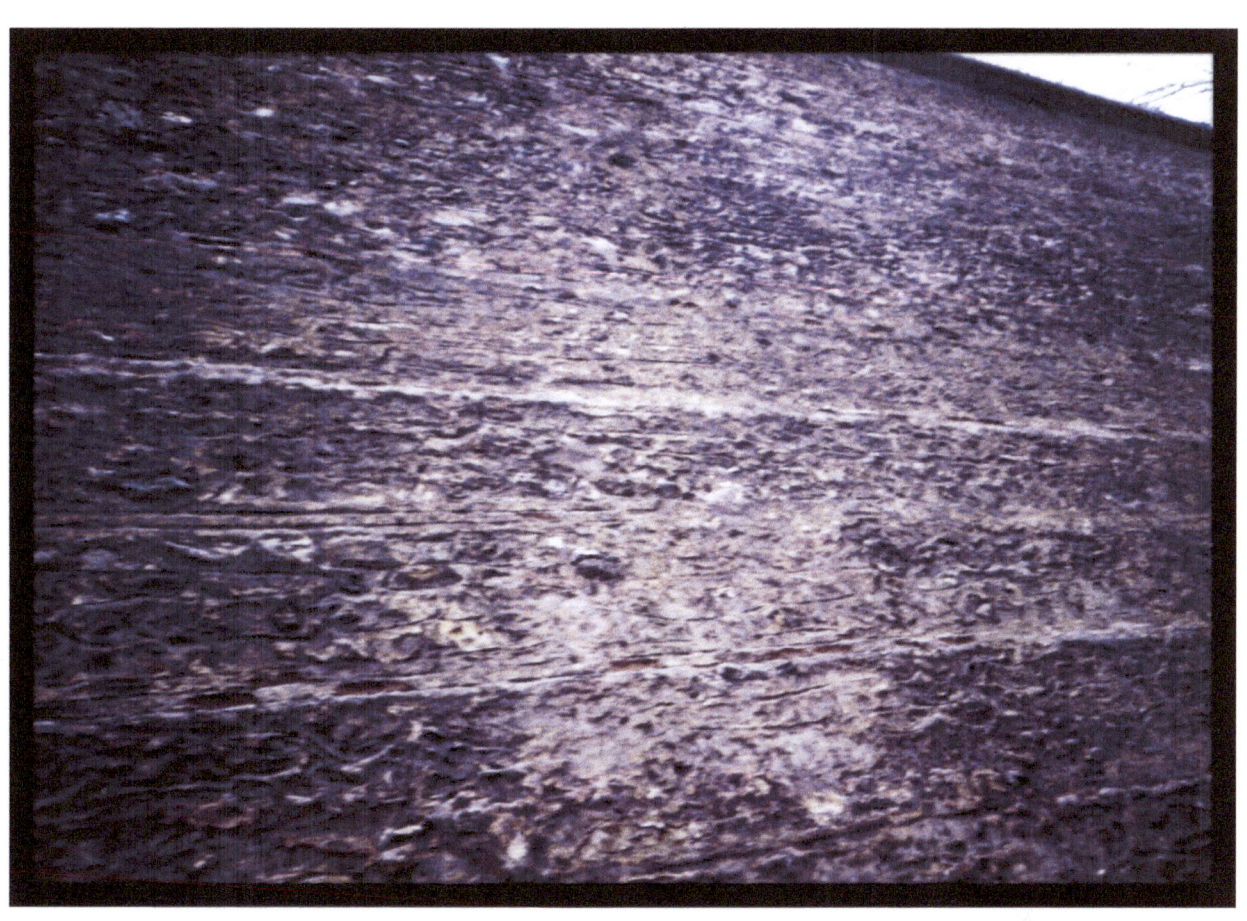

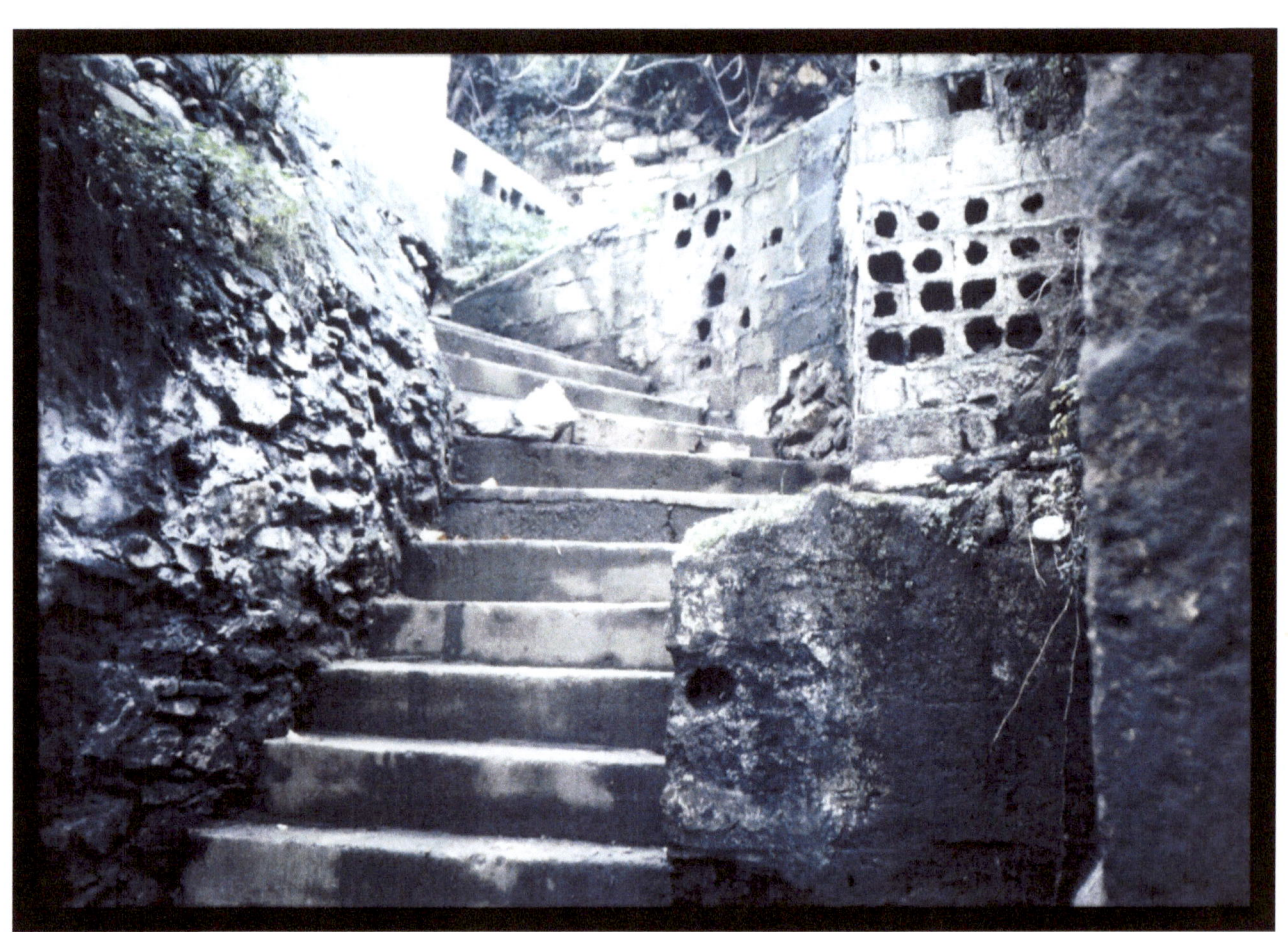

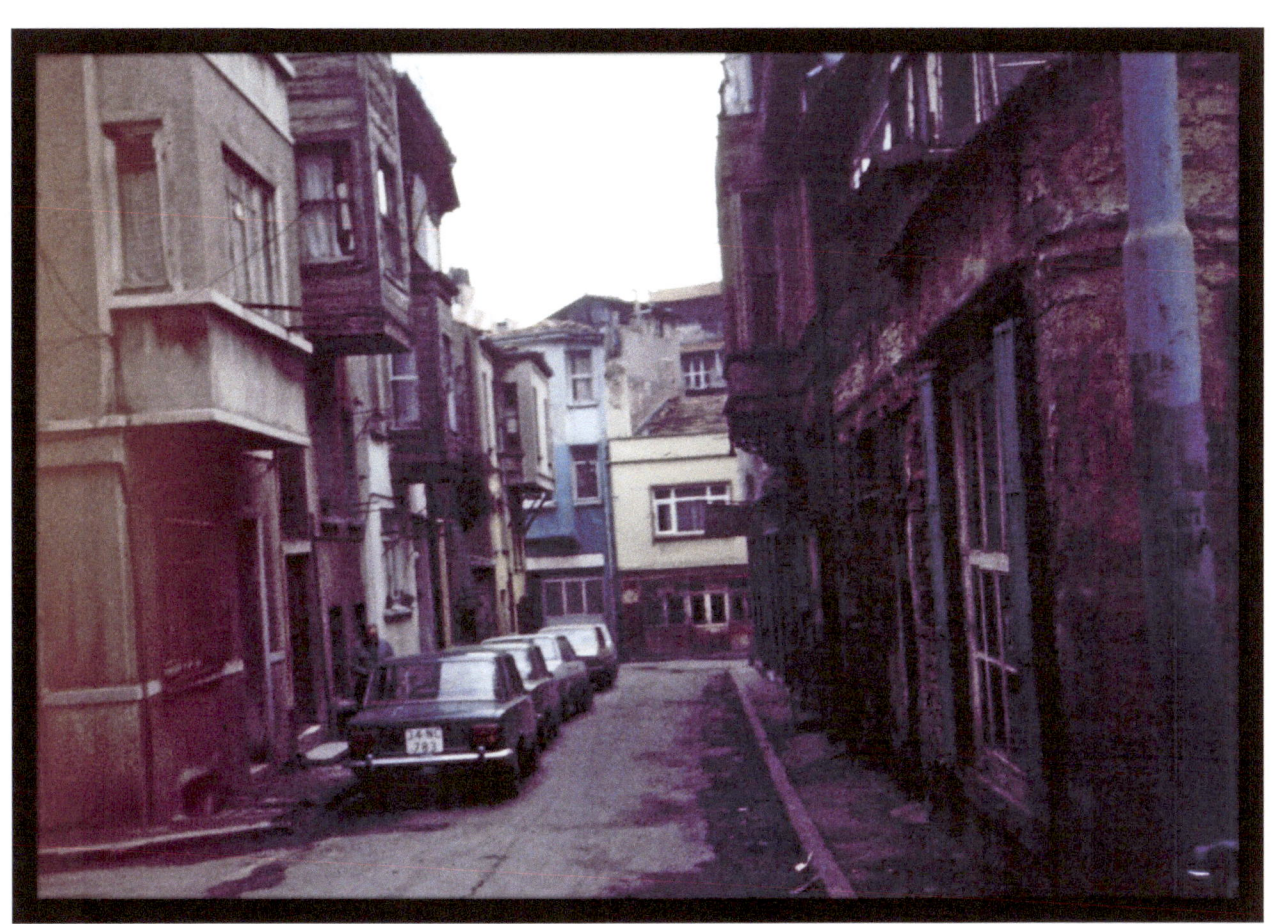

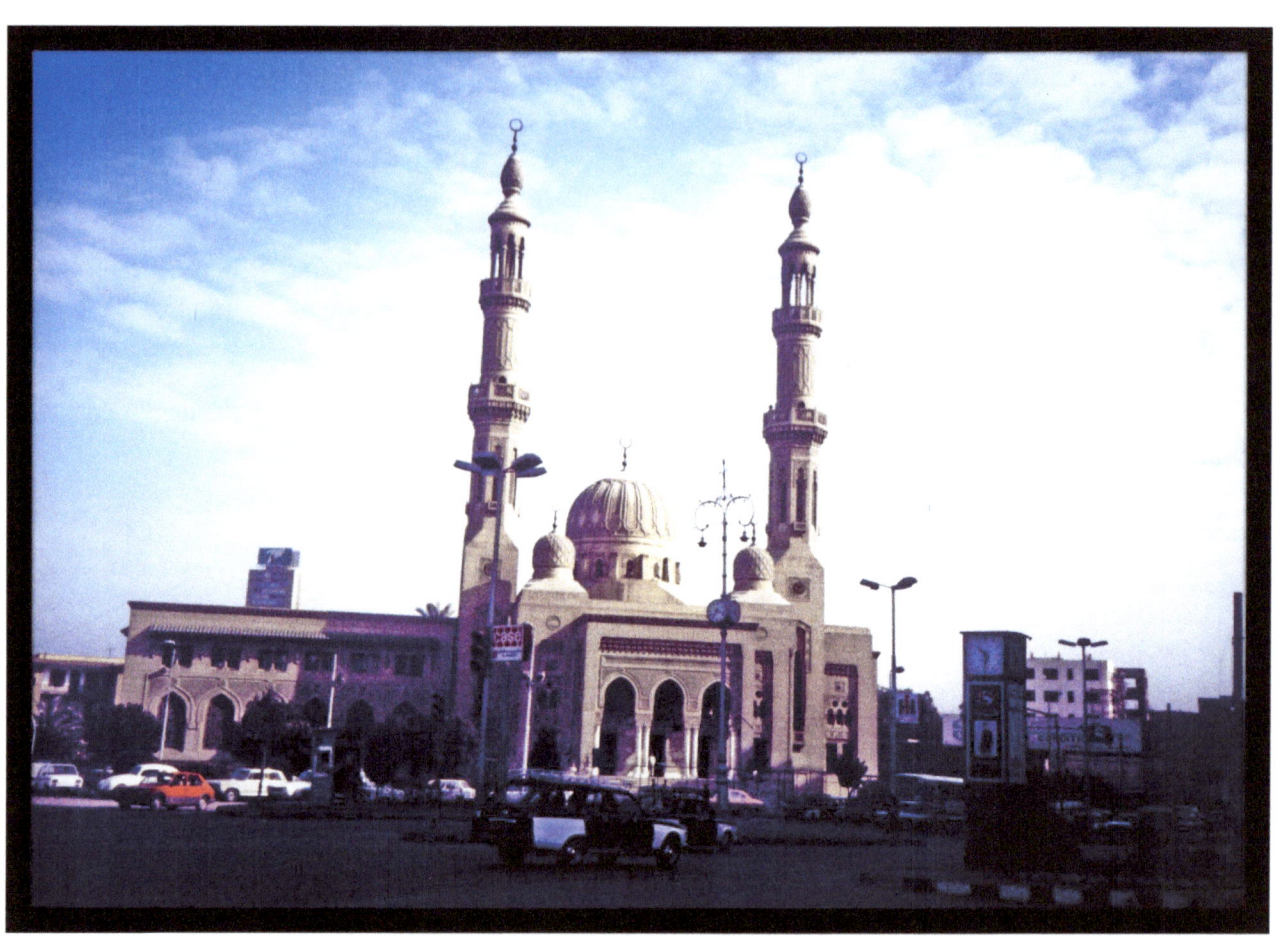

www.ingramcontent.com/pod-product-compliance
Lightning Source LLC
Chambersburg PA
CBHW051146220526
45473CB00003B/670